BAGGAGE

ALSO BY ALAN CUMMING

NONFICTION

Not My Father's Son

FICTION

Tommy's Tale

BAGGAGE

TALES FROM A FULLY PACKED LIFE

ALAN CUMMING

CANONGATE

This paperback edition published in Great Britain in 2022 by Canongate Books

First published in Great Britain in 2021 by Canongate Books Ltd,
14 High Street, Edinburgh EH1 1TE

First published in the USA in 2021 by HarperCollins

canongate.co.uk

1

British Library Cataloguing-in-Publication Data
A catalogue record for this book is available on
request from the British Library

ISBN 978 1 83885 667 0

Designed by Paula Russell Szafranski

Printed and bound in Great Britain by Clays Ltd, Elcograf S.p.A.

For my granny,

who made me realise it was okay to be different

CONTENTS

BAGGAGE

PROLOGUE

Shakespeare calls memory "the warder of the brain" and despite the fact that it is Lady Macbeth who brings up this idea while bulldozing her husband into murdering their current house guest, I find it very comforting.

The notion that my increasingly spotty reminiscences of tumbling through life will somehow protect me, like a cerebral condom, from repeating old, negative patterns or embarking on perilous new ones that my gung ho, adolescent brain would otherwise have dived straight into has, for me, coloured the Bard's fiend-like queen with an Oprah-like hue.

It makes sense that what we have experienced in the past, and how we have analysed and grown from it enables, or at least helps us, to have better judgement. Right? That's what we call the benefit of hindsight. But what if your memory isn't so accurate? What if the stuff supposedly protecting your brain is actually deluding you into making the same mistakes again and again? Even a cerebral condom can break, right? I know I have, on several occasions throughout my life, repeated the exact same patterns of behaviour that previously made me unhappy to the point of despair. So much for the warder of the brain, huh?!

Every day more experiences and lessons are poured into our

memory banks, rearranging and augmenting our views and actions. And if we accept that sometimes we simply choose to ignore our memory's lessons, then we must also agree that memory itself, not just our relationship to it, is ever shifting.

Have you ever wondered if you remember an incident from your childhood because you actually recall it or merely because you've heard others talk about it, or seen a photograph of it? My first memory is of a leaf falling down from a tree and landing beside me in my pram. I do genuinely remember seeing that happen but did it really?! Do I perhaps remember it because my mum once mentioned something about a leaf landing in my pram, or I remember seeing an old photo of me sitting in my pram beneath a tree on an autumn day? But did what I recall actually happen? Did my mum really once talk of it? Was there ever such a photo? Truly, how reliable can any of our memories be?

One single memory can never be a true touchstone, and perhaps even a collection of remembrances of the same event—both ours and others', as faulty and varied as they all may be—is not the true function of memory, either. Rather it is what we do with those memories, how we let them accumulate then process through our minds so we can learn from them. Isn't that really what memory is, or should be? Not just for recall but for growth? The repetition of memory is wisdom, but how we act upon that wisdom is the making or undoing of a good life.

Nowadays I see memory differently: it's not something to be dragged out of the past and dropped at my feet like some subconscious carcass. Now I look forward to meeting up with people I haven't seen in decades and reminiscing, for I know that they will unlock doors in my mind, and I will relive moments we had together that I otherwise might never have accessed again. I have learned that memory is collective and now memories are a gift awaiting me in the future, not the past. Each time a new one is coaxed into the light from the unchartered mists of my mind, I am buoyed and fascinated. Even the bad ones are another piece of the jigsaw of the life I inhabit. I welcome them all.

Here's how I think about memory today: picture some spaghetti cooking in a pot of boiling water and imagine the entire contents of that pot are my life experiences. Now picture the spaghetti being drained through a colander, and that colander is my brain. What is left, the drained spaghetti, is my memory.

Yes, huge swaths of what we've lived just drain away, but I like to think they're the boring bits, the routine, the day-to-day minutiae or the stuff we just didn't register all that much at the time. What's left—the spaghetti—are the remarkable bits, the bits that arrested us. And what makes life interesting is that we all get arrested for different reasons, by different things.

This gratuitous culinary metaphor also functions as a disclaimer to remind you that perhaps not every detail of what I am about to tell you will be completely and utterly accurate. But how could it be? My head's full of spaghetti!

elementary

Whenever anyone asks me how I am, I always reply, "Still alive!"

Each day is a prize for me. Not a gift, mind you. A gift is given but a prize must be won.

There is absolutely no logical reason why I am here—in this life, in this house, in this country, writing this book, having been *asked* to write this book. None. The life trajectory my nationality, class, and circumstances portended for me was not even remotely close to the one I now navigate. But logic is a science and living is an art.

For years people would tell me I was brave or courageous, thank me for having inspired them or making them felt heard or seen. What they meant was that by living an open life as a queer man—and a famous one—I was somehow empowering them. I felt fraudulent being so vaunted for merely enjoying living my life, but I began to comprehend the utter thirst so many have to feel represented, especially when they do not have the option to express their true selves. And I could relate, for I too had a secret.

My first memoir was written without guile and out of utter need to tell my tale, to be heard, to be seen. I wrote of my experiences as a little boy dealing with a very disturbed and dangerous adult man whose splintered psyche rained down such physical and emotional violence it startled even me as I recounted its horror on the page. That man was my father. But the title of the book, *Not My Father's Son*, was a gesture of succour, an assurance that I had not only managed to transcend those early days but indeed, in spite of them, bloom.

Writing compounded my healing and learning. Setting experiences down meant I had to analyse and quantify them. It was the ultimate breaking of a cycle, for in sharing the breaking of mine, I have empowered others to shatter theirs: every single day still, so many years later, I hear from people that my words galvanised them— to confront their abusers, to confront their memories, to reveal and reckon with what had been their shame. I learned the power of my words. I was reminded of the absolute duty of authenticity. That in telling my story, by being fully and openly me in all areas of my life, I could empower so many was initially frightening, like a wildfire I had started but could not control. But if the utter liberation I felt in telling my truth could be manifested in others' lives, I felt at peace. I felt, in fact, I had found my calling.

However, there was one gnawing downside to the wave of positivity that washed over me, and one I hope this book will help redress. After the publication of my memoir, everywhere I turned I saw myself held up as an example of having triumphed. I had overcome my demons. The nervous breakdown was long behind me. I had beaten back the tide of childhood despair. I had conquered my father and he was gone, never to return, like some banished ogre in my fairy-tale life.

Nothing could be further from the truth. I may have transcended and bloomed, but I have not won. There is no prize there.

I had thought, foolishly perhaps, that writing about my abusive father would somehow conclude and resolve the troubled legacy he left me. By discussing him I found peace, but not closure. Instead, he was brought crashing back into my life and is now much more present than at any time since those dark days of my childhood. And that is as it should be. He is my father, after all. He is half the reason I exist. He will forever be a looming tower in my psyche, but now he merely provides shade, or is the occasional storm cloud in the clear sky I look up to.

The difference is he is here now on my terms, not his.

I dream of him often. One particular dream centres on the saw-mill yard that lay behind the house I grew up in, on the country estate where my father was head forester. The sawmill is surrounded by great stacks of tree trunks awaiting their slicing, and pallets of posts and other cut lumber. There are store sheds full of chain saws and strange tools hanging from the rafters and other buildings housing tractors and machinery. In the centre of it all is the Celcure plant.

Celcure is a compound of copper and other chemicals that, when saturated into wood, makes it impervious to fungus, insects, and the vagaries of weather, and thereby destined for a longer, stronger life. The Celcure plant is a sparkling new addition to the yard and—unlike me, permeable and weak me—is my father's pride and joy.

The Celcure plant is a large open-ended cylinder in the middle of the yard with little railway-like tracks leading into it, on which a series of trolleys are packed with posts and other cut wood, locked in place with metal chains. The whole caravan is pushed by a forklift into the depths of the cylinder, the door is closed, and vacuum sealed by pulling down a huge lever. Then all the air is sucked from the cylinder, the green coppery liquid fills the chamber, the pressure inside is increased, and the Celcure pervades the wood.

In my dream, though, something has gone wrong. I see the lever of the pressure lock being pulled open by one of the men who works for my father, but the forklift cannot pull out the carriages packed with the dripping green wood because some of the posts inside the cylinder have slipped their chains and fallen off the carts, causing a blockage. Another worker is called over who tries to reach along inside the green, slimy dripping side of the cylinder but the offending posts are out of his reach. My father is summoned. I see him walking up the yard towards us, a charismatic figure, the tacks in the soles of his work boots clacking on the tarmacadam. He spits without break-ing his stride. The men tell him what has happened, and I see him bridling his annoyance. He shines a flashlight down inside the dank tube and surveys the damage. And then he turns to me.

I realise my father needs me. I am suddenly and unusually valuable to him. I am small, the smallest boy, always, and it is now my job to crawl along the space between the edge of the cylinder and the wood and pass out the posts that have slid out from their stack. My father is kind to me. Kind in that he treats me like one of his workers, explaining to me what I have to do but without anger or telling me I am worthless, as is his norm. I feel bathed in his approval and I want to perform well for him.

The space I have to crawl along is very small. On one side there is the curved wall of the cylinder, with its cold brown-and-green sludge. On the other, to my right, the stacked wood is wet, and the smell of the chemicals stings my eyes. I am scared and I ask if I really have to go inside this dark tunnel. My father tells me not to be scared and yes, I have to as I am the only one who can save the situation. He makes me feel special.

Just as I begin to clamber along the cramped sliver of the cylinder, I think of something. I strain my head back to look at my father and ask him to please promise not to close the huge vacuum-sealed door on me. I have had nightmares about him doing so, switching on the Celcure plant machine and then I die a gruesome death: the air sucked from my body before being drowned in a sea of toxic green. But I do not tell him about the nightmares, as I know he will mock me. He scoffs and assures me he will not shut the door. I believe him and continue propelling my little body into the wet dark. All the time my father's flashlight is weaving across the tunnel and I hear his shouts of encouragement as though he were cheering me on from the sidelines at a school football match.

The copper-green sludge gets in my hair and my mouth, but I persevere. I will perform this task with aplomb, and he will never hit me again. I reach the fallen posts, but they are jammed too tightly, and I am too weak to move them. My father's tone changes. He begins to sound like his old self. He calls me a sissy.

I realise what is going to happen and I start to slither manically backwards towards the opening of the cylinder, but it is useless. The daylight is already starting to ebb and then everything goes dark and deathly quiet, except for some dull faint laughter that I recognise as my father's. He is joking with the other men about having broken his promise and closed the door of the Celcure plant on me. He is disposing of his useless son once and for all. And then I wake up.

The thing about this dream is that it actually happened.

He opened the door again, of course, after just long enough to ensure I became hysterical with panic. The sting of his words, "Do you not know how to take a joke?" was followed quickly by the stinging of my ear and head as his hand made contact, and through the dizziness that followed I heard my orders barked over his shoulder as he walked away.

I spent the rest of the day taking every single post off the carts by hand, hunching over as I progressed farther inside the cylinder, darting a look fearfully behind me every time in case he appeared and shut the door on me once more.

No one ever fully recovers from their past. There is no cure for it. You just learn to manage and prioritise it. I believe the second you feel you have triumphed or *overcome* something, anything— an abuse, an injury to the body or the mind, an addiction, a character flaw, a habit, a person—you have merely decided to stop being vigilant and embraced denial as your modus operandi.

And that is what this book is about, and for: to remind you not to buy in to the Hollywood ending. At some of my greatest career highs I have been my most unhappy and confused. At my most celebrated I have felt the lowest self-esteem. I am a survivor, but I am not cured. And as much as I espouse and propagate the notion that *anything could happen* as a mischievous and exciting mantra to live by, I also accept that it therefore must follow that anything could happen *again*. I could go under. My life could fall apart. That is why I see each day as a prize.

In the chapters that follow I will share with you the shape my life has taken as I've learned to live with my baggage. This is a book about my career, my struggles with mental health, my many forays into love and sexuality and everything in between. Ultimately it is a story between two marriages and how I've navigated and found peace with the journey life has taken me on.

But like the proverbial onion, there are many more layers beneath, years of unravelling the detritus of a prescribed life. I may have broken the cycle, I may have stopped taking my prescription, but I still have some residual virus in my system. And the best way to heal it is to admit it will always be there. I have great access to darkness, but I choose to stand in the light. Life is pain management and a slow march towards death, but here's to having fun while we're marching! Talking of which . . .

I have been coupled, consciously, for the majority of my adult life. I've been engaged, domestic partnered, I've worn rings and even been tattooed to represent the pledgings of my troth. And every time I thought it would be forever, at the time, for a time.

I've also been married twice, and those unions are the bookends of this tome: the collapse of my first, the ascension to my second. But despite the proliferation of alliances in these pages, I don't look back at any of my previous relationships as failures—though some of them were nothing short of disastrous and caused lasting damage that was hard to measure. Some, though, have evolved into beautiful, life-long friendships. Indeed, even some of my *very* short-term dalliances have gone that way. But we shouldn't be surprised if a one-night stand should yield a lifelong intimate friendship, for what is a dalliance but an alliance that begins with a big *D*?!

No, I choose to see this proliferation as a sign of optimism and hope. Even after being beaten down lower than I thought possible, I always bounced back. I still looked for love again.

I am a completely different person in the opening pages of this book to the one when the story closes, and more different today as I write it all down. One of the great things about getting older is recognising patterns: in circumstances, in your behaviour and choices, and in those of others. It's all just the same show with different costumes but the great thing is you get to change parts. You even get to change the ending. Unlike Cleopatra, age may have slightly withered me, but like Jacques in *As You Like It*, I have gained my experience.

And ultimately—something that Hollywood did get right—it is all about love, actually. Just make sure you find the right kind for you, with the right rules. And make sure they're kind. Above all, make sure you're heard, and seen. And be vigilant: nothing is forever, so enjoy it while you can.

suspensory

2

It was early in the spring of 1994. I was twenty-nine and on top of the world. That world was about to fall apart.

I had been married (to my wife) for nearly eight years. The previous summer we had bought a big house in north London with a garden and many empty rooms that we hoped would soon be filled with our progeny.

I'd recently played Hamlet in London's West End to great acclaim, followed immediately by the Master of Ceremonies in *Cabaret* (save your applause, this will keep happening). I was showered with plaudits and awards and gushing profiles in the Sunday supplements. I was the new, shiny, Scottish wunderkind.

I was also desperate, empty, anorexic, and on the verge of a debilitating nervous breakdown.

A daze had enveloped me for the previous half a year. A haze that had descended when I began to contemplate becoming a father. A maze of wrong turns and blocked paths that obfuscated the answer to my burning question: what kind of father would I be?

By spring something had stirred deep within me and answered that question—that I must *never* become a father. That startled me. It certainly startled my wife, with whom I'd been frantically trying to get pregnant for the previous six months. And when I say frantically trying, it was the whole nine yards: no drinking to enable the strongest sperm; rushing home to fornicate—and hopefully procreate—at the merest hint of ovulation; legs up against the wall afterwards (hers, not mine, though I did in solidarity; I've always been a yoga man).

And there was more, worse: I stopped eating. Enough, anyway. I got worryingly skinny and it was the only thing that gave me any pleasure because it was the only thing in my life I felt I could control. It makes sense. It's sadly quite logical.

I had been far from well for quite some time. I was definitely depressed, that was for sure. Deciding what to wear each day could be an insurmountable task, and then my shame and guilt at my ineptitude would reduce me to prolonged, stinging tears—and all that before I'd even got downstairs to the kitchen and began negotiating breakfast. I was totally exhausted. Hamlet and the Master of Ceremonies are not the ideal roles to do back to back, unless, of course, you are actively *trying* to have a nervous breakdown, and then the combination of youthful Danish torpor, betrayal, and suicide combined with drug addiction and the rise of Nazism is just the ticket. I actually rehearsed *Cabaret* during the days while performing *Hamlet* at night in the same theatre. I think the two performances may have borrowed from each other a little too much.

My marriage was suffering, to say the least. Aside from dealing with my volte-face in the fatherhood department, my wife now found herself shackled to a lachrymose zombie with an eating disorder, not the man she married. She needed answers and I just didn't have them. Her understandable frustration and anger made me recoil ever deeper into my thinner and thinner shell. Something was obviously going to have to give, and that something was obviously going to have to be me. But not quite yet, for something extraordinary happened.

Hollywood called.

Yes, *Hollywood* called, and kind of saved me, though I didn't realise it at the time. I didn't even realise it was Hollywood at the time. *Circle of Friends* was indeed a Hollywood movie in that it was financed by a studio in Los Angeles, but at the time it felt very much like a small, European film. For my screen test I had to go to the BBC studios in West London on my day off from *Cabaret*. Riding the tube from Finsbury Park to White City on a rainy London Sunday is hardly the same as being discovered at the lunch counter of Canter's Deli, so forgive me if you think I was naïve or am being disingenuous about my career trajectory.

A week after *Cabaret* closed at the Donmar Warehouse, I left London and flew to Ireland. And it was a flight. It was a prison break.

In the film I played Sean Walsh, a creepy clothing shop clerk with designs on his boss's daughter, played by Minnie Driver, who in turn had the hots for Chris O'Donnell's all-American Irish boy. Chris, fresh from the success of *Scent of a Woman* with Al Pacino and *The Three Musketeers*, was being pitched as the new Tom Cruise. Minnie was making her feature film debut, though we had met the previous year when we starred together as goofy star-crossed lovers in the short film *That Sunday*. Although Chris and Minnie were the leads, *Circle of Friends* was very much an ensemble film, with Geraldine O'Rawe and Saffron Burrows playing Minnie's convent school friends, and Aidan Gillen and Colin Firth as their suitors. There was also a supporting cast of some of Ireland's most beloved actors. The atmosphere on set was egalitarian and fun and devoid of the usual hierarchy that can abound. For all of us it was a really special experience.

We shot mostly in County Kilkenny, and I was billeted with some other cast members in an old, allegedly haunted, converted abbey in the little village of Thomastown. We'd meet in someone's room at night and drink wine and tell stories and play games, or maybe go to the local pub and sing and dance with the locals. Once or twice I even bashed on a bodhran, badly.

Playing Sean was the first time I realised the joy it is for an actor to come to work and be made to look *worse* than you already do! Normally it's the other way round. Way, *way* round!

Once, many years later, I went to a lawyer's office to sign the papers for a new apartment I'd bought. At the time I was appearing in *The Good Wife*, the CBS TV show centred on a legal firm, and I was amazed how the glass-walled offices I was visiting were so like our onscreen version. But there was something different. I couldn't put my finger on it at first but soon it dawned on me: the people! Their clothes were less stylish, their hair frizzier, they had shadows under their eyes. In short, they looked like *real* people. None of them had ever seemingly seen a lint roller, let alone an under-eye mask! I'd forgotten that real life on TV is a very different thing to real life in real life. Another time Valerie Jarrett, special adviser to President Obama, came on to *The Good Wife* to play herself. Because of her real job, she had Secret Service protection, so there were four actors hired to play her officers in the scene. They were tall, athletic, and handsome, bedecked in black Armani and very well groomed. Standing off to the side were her real special agents—shorter, flabbier, paler—and looking rather cowed by their fictional counterparts.

Sean Walsh had greasy hair, brown teeth, and dark circles under his eyes. Conversely, I couldn't remember when I'd felt more relaxed or healthy. I was eating more, sleeping more, enjoying the fresh Irish air. One day I even heard someone singing and realised it was me. That hadn't happened for a while. But I knew in my heart this was all a mirage. Outside the bubble of the film, my life was still in tatters. Here on location I was safe. The bonhomie and the positivity that surrounded me I used as nutrition for my sick soul, sustenance for the inevitable reckoning when I returned to London.

I started a journal and tried to commit my feelings to paper, an attempt to unravel why I'd been so unhappy and confused. I was utterly exhausted from my recent theatre marathon and I knew that must have taken a toll on my psyche. Playing Hamlet had also triggered many long-dormant feelings for me, and the new level of media interest that had engulfed me of late left me anxious and self-doubting. Being probed about my upbringing and my family and my personal life made me incredibly uncomfortable but, paradoxically, overly candid, too. Michael Church in *The Times* wrote:

He spent his childhood on a remote Perthshire estate, where his father was a forester, and his elder brother "Laertes to my Hamlet" was better at everything than he was. He roamed the woods at night, addressing imaginary multitudes, with just his dog for company. He despaired of ever measuring up to the prevailing macho standards.

More pertinently, he grew up amid parental strife, a state of war in which he still takes sides (with his mother). He now finds himself harbouring Hamlet-like feelings about his mother's new companion. He doesn't buy the full-blown Freudian line on Shakespeare's closet scene, but he does observe, in the throw-away manner with which he delivers important thoughts, that his current job is "cheap therapy".

Meanwhile, the part of Ophelia in this production is played by Hilary Lyon, who just happens to be Cumming's wife. The savage intensity of the "get thee to a nunnery" scene, and this Hamlet's piercing grief over Ophelia's corpse, might suggest some therapy is going on here too. "Well, it is upsetting, it is not just Ophelia in the grave. And the fact that I have been horrible to her . . ."

And then I had gone on to *Cabaret*, where I dug deep into my well of untapped desires to create the character of the Master of Ceremonies. Was that fusion of sexual freedom and bacchanalia I embodied in *Cabaret* so soon after delving into my damaged familial past the reason I now doubted so much—fathering a child, even staying in my marriage at all?

I was also not far off thirty. Perhaps this was just my Saturn returning and the resulting jangling in the spheres was instigating the reassessment of the future I had allowed to be paved out in front of me.

Still, I knew there was more. There was something else. But I wasn't ready yet. I wasn't strong enough to go there. I didn't know it at the time, but I had blocked out large swaths of my childhood. I knew bad things had happened but there were few specifics. I was walking down the corridor of my adult life and they were hidden in a room I'd long ago vacated and closed the door behind me. Not locked, as it turned out, but the DO NOT DISTURB sign was definitely on.

It would be several months before I'd begin to remember specific details of the violence and abuse I had endured at the hands of my father. At the moment he was just a black cloud hanging around me, unfocused and vague.

What I did begin to see, tentatively and definitely unaccustomedly, was that I was okay. Of course, I clearly wasn't okay, but I accepted that it was okay for me not to be okay. I didn't have the answers. I didn't know why, suddenly, my seemingly perfect life no longer made me happy, why everything about the future in that life actually repelled me. But I also saw that if I needed to take some time to find out why and how I had come to feel that way, I should be allowed to take it. I had lived my whole life trying to avoid inflaming those close to me. It began with my father, of course, and as I entered adulthood, I continued the practise by making others' needs and happiness paramount. My happiness, my worth was predicated on my success at appeasement. I was a life chameleon, a walking emotional spirit level. It was my familiar. But it meant that at twenty-nine I was so devoid of introspection I did not even have the vocabulary to ask for what I needed most: some time for myself.

And then Hollywood called again!

emergency

3

I wasn't fully conscious the first time I set foot on American soil. Also, I got there by horse.

Okay, first of all, I was *actually* conscious. I'd had a few glasses of wine, but I was functioning. I just wasn't fully there, you know?

And as much as I would have enjoyed hurtling through the Rockies at the reins of a four-steed stagecoach or hanging on to a burly gaucho as we barebacked across the Rio Grande, I did not in fact actually *travel* by horse. But the reason for my trip was indeed an equine one.

Not just any old horse, though, but none other than Black Beauty, the eponymous hero of Anna Sewell's 1877 novel as well as the 1994 Warner Bros. live-action movie version, for which I was now being asked to supply his voice! Yes, that was me. I am Beauty. Or at least, I was. The film was being faithful to the book in having the horse narrate the story. Everything had been shot the summer before and now I was to add my voice to the nearly completed cut in a mixing stage at Pinewood Studios, on a break from shooting *Circle of Friends*.

I had never done anything like this before. I mean, I had done plenty of voice work—audiobooks and stories on the radio for the BBC—but Black Beauty was certainly the first live animal I had ever voiced. He would certainly not be my last—oh no! I have since voiced a cat named Persnikitty in *Garfield: The Movie*, a Yorkshire terrier named Dante in *Show Dogs,* to say nothing of my animated-animal oeuvre: a goat opposite Sean Connery, a koala bear, the White Rabbit in an *Alice in Wonderland*–themed musical episode of *Dora the Explorer* opposite Jewel and Mel Brooks (together at last!), a spider in *Michael Jackson's Halloween* (as weird as it sounds), a bear for the BBC, and a poodle in an episode of *Arthur* (for which I was nominated for a Daytime Emmy. Robbed!). I've also voiced a Bog King for George Lucas, a Smurf (twice), Hitler, the Devil, Prince George's valet, and a lecherous and foul-mouthed HIV+ man in a wheelchair. (It has not escaped my notice that I seem so much in demand for roles predicated on my not being seen.)

Back in Ireland, across from the converted abbey in Thomastown where we were filming, was a field where a few horses grazed. A couple of times I'd tried to woo them to come over and be petted, but they, like Minnie's character in *Circle of Friends,* were immune to my charms. But the day after I returned from London and the *Black Beauty* recordings, I saw, standing alone in that field, a black horse. Not only that, a black horse with a white mark on its forehead, just like *you know who.* I hadn't noticed him before. And now here he was, shuffling across the grass towards me, and in an instant I was nuzzling my very own black beauty. What did it mean? Was it a sign? Of what? That a black horse would play a more portentous role in my life than a few days recording in a darkened studio?

When *Circle of Friends* wrapped, I returned to my life and wife in London and faced the music. It was obvious to me that I was not ready to pretend everything was all right. I felt stronger, yes, but I also felt a storm was coming. I had to prepare for it.

I told my agents I was taking a few months off work and worked up the courage to tell my wife I wanted to move out of our home, rent a flat somewhere, and just wait for whatever it was that needed to happen. I didn't know if I would ever go back, but I knew I had to go. It felt like I was in one of those horror films where the hero goes off into the woods to lure out the creature for the final showdown. Except the woods for me was a dark bedsit in Primrose Hill and the creature turned out to be a tide of awful childhood memories.

Before all this could happen, however, I had to fulfil one more work commitment: *Butter*, a short film that would mark my directorial debut. It was the story of a successful woman with an eating disorder having a bit of a breakdown. Would you believe that I also wrote it?! And that it was to star none other than my wife! It's all in the timing, as they say.

I'd written *Butter* originally as a monologue a few years before when I was a member of the Royal Shakespeare Company, and my castmate Jane Maud performed it as part of the RSC fringe festival. It was inspired by something Jane had said to me that became a line in the finished film, bemoaning the feast of delicacies she was now saddled with since the paramour whose visit she had bought them for had stood her up at the last minute:

Butter! Do you have any idea how long it is since I last tasted butter? Months! Literally, months!

My friend Dixie Linder, a then up-and-coming film producer, encouraged me to turn the monologue into a screenplay that she could produce. So as soon as I got back from Ireland, we got started. Dix had assembled an amazingly experienced and talented crew; Kenneth Branagh let us into his *Frankenstein* editing room to cut our little film in their downtime on a new, digital system called Lightworks (a system destined, alas, to become the Betamax to the AVID system's VHS but which was cutting-edge at that moment); the supporting cast included my *Cabaret* co-star Jane Horrocks, Helena Bonham Carter, and Richard E. Grant. It was a dream come true for any director, let alone a first-timer.

Butter is only fifteen minutes, but it is packed with portent and significance for me. I was clearly screaming for help in writing about a successful person with an eating disorder and huge self-worth issues. It is also my final collabouration with my wife. We had worked together many times—most recently she had played Ophelia to my

Hamlet—and had known each other since our days at Carnoustie High School, though there only tangentially. We were sometimes dubbed "high school sweethearts" in the British press but that was far from true. She was four years older than me, and during high school that is a lifetime. But I knew who she was. She was the star of our high school opera, and then later when I went to drama school, she was the star again—sophisticated, experienced, having been to university but now studying acting. She was daring, too, baring her boobs as Lady Macbeth in her final year in drama school, and destined for great things. I was seventeen, tucking my sweater into my jeans and my jeans into my suede Tukka boots. If we hadn't both been to the same high school, I don't think she would have given me the time of day. We didn't start going out until a couple of years later, after she had graduated and we'd ended up together in a show at the Edinburgh Festival fringe called, rather prophetically, *Off the Rails*. That was in 1984. Several lifetimes ago. It was now 1994. The dynamic had changed.

Most couples have a power dynamic. We either inhabit or play roles that are familiar to us in our unions. Of course, these are not rigid: hopefully we evolve, we grow. Through time and circumstance our once-perceived roles can shift seismically. My wife and mine did almost immediately. Within a few months of us being together I was the student allowed out of drama school to make my professional debut in a play, then a film. I was no longer just the pretty boy with the worldly, older girlfriend. I became the star. The phone rang for me. Before long she was Alan Cumming's girlfriend. Then Alan Cumming's wife. With *Butter*, I was closing the circle and bringing our dynamic back to how it had first been when we got together a decade before: she was again the star.

———

The release date of *Black Beauty* was fast approaching and the picture about to be locked, but there were a few last-minute changes to Beauty's dialogue, so I was summoned to Hollywood to perform them. Nowadays, of course, there would be no need for such opulence. A quick trip to a studio in the centre of London and a half hour's read via satellite to Tinseltown would suffice. I'd probably be able to do it on my iPhone. Several times recently I have lain under the quilt in my bedroom and said a few lines into my phone that magically appeared on television a few days later.

But this was 1994. Internet was still in its infancy. So on Monday, June 27, 1994, a week after *Butter* wrapped, off I went, like Pip in *Great Expectations*, to the big, bad City of Angels.

As I walked down the jetway of the LA-bound Virgin Atlantic plane, for the first time in my life I turned left into first class. Just then, I heard someone call my name and turned to see Ruby Wax, beaming her megawatt smile, curious to know to where and why I was travelling. She was en route to California to interview Tammy Faye Bakker for her show *Ruby Wax Meets*, but as it was on the BBC and publicly funded, the budget did not stretch to first class. Ruby was turning right.

To my utter delight I was plied with champagne and hors d'oeuvres, sleeping suits and amenity kits, and asked if I'd like a shoulder massage or manicure—all before we had left the ground! And once we were airborne my table was set for a delicious silver service lunch. Soon I was supping and scoffing my way across the Atlantic.

It felt like a fever dream where I had been swooped up into a luxurious bubble—a magical suspension of my earthly life where every turn portended despair. Here I was, light, giddy even, definitely slightly squiffy, on a journey into the unknown. Everything took on an enchanted hue. My glasses of water and wine were refilled religiously. Out of the window I marvelled at the glistening beauty and the closeness of the ice floes. *This is the life*, I thought.

But then I began to ponder if transatlantic planes always flew so low. My reverie was broken by the captain announcing we were about to make an emergency landing in Reykjavík as someone on board needed urgent medical attention. Dream deferred.

Suddenly I was in a disaster film. The tension in the cabin was palpable. My tray of delicacies—as well as my delicious wine—was snatched away and soon we were on the ground. Medics rushed on board and, in a whirl of gurneys and oxygen machines, someone was removed, alive or dead I couldn't tell. Next, we were told we too must temporarily deplane. I think that was the first time I had ever heard the word "deplane." I didn't like it. It has not grown on me. We don't ask people to detrain or debus or decar, do we?

But as I did so I ran into Ruby, her eyes darting over my shoulders to the forbidden palace of the upper-class cabin.

"You may be in first," she said slyly, "but I got a picture of the stiff!"

She proffered a Polaroid (remember, it was the nineties) of an elderly man strapped to a stretcher, clearly snapped as he was wheeled past her on his way off the plane. She went on to show me an array of sneaky pictures of other passengers sleeping, mouths agape, heads lolling. This is why Ruby was so popular in the United Kingdom. She said, and in this case did, all the things British people wanted to but would never dare. But when a brash Yank did it on their behalf they could laugh with impunity and at the same time slightly scoff at her gaucheness.

Ruby wasted no time in making lemonade out of our situation and instructed her film crew to follow us as we whiled away the time in the various gift shops of the Reykjavík airport. The footage never saw the light of day, thankfully, but I distinctly remember us cracking up at souvenir fossilised seagull poop on a plinth. Yes, really.

Eventually we were instructed to return to the aircraft—or would that be "replane"?—but told that due to the regulations concerning the number of hours pilots can fly, we wouldn't be able to make it to Los Angeles that day and instead would touch down in Portland, Maine, where we'd spend the night before continuing on to LA the following afternoon. I was thrown into a panic. This was Monday. I was supposed to be recording in a Warner Bros. soundstage on Tuesday as *Black Beauty* had to be locked by Thursday, whereupon I would be deposited back on a plane home to Blighty. But now I wouldn't arrive in California until late on Tuesday and so would not be able to work until Wednesday! Also, where in the hell was Portland, Maine?

When we landed, we deplaned once again and were guided to buses bound for our various hotels, each one corresponding to our class of onboard travel. It was the very last days of the Raj. I got chatting to the boys from Ruby's crew and in all the hullabaloo, and also perhaps because of the heavy pouring of the flight attendants on the Reykjavík/Portland leg of our epic journey, I got on the wrong bus, the bus headed for the budget accommodation instead of the presumably swanky digs I had been destined for. Ruby, strangely, was missing in action and somehow found herself on the bus that was bound for my hotel, where she ensconced herself in a night of luxury that originally had my name on it.

So, there I was on the wrong coast, in the wrong city, on the wrong bus going to the wrong hotel! Even in my Chablis-infused glow I couldn't help feeling it was all a metaphor for my life at that moment. My entrée into the land of moviemaking was turning pear shaped. I began to spiral. The studio would have to abandon my last-minute vocal changes and my failure to appear would be deemed negligence on my part, which would naturally lead them to charge me for the massive cost of this swanky flight and the hotel room in a place called Studio City I would *not* be sleeping in tonight. It's funny now to think there was a time in my life where I would think that way, that everything was my fault. But just as my worst-case scenario started to crescendo—probably to my death after bankruptcy and public humiliation—I had a moment of clarity, a kind of clarity that has thankfully revisited me many times over the years when I've found myself in similar situations:

There's nothing I can do, I thought. *I have no way of letting the* Black Beauty *people in Hollywood know. I can't get there any faster, so I may as well enjoy myself in this moment and hope for the best.*

Now one glance at my smartphone would provide a plethora of contact numbers I could call for help, or one press of a button could send a voice text to my agent or manager or assistant and any number of people who would probably not only be aware my flight had been delayed but already have emailed alternative arrangements to my inbox. But that is now, and this was then. I had no mobile phone and believe it or not, I had no contact numbers. It seems a rather cavalier way to travel, but why would they have given me contact numbers when I couldn't contact them anyway? That's how it was done in those before times. People used to just get on planes and assume there would be someone waiting for them at the other end.

I could have called my agents from my room in the (budget) hotel, but it would have been the middle of the night in London. All I had, as a contact in case of an emergency during my absence, was the number of the hotel where I was supposed to be staying in a place called Studio City, which sounded to me like a made-up name, a joke I wasn't in on.

Ruby's crew persuaded me to join them for dinner, citing, quite rightly, that staying put in a drab motel room would not make the situation any better. When we returned, the front desk clerk told me, rather scoffingly I remember, that no, there hadn't been any calls for me, so I went to my room and lay down, stared at the ceiling, and reasoned that, oh well, I'd just get back on the plane the next day and hope for the best. Warner Bros. would understand.

I was just wondering about the number, and indeed the actual existence, of the brothers Warner, when the phone rang.

"Hey there, is that Alan Cumming?" a rather laid-back-sounding American gentleman drawled.

"Yes," I squeaked. I felt like Matt Damon in *Saving Private Ryan*, and the voice on the other end of the line was my Tom Hanks.

"Good! We hear you've had a little delay," he continued, seemingly unfazed by my blighted trek.

"Yes, we had to land in Iceland because an old man died." The relief of being rescued was making me babble. "And then the pilots had flown too many hours so we couldn't go all the way to Los Angeles and so we had to land in Portland. But it's okay, I'll be in LA by tomorrow early evening, cos we're leaving here in the afternoon and—"

"Alan, listen to me!"

Was Tom Hanks shouting at me?

"You are not, repeat, not, to get on that plane tomorrow. There is a car outside your motel right now. . . ."

I peeled back the grubby net curtain and saw a limo idling below.

"What?!" I gasped. "How did you know where to find me?"

Suddenly it wasn't Tom Hanks in *Saving Private Ryan*, it was Liam Neeson in *Taken*!!

"That isn't important. What is important is that you get in the car, immediately, and get on the United flight to LA that leaves in fifty-five minutes. Your driver has all the details."

"But what about . . . ?" I began, but he shut me down with a "Now!" and I was up, grabbing my bags and off down the corridor.

At reception I saw one of Ruby's crew and hurriedly explained to him what was happening.

"Tell Ruby I bequeath her my plane seat in posh!" I yelled over my shoulder. "She's had the hotel; she may as well have the whole hog!"

Outside I leaped into the car and the driver handed me an envelope with my tickets. At the airport I was whisked onto the plane for a slightly less opulent experience—though there were more drinks—and before I knew it, I was opening the door of my room in the Sheraton Universal Hotel in Studio City, which turned out not to be a made-up place at all, but a sort of actual, small city where, well, all the studios are. Duh.

The next couple of days are a blur—and not just because my recollection is dimmed by the quarter of a century and counting that lies between them and me now. They were a blur then, too.

Being driven through the gates onto the Warner Bros. lot in Burbank was a very meta experience: I felt like I was in a Hollywood movie, and I also was! I read a few small changes to some of Black Beauty's lines. There was a lovely PA who took me on a tour of the

Hollywood sights, which included Universal Studios. There I saw up-close the mechanical Jaws I'd seen so many times on television back home, and as it reared its ugly head from the water I gasped in recognition as much as fear. I was jet-lagged, of course, but I wore my blur as a protective denial. I knew that in only a few days I'd be back home on the other side of the world, living in a flat alone, not working: two things I'd never done as an adult. One evening I took off in my rental car in search of the city centre, which was a foolish errand on many levels. Nobody should make a journey on the 101 freeway their first-ever foray into the LA driving culture, let alone as their first time driving in the United States, or in an automatic when they were used to driving a manual, on the wrong side of the road and with the steering wheel on the wrong side of the car, at night and with no directions. This was the perfect metaphor for my life right then. I was lost. Almost wilfully lost. But nobody died. And I discovered that Los Angeles has no centre. Another layer for the metaphor.

On the third and final night of my trip, Caroline, the film's director, threw a dinner party for me at her beautiful home in Burbank, to which she invited Eleanor Bron—whom I knew from having wept into her bosom eight times a week in iambic pentameter

the previous year when she had played my mum, Gertrude, in *Hamlet*. She was in LA filming *The Little Princess* and had also played Lady Wexmire in *Black Beauty*. It was a joy to see her again. For a few hours that evening I was with friends, old and new, and I felt safe and at home.

Both Caroline and Eleanor have asked me since why I didn't confide in them about what I was going through during that first trip to Los Angeles. But I couldn't. I had thought of little else for every waking moment for as long as I could remember, and four days away from it all in this, literally, New World gave me the breathing space and the shred of confidence I needed to go back to Britain a little stronger, a little more sanguine. After all, if I could find my way back to the Studio City Sheraton, I could find my way back to myself.

A few years later, I was a guest on Ruby Wax's dinner party-style talk show. Around a table in a studio I broke bread and chatted with Ruby, the actress Olympia Dukakis (RIP), and the playwright Martin Sherman, whose harrowing and brilliant play *Bent* I would perform in the West End seven years later. As the meal progressed, Ruby and I regaled the others with the story of our shared, ill-fated trip to Los Angeles. We laughed at how she had blagged her way onto my bus and nabbed the swanky hotel room and then my seat in first class for the final leg of the journey, and I wondered aloud what had become of that poor man whose medical emergency had led to the unexpected turn of events.

Incredibly, Ruby knew the answer! On her return to London she'd had dinner with her husband's father, who mentioned he knew someone who had recently returned from a stint in a hospital in Reykjavík. Her interest piqued, she began to question him and discovered that, in fact, the man she had snapped in his oxygen mask being wheeled off the plane, headed, we were sure, to his Icelandic demise, was actually her father-in-law's best friend! What were the chances?! Apparently, he had not only survived and returned to London fighting fit, but his health scare was not nearly as dramatic as any of us had imagined.

"I was on some new pills from the doctor," Ruby, putting on an upper-crusty accent to impersonate the gentleman in question, announced to the table.

"I had a glass of red wine before dinner, next thing I know I wake up in hospital in bloody Reykjavík!"

mortality

4

I moved in to the bedsit in Primrose Hill with a suitcase and sat on the squeaky, wrought-iron bed and waited. Only a few close friends knew where I was. I'd been so reclusive for the past year it was quite easy to disappear from my life. I was ready to exorcise my demons—and it was an exorcism of sorts. I felt I was about to have the fight to the death that my father had always wanted.

It began almost immediately. A virtual reality flip book of patriarchal violence flooding my vision

A sudden unexpected blow to my head. I stagger backwards with the force. The shock gives way to pain. Thereafter and always the humiliation, the ringing in my ears. A kick from behind as I'm carrying logs in for the fire, they fall to the ground with me, and as I scramble to gather them he strikes again, the hatred in his eyes, again, again. I'm older, he holds back less, I fly through the air, the panic, the pleading for him to stop. Move that tractor. I don't know how to drive. Move it! I can't even reach the pedals. The endless repeated dance of being punished for my failure to accomplish what I am incapable of. I can't swallow for the grief. Like my mother said so long ago, he has gone too far, again and again, the fear, the utter fear that this time he may go just *past* too far. Repeat, repeat, repeat until the only shock is if it does not happen.

And now not just the violence. Now the terror, the inevitability of the awful. The constant possibility of his savagery is exhausting. This is where my father, my domestic terrorist, derives most pleasure. I can smell it on him. Eventually he will break my spirit completely and I will long for him to hit me just to make it end. Then the all-pervading shame that ensures both my silence and the continuation of his abuse.

I did my best to process and collate the onslaught of these memories, and at the same time try to assuage the utter shock I felt that they had happened at all, that this had actually happened to me. I was a warped man, a construct of my father's violence and my suppression of it. A Frankenstein of fear and shame. No wonder I had wanted to change my life.

On waking one morning I discovered the shadow of suicide had glided into my periphery. An option, a potential gift. I tried not to move too much or too quickly in its presence, lest any sudden transfer of my weight or thoughts might unleash its power. As a child, dealing with my father's constant sadism, I had flirted with the idea of suicide. But it wasn't my life I wanted to end, just my situation. And I felt the same again now.

One of the few people I was able to see during that time was a friend who, like me, had recently found his world turned upside down. I remember a long lunch I had with him in a little Polish restaurant in Primrose Hill, where we brought each other up to speed on our respective tales of woe. At one point the waitress came over and asked us, "Are you both okay?"

"No, actually," he said, not missing a beat. "He's having a nervous breakdown and my wife's fucking another guy!"

———

Sometimes when you least expect it, and very often inadvertently, people do you a huge favour. Once, on a road trip across Canada, my boyfriend at the time told me I shouldn't buy a lamp I'd spotted in the little vintage store attached to a service station where we had stopped. Things were rather shaky already, but I remember thinking to myself, *You don't get to tell me what I can buy.* We didn't live together, and the lamp wasn't going to impinge on his space in any way aside from how much room it would take up in my VW van that we were using for our trip. Also, it was eight dollars! And eight Canadian dollars at that! A bargain! I bought it, and in that moment, I knew our relationship was over. The lamp has died now, too, but I kept its glass shade and it hangs on my wall to this day, a totem of my independence and a reminder to trust my instincts: the boyfriend is now a friend and one of the closest people in my life. We are better as friends. And nobody—aside from my business manager—gets to tell me what I can or cannot do with my eight dollars.

And my wife must have known that when she told me she didn't believe the stories of my father's abuse, and worse, that I was using them as an excuse to leave her, our marriage was truly over. It was the gift she gave me, of clarity. To me, it's indefensible to immediately question anyone's story of any kind of abuse, especially when you know you are one of the first people they have ever opened up to. At that time, I *had* to be believed. It was as insane for me to say those words as for another to hear them. I had just opened these floodgates of shame and guilt and confusion and fury and sorrow and was asking for the first time *why* those things had happened to me, so the idea that I would not be believed by the person closest to me in my life sent me reeling. I retreated into a cave of doubt, fear, and all the other dark detritus that abuse leaves behind it like some lifelong PTSD snail trail.

I understand now why she responded this way, for she was also hurting. I had destroyed her life and she needed to punish me. She was at the very apex of her pain at my rejection of the life we had created, and the primal knee-jerk, the only way she knew to hurt me, was to deny my pain. So she belittled my story, one that was humiliating to share and incredibly raw. I understand that today. Back then, I understood only that I could never dare be vulnerable around her again.

And I knew how to do that. My entire childhood was one long exercise in masking vulnerability. I could never please my father, so I did the best I could not to irritate him. The more I made myself invisible around him, the less chance there was he would hurt me. And now I needed to do the same thing as an adult with my wife.

By autumn I was ready to come back to my life, to come back *to* life. I was also ready to face my father. But before that my wife gave me an ultimatum: come back or it's over. I went back and told her it was over. She immediately took her wedding ring off and laid it on the coffee table between us, a final power move. For a long time afterwards, I carried mine in a pocket of my wallet, not quite sure what to do with it, until one day my wallet was stolen, and I felt relieved.

―――――

"So, Alan, why are you here?"

Those were the first words I heard on the morning of my thirtieth birthday, and they came from the mouth of my divorce lawyer, sitting across the desk from me in her office in Islington. The irony of such a milestone meeting on such a milestone day had not gone unnoticed by me, yet I did not expect her opening gambit to be so piercing. This was a lawyer, after all, not a therapist.

"Well . . ." I stammered. "I obviously want to get divorced." She nodded and held my gaze.

"And I really don't want it to get ugly."

I actually meant I didn't want it to get ug*lier*, or ugly again. I truly didn't.

By now I saw my marriage as collateral damage—ultimately necessary but completely shocking to both of us, and shock can make us do and say some awful things.

"I'd just like it to be kind," I added. These were nice intentions, you must admit, but anyone who has been through a breakup knows that nobody leaves unscathed. I have had, alas but ultimately hooray, more than my fair share of breakups—some parasitical and vengeful in terms of money and property and dissolved through lawyers, others just two people disentangling emotionally—but all painful, all with stages of hurt and outrage and becoming people unrecognisable from who we had first met.

The lawyer smiled and opened a folder and began questioning me about the nitty-gritty, the minutiae of bank accounts and assets and names on forms that are all that remain when love no longer functions.

Nobody actually wins in a divorce. There can be no real victory when what you win are the spoils of a death. And that's how my fourth decade started, with the death of something. Though actually it was my third decade that ended with the death of something, and that something was the old me, the trapped me, the little boy who'd shut down his emotions to survive abuse and terror, the teenager who'd run as soon and as fast as he could to a new life in Glasgow at drama school; the man—the young, too young man—who'd entered a marriage because it made him feel safe and secure. What he didn't realise then was that shutting down emotions, running away, feeling secure because he was in a relationship that felt familiar, were all the ingredients of a recipe for disaster. For a death.

But as so often happens, death and birth are beautifully entwined and so my fourth decade was a birth: the me that was able to express his own joy. By the time autumn came I had gone with my brother to our childhood home and confronted our father about his abuse of us. I returned to work, to shoot *The High Life*, a sitcom I had written with my college friend Forbes Masson. Laughter is indeed a great medicine and I learned to laugh again during that shoot. I was still shaky, like a little fawn finding its feet. I was starting a new life and making all my own decisions. I was finding out who I really was, not who I was trying to be for others.

astrology

5

By dint of birth date, I started school at four, and so grew up being at least a year younger than all my peers. In those days, certainly in the rural area of Scotland where I lived, there was no nursery or kindergarten. The first day I wasn't at home alone with my mum was my first day of primary school.

As often happens with the second child, my parents forgot to take the requisite photo of me on this milestone day in my life, so they took one on my second day instead. However, I had forgotten to change back into my proper shoes after games on my second day and came home wearing my plimsolls (canvas shoes with rubber soles that every child of my generation wore for gym until sneakers came into vogue), and that is why I am wearing them in my pretend-first-day-of-school photo. I guess I learned to fake it for the camera early.

The thing about being a year younger than all your classmates is that if you are even remotely bright you can be mistaken as some sort of child genius. It was kind of great! But ere too long puberty descended, and this wunderkind fell from grace and became merely the short one with the high voice whose saving grace was his cool best friend who had a hairy chest, smoked, and got engaged to a college student while still at high school! His name was Alan, too.

But not only was I younger, I was a late developer—a combo from

adolescent hell! I remember the indignity of being in the changing rooms of our school gymnasium and having the awful realisation that I was the only boy in my class with no pubic hair.

I *longed* for pubes. Their absence was my youthful obsession. Ironically, for the majority of my life since I have been pretty indifferent to them, but recently they've become rather perplexing again. I mean, who needs a visual reminder of their age in the form of a gray or white pube? Nobody wants even the whisper of decrepitude in the vicinity of their penis. And now that I have taken a renewed interest in them, I have to report that with their tight perm vibe going on, pubes are a bit, well, eighties.

Back to my teen years. Eventually it happened: a pubic hair appeared! I was so proud, for now I was a man. Soon more would come and join it and I could enter the showers facefirst and proud.

But then, one day not long after, as I absentmindedly took a pee in the upstairs loo of my parents' house, the unthinkable happened. I looked down and there, floating like a corpse down the River Styx of my sexual awakening, was my pube. My one pube had fallen out! I was devastated. My life was over. I felt I was destined to always be a boy soprano with bald genitals, the butt of a lifetime of jokes and pitying glances as I attended my school friends' weddings and funerals.

I'm happy to report that my hormones eventually kicked in, but it was a long time before I even approximately looked my age. As a young actor, I played teenagers well into my midtwenties. When I married for the first time, I was filming a TV show playing a seventeen-year-old.

It used to be embarrassing to me how young I looked. Of course, the older one gets, the more pleasant it is to be thought of as younger than we actually are. *Still got it* is the most vaunted of aphorisms in my book these days. But my youthfulness was absolutely to my detriment when I left high school. We didn't really graduate in Scotland then— not high school at least. We graduated from university or college, with the appropriate pomp and gowns, but we just sort of *left* high school. Graduations and proms and reunions were so much not a thing when I was growing up that when I went to Hollywood many years later to make my first film there, *Romy and Michele's High School Reunion*, I actually had to ask someone to explain to me what a prom was. Also, I thought you pronounced the city where the film was set, Tucson, with a hard *c*—Tuckson! Fun fact!

Because I'd gone to school when I was four, I was only sixteen in 1981, and even though I had passed all the exams I needed to gain entry to university (or drama school in my case), none would take me because of my age. Wisely, the Scottish seats of learning would not admit anyone younger than seventeen. That was a whole year away! What was I going to do? I had spent my summers and weekends working for my father on the estate, but I could not stomach the idea of working for him full-time for a whole year. School had always been my respite from his brutality. Any bullying or problems I encountered on school grounds paled into insignificance against the cruelty I endured at home.

It was my mum who showed me the posting in the newspaper for a junior editor at a publishing house named D. C. Thomson & Co., based in nearby Dundee.

"You've always been keen on English," she said encouragingly.

We both knew I had to do something. My father had made my options very clear: find work or else leave the house. I was sixteen. As much as the idea of living away from my father was appealing, even I knew I was not ready.

At the interview I had to complete a very long application form that included questions about my religion and my father's occupation. Then came general knowledge, spelling, and grammar tests to ensure, among other things, that I knew the difference between "wait for" and "wait on"—the latter only in a restaurant, FYI. The whole thing was rounded off with in-person interviews with various editors who asked me things like what was the last film I had seen and what I had thought of it. I was pretty syntax savvy as well as chatty and opinion-ated, so I passed with flying colours and got the job!

A few weeks later I reported for duty to the fiction department in Meadowside, the company's headquarters. (The meadow was long gone, though the building did look out onto a beautiful graveyard known as the Howff.) I was sixteen years old. I'd never worked for anyone but my father, and here I was in the big city of Dundee in a massive old red stone building buzzing with the worker bees who produced the various magazines and newspapers that made up the D. C. Thomson empire. I felt like I was in some silent-era movie come to life: the country boy sent out to make his way, suddenly faced with the mores and machinations of the big city. While Dundee is hardly a heaving metropolis, it had streetlights and shops, so considering where I was from, it was culture shock.

I loved the fiction department. My first job was to answer the phone and say, "Hello, Fiction!" which, to me, meant everything I said after that could be a stonking tissue of lies! I also had to copyread the stories that appeared in some of their papers and women's publications, mostly romantic flights of fancy full of references to ladies with flaming hair and brooding gentlemen in breeches.

But in addition to copyreading and editing if the stories ran long, we sometimes had to do some rather complicated typeface calculations in a unit of measurement called ems, to make sure the stories fit the columns available in the newspaper. This was when I truly realised I am an artist and not a scientist. My brain does not work well with straight lines. My idea of hell is an Excel spreadsheet.

Once, when I was charged with this part of the process for the final instalment of a rip-roaring serial of passion and valour, I became completely confused, and the galleys of that night's paper came back from the printers with one short paragraph of the story followed by several long columns of nothing. Zilch. Just blank, white newsprint. I had totally screwed up my ems! It was panic stations! Hilary Lyall, the rather strict and prim lady who ruled the fiction department roost, lost it. There was nothing to be done except abandon the whole thing and begin the next story a day early. So all the poor readers who had been following this churning tale and were looking forward to an exciting climax as they read that night's paper on the bus or at home in the bath were left hanging, never to be sated. I may have permanently disturbed the psyches of many Dundonians, who never experienced the happy ending of our hero's inevitable pressing of his manhood onto some unsuspecting damsel.

I was still living at home, but I was now a working man and contributing to the household, and with that came a new, if not respect, then détente, an abatement of my father's rage. Don't get me wrong, he was still terrifying, but I now had grounds to be more absent, to create a bit of a life of my own. And so, I started to do a spot of manhood pressing myself.

I still didn't take any chances, though. My father's critical eye and obsession with my appearance had not changed with my ascension into working manhood. He insisted I wear a tie to my job (it wasn't required), along with a dress jacket and brogues. I acquiesced, not wanting to jeopardise my newfound freedom. But I always took different clothes with me in my backpack, and I kept another bag hidden behind a tree, down a lane I cycled past each morning. In that bag were my latest prized possessions: black suede pixie boots, de rigueur for a young man about town in the early eighties. I'd take off my tie, change my jacket, and slip into my boots, stashing my former outfit in the bag behind the tree then hopping back on my bike to pedal for my life. This was a dangerous game to play with a man as volatile as my father, but I grew to enjoy starting each day with a frisson of danger and insurrection. One must suffer for fashion, after all.

I had begun to do plays with the local theatre club towards the end of high school, and now I expanded my artistic reach and joined the Carnoustie Musical Society for its production of *My Fair Lady*. I was cast as Freddy Eynsford-Hill, the young upper-class twit who becomes besotted with Eliza after seeing her swear at the races. (Yes, that's actually what happens.) Everything was going swimmingly until, a few weeks before the show was set to debut, the man playing Colonel Pickering—the show's moral compass, voice of reason, and

best friend to the Dr. Frankenstein-like Henry Higgins—fell sick and had to pull out. It was drama with a capital *D*! Would we have to cancel the show? Who could possibly learn such a pivotal role in the few evening rehearsals remaining? Yes, you guessed it. I was plucked from, not exactly the chorus, but certainly the juvenile department and flung onto centre stage with a couple of mutton chops glued to the sides of my face, a series of poorly drawn ageing lines, and a *lot* of talcum powder in my hair. I saved the day, and I was not yet seventeen years old! Colonel Pickering is probably *still* the oldest character I have ever played—if you rule out God and the Devil. Yes, I've played them both.

I just want to point out that this was not a high school production. And unlike the plays I would go on to perform in at drama school, where a teenager playing an octogenarian Chekhovian old retainer would not raise an eyebrow, there were many people in the Carnoustie Musical Society who were age appropriate to play Colonel Pickering. But they asked barely-seventeen-year-old me. I think it was the first time I realised I boxed above my weight when it came to acting, or certainly old-man acting.

Carnoustie's Station Hotel bar was the hostelry of choice for post-rehearsal libations, and it was there that I made several bad decisions, most of them involving both my endemic, youthful need to people please and my then passion for gin and bitter lemon—a drink I thought at the time to be the epitome of casual sophistication, but now is so triggering I can barely even say its name aloud without some shuddering of my innards. Suffice to say the only time I have had gin since was when filming a TV travel show about Scotland's Hebridean islands, where I visited a gin distillery on the Isle of Harris and could not avoid imbibing a few (on-camera) sips.

Things started to heat up in the fiction department when I was given the task of writing the horoscopes for the *Evening Telegraph* in Dundee. Yes, that's right. A sixteen-year-old country boy who probably looked about twelve entirely fabricated the daily horoscopes of a bona fide newspaper!

I took this task very seriously. I thought each fake prediction through with care and was incredibly vigilant not to take the easy road and make my horoscopes all about potential love and romance. What if, the earnest younger me thought to himself, an old lady who lived alone with her cats was reading these horoscopes each day? I couldn't live with myself if I thought I might be amorously teasing a lonely geriatric. She (the old lady with the cats) became my touchstone for both the tone and content of my column each day. I would crib phrases from other magazines and newspapers that involved actual astrological happenings such as "Uranus is in retrograde", but I'd follow up with my own flourish—"so why not think about a few new additions to your wardrobe?" Or "Saturn is returning, so now isn't the best time for a spring clean!!"

The fiction department was only ever meant to be a stepping-stone to greater literary challenges. It was a nursery where young green things like me were watered and nurtured and when we bloomed, we were placed on the editorial staff of one of D. C. Thomson's many publications. Of course, exactly where we would be posted was the subject of much speculation, especially to me and my friend Jackie Brown, who had joined the company and entered the world of fiction shortly before I arrived. Would it be one of the several magazines geared towards the teen market whose glamorous, young, mostly female employees we saw bouncing by us in the corridors in their garishly coloured puff skirts, red plastic earrings, oversized sunglasses, and yellow Walkmans clipped to their skinny waists? Those magazines had titles like *Patches* and *Blue Jeans* and, most desirable of all, the colossus towering over all other teen girl titles, *Jackie*. The star reporter of *Jackie* was, of course, a girl actually named Jackie, who did stories under the byline "Jackie from *Jackie*", and we watched her giggle through exciting visits to the zoo and meetings with pop stars. And Jackie from *Jackie* was no flash in the pan. Jackie from *Jackie* went on to become the anchor of BBC Scotland's nightly news show for thirty years.

Jackie Brown from Fiction and I awaited our magazine postings with a mixture of great dread and hopeful optimism. The dread part was that we would be cast out to what we perceived as Siberia, the Kingsway branch of Thomson's, and onto a homespun old-lady-type mag like *The People's Friend*, where we'd have to edit recipes and knitting patterns and interview people who hosted TV gardening shows. Also, the Kingsway is a ring road that circumnavigates the north part of Dundee, and was therefore far away from the shops and restaurants that were within walking distance of Meadowside.

The day finally came when our fate was revealed . . . and we struck gold! We were both placed on a *new* magazine! A pop and TV magazine for boys and girls named *Tops*. We looked those skinny, noisy-bangled girls square in the eye now! Who needed *Jackie* when you were *Tops*?

I was sixteen years old. Can you imagine how truly exciting it was to be a part of a new national magazine project and to be able to actually make our mark on it? And make our mark we did! Harry, our editor, made sure the smallish editorial team was all visible to the reader. Jan, the girl who sat across from me, had her own page (named "Jan's Page", natch); a hilarious, short woman from Glasgow named Margaret Robb, who is responsible for my lifelong love of curry after taking me for my first at Gunga Din on Dundee's Perth Road on Friday lunchtime, was featured in the editor's letter each week as "Small Margaret"; a very tall man (also named Alan) to my left on the bank of desks in the communal office was referred to in the magazine's pages as "Tall Alan". I was the keeper of the readers' letters section, the first two pages of the magazine, and I signed off my little message each week as "Young Alan".

But amid the fun, camaraderie, and excitement of all this there lurked an ominous sign that maybe we weren't as fabulous as we felt: the address that the readers were given to send me their letters was 185 Fleet Street, London, England EC4A 2HS.

We were all in Dundee. Dundee, deep in the heart of Scotland.

The entire sprawling operation of the D. C. Thomson empire was in Scotland, mostly in Dundee, with a Glasgow office where the *Sunday Post* newspaper was produced. So why the London address? Because, I imagine, the idea of such a large publishing house with so many national titles not being based in the United Kingdom's capital and vortex of the publishing world was inconceivable. Being located in Scotland somehow signalled us as lesser than.

The London office was basically a mailbox, with all the magazines in Dundee having their bags of mail sent up from down south daily. It felt like we were pretending to be English, but back then I didn't really mind. It felt glamorous and cosmopolitan that kids thought of me receiving their letters on Fleet Street, the ancient home of both journalism and Sweeney Todd. But there was also something shameful about it, something I began to see as a constant in my young life, and something that I would continue to be reminded of: Scottishness must be hidden; we must obfuscate it even with a postcode.

The first edition of *Tops* hit the newsstands on October 10, 1981. "TOPS is tops for pop and TV!" the banner above the title screamed. There were ads on television for it, Adam Ant was on the cover and you got a set of flicker stickers free with every copy. Work instantly became more and more exciting. I got to interview pop stars, mostly on the phone. And I mean *the* phone. Harry the editor had his own on his desk, but the rest of us had to share the one communal phone that lived on the windowsill overlooking the Howff. We only were allowed to use it after 1:00 p.m., as long-distance calls were cheaper then. There was also a phone booth in the corridor (that we shared with all the magazines on our floor) where we could conduct interviews in a little more privacy, never forgetting to follow the protocol set out in the D. C. Thomson rulebook: "Speak quietly and say 'yes please'!"

Occasionally big bands would pass through Dundee and perform at the local concert venue, Caird Hall, and sometimes I was asked to go all the way to Edinburgh and see a show and even go backstage and interview the stars.

The first time I was sent on this odyssey I encountered a corporate blockade in the form of the D. C. Thomson driving test. I had recently passed my actual, real-life driving test in the nearby town of Arbroath, and although it had not been a total triumph—the instructor turned to me at its conclusion and said, "Awright, son, I'll let you off with it!"—I was still legally allowed to drive a car. However, Thomson's was a realm unto itself and my British driving licence meant nothing to them if I was to be entrusted to drive one of their company cars. So, I had to endure a Thomson's test. It went fairly well, I thought, until the Q and A portion, when I was asked if I could change a tyre. George Washington-like, I confessed I could not and thereby ruined my chances of automotive autonomy.

However, I hit upon the plan of bringing along my school friend Alan (he of the hairy chest, the older fiancée, and now car ownership) when I was sent to interview Mike Oldfield, the progressive rock/classical musician best known for the spooky *Tubular Bells*, which was used as the opening theme for the even spookier film *The Exorcist*. What must that poor man have thought, having just come offstage and having to sit opposite an awkward child asking him banal questions while his tall hairy friend circled them both, flashing away? (I should point out that hairy Alan is not nor ever has been a photographer.)

I was completely in awe of Toyah Willcox, who was a sort of early-eighties English Lady Gaga, and rather intimidated by Sal Solo, the shaved-headed lead singer of the New Romantics band Classix Nouveaux, who asked me back to his hotel room and had me interview him as he took a bath. Ever the professional cub reporter, I ignored what now seem the very clear signs, nay billboards, being flashed at me, and remained perched on the edge of the tub with my notepad and determinedly asked my questions. Sal, though, was the perfect gentleman. I was very happy and not entirely surprised to discover, during research for this book, that on a trip to the northern Italian town of San Damiano with his chum Nick from fellow eighties band Kajagoogoo, Sal found God and is now the music coordinator of a Catholic church in Florida.

But perhaps the greatest legacy of my time at D. C. Thomson is the substantial amount of photo story modelling I did for *Jackie*, *Blue Jeans*, and *Patches*. Photo stories were something of a phenomenon in those days. They were essentially comic strips with photographs instead of drawings and the lynchpin of many of the teen publications. Most of the models used were employees or friends of employees of D. C. Thomson, and as there were relatively few young male employees, I was in high demand, despite my childlike countenance. I was usually the other man, pining for my ex across the dance floor as she slow danced with her new beau.

I continued my photo modelling career even after I had left my publishing career behind, starring in my own vehicle called *Dance Yourself Dizzy!* for *Blue Jeans*, about a young man named Jim, obsessed with the *Kids from Fame* television show, who thought if he learned to dance like his hero, Leroy, his luck would change with the ladies. (Perhaps the fact that Jim was obsessed with Leroy was part of his problem.)

There was also a touching tale in *Jackie*'s 1984 annual edition in which I played a stable boy whose pony worked as matchmaker and found him the perfect girl.

Incidentally, whenever I am browsing around a British charity shop, I always take a close look at the book section to see if there are any

Jim was led a merry dance in his efforts to become a second Leroy!

Dance Yourself Dizzy!

straggler copies of this rather embarrassing tome so I can snatch them up to keep them from seeing the light of day. Of course, the nasty internet means that even though I have bought several well-eared copies and secreted them, my photo story modelling career is impossible to deny.

In the spring of 1982, I took a day off work and travelled to

Glasgow to audition for drama school. My mum came with me for moral support. I had to prepare two speeches, one classical, one modern. The modern was from an Irish play I had performed recently with the theatre club, *Lovers* by Brian Friel, and for my classical I chose the "Look here upon this picture" speech from the chamber scene, Act 3, Scene 4 of *Hamlet*. I could never have imagined that just eleven years later I would be playing Hamlet in London's West End.

I had no idea what to expect. I had never auditioned for a panel like this before. I had never been to Glasgow before! I had only recently discovered that there was such a thing as the Royal Scottish Academy of Music and Drama, where you could actually go and study acting. When I'd had to choose the subjects I wanted to do for my O-level exams, at the top of the form there was a space for intended profession. I put "actor or journalist". I remember in my meeting with the careers officer that nothing was said about the "actor" inclusion. All the helpful officer told me was to stick to my English classes. I did. And now I was, technically, a journalist. Tick.

But the fiancée of my hairy friend Alan was called Carolyn and she had gone to study drama at the Academy, so I wrote off for a prospectus and suddenly a whole new world of possibility opened up for me. (Also, not long after, Carolyn put her acting chops to good use when she played my love interest in the *Jackie* annual pony photo love story!)

I read and reread that prospectus like a spy who was about to go undercover, so on the day I finally walked through the Academy doors and was shown around by a lovely student named Margaret-Ann, the place felt almost familiar, like it was the place I was meant to be.

I had discovered I was quite good at it (acting, I mean) after doing a play in high school and it was the first time anyone, strangers, had told me I was any good at anything. And so I stuck with it. At first, I thought people were only complimenting me because I was able to do something they couldn't or would be too afraid to try—and I think the former is in some sense true. Some people just aren't very good at acting and never will be. I suppose they could get some help and become a little less bad, but why bother? It's obviously never going to be their thing, and, well, life's too short. Or put it this way: some people are double-jointed or can ride a unicycle, and some people can act.

But after that first school acting foray, I realised that my school friends and various parents and teachers weren't just giving me false flattery or some version of "I wish I could do that". There was something about *me* acting, and the way that I did, that they responded to. I could connect with them when I was onstage. I didn't really understand why at the time, and I suppose one of the reasons I carried on acting was to try to find out. All I knew was I could do something special and I'd never experienced anything like that before.

As I ran down the Academy steps after my audition, my mum was waiting for me. Although she didn't really understand what the course was about or even why I wanted to do it, she could tell that it meant a lot to me, and the very fact that she had come to Glasgow with me showed I had her full support. My father was another matter. The only reason I had been allowed to apply at all was because the drama programme offered a BA, in conjunction with Glasgow University, and those two letters seemed to dazzle my parents like rabbits in academic headlights, and somehow made the outrageous and dangerous idea of their son becoming an actor easier to bear. The phrase "something to fall back on" was oft used, though a degree in dramatic studies does have limited fallback potential.

I don't know what I would have done had I not been accepted for drama school. I didn't have a backup plan for the rest of my life. I suppose I could have stayed on at D. C. Thomson, as my journalism career was going rather well, and I liked it. But I liked acting more. There was something about the doing of it that made me feel *alive*—well, since we're all obviously alive, I suppose *more* alive, heightened, energised. I guess pretending to be someone else is both a way to show others who you are and at the same time not fully have to present your true self. It's a constant duality of utter truth and utter deceit, and for me that was and is completely thrilling and addictive. And addictive is quite apposite actually, because I'm struck by how in trying to describe what it feels like for me to act, I want to reference the tingling, the rush, the giddy point of no return that we all get from our respective drug of choice, be it cigarettes or cocaine, tequila or chocolate, coffee or sex. Acting has been like that for me since the very beginning, and it still is.

I was accepted. A letter was waiting for me from the Academy when I got home from work one evening a week or so later. And it wasn't just a letter of acceptance, it was an escape, a new life, a miracle.

I handed in my resignation and was immediately summoned to the managing editor's office. He was a former member of the RAF named Gordon Small who ruled the women's and teenage magazine department with a rod of steel. I was only ever sent to his office to show him the dummy copy of each issue of *Tops*. The fact that the youngest and lowest on the editorial ladder was sent to present the managing editor with the fruits of that week's labour before it was sent to press gives you some indication of how intimidating he was. I walked along that long corridor each week, the sheaf of pasted-up papers under my arm, like a man condemned. Next door was an office reserved for one of the actual Thomsons. There was a Thomson brother in the same office on every floor of Meadowside and in order to differentiate which one we were referring to, we had to call them by their first name, so ours was Mr. Brian, the spectre of whom really did frighten me. For D. C. Thomson was a very conservative institution: unions were banned, and the founding Thomson famously refused to employ Catholics. It wasn't until ten years after I left that the male and female layout artists were allowed to integrate.

"Alan, I hear you're intending to leave us to pursue acting," said Mr. Small, looking over the top of his half-frame glasses. I nodded meekly.

"Well, Alan, I would like to ask you to reconsider. We have been impressed with your progress here, and with continued hard work, I believe, in a few years, you might, *might* be able to become an assistant editor." He dangled this bait in front of me for a few silent seconds.

"What do you have to say to that, eh?"

I told him I was grateful, but my mind was made up.

A military man knows when to surrender and he duly did, wishing me well and thanking me for my service.

Young Alan signed off and said good-bye to the readers. On my last day we had a going-away party, appropriately in the bar of the Dundee Rep theatre. One of the *Tops* layout designers made a poster for this event, billing it as "Young Alan's Dramatic Departure" complete with quotes like "Puts the 'A' in Showbusiness—*The Standard*"! I still have this poster framed in my study.

At one point in the evening I came back from the loo to find everyone in my group holding up masks with my face on them. It was one of those discombobulating tributes that don't really make any sense but are utterly memorable and quite moving nonetheless.

I got drunk, I hugged everyone, and at the ripe old age of seventeen and a half I was a retired journalist about to embark on my second career.

lucky

6

Circle of Friends, it seemed, was going to be a hit. In America at least, and as we know, that's all most people—especially Americans—really care about.

So, in late February 1995, I was asked to be a part of the film's press junket and attend the premiere in Los Angeles. My first, fumbling visit to the City of Angels had been a mere eight months before, but in those intervening months I had stumbled into a completely different life, and, as the night must follow the day, I was a completely different person. Obviously, ending my marriage and then embracing the toxic tendrils of my childhood would foster some major change, but soon a kaleidoscope of magical, life-affirming events began to engulf me.

First of all, there had been the confrontation with my father. My brother, Tom, accompanied me on the odyssey to our childhood home and we supported each other through the terrifying, but ultimately liberating, encounter. As we drove away from the scene of our father's crimes, I felt something unusual and new in relation to him: superiority. I knew he could not possibly have done what my brother and I had that day. We had faced our worst fears. Our father could never do that. For all his machismo and swagger and intimidation, he was at his core a coward, deeply afraid of danger, pain, and, especially, honesty. So the walk we took together along the driveways of the country estate we had grown up in, while empowering for Tom and me, must have been excruciating for my father. There was nothing about the encounter he was well equipped for, least of all being comfortable let alone intimate with his children. It was literally my father's worst nightmare.

We had not merely faced our demon; we had also invited him to engage about *why* he might have behaved the way he had. In our hearts I don't think we really expected an answer. The act of standing up to him was empowering enough. I have feared nothing since. He never contacted me again after that day.

Remembering abuse means reliving it, but also simultaneously being thrown into a state of shock, and shock of two kinds—that this awful thing even happened to you, and also that you were incapable of acknowledging it for so long. I now understand I hid my memories away to protect myself. When I was unable to move forward in my life, my body spewed them all out.

Afterwards, my brother dropped me off at Edinburgh airport. We hugged a long, exhausted but elated good-bye. Then, when I landed at Heathrow, another catalyst for my newfound happiness was waiting. Even though it was very early days in our relationship, she had insisted on coming to collect me when I'd told her the purpose of my visit. I cried in her arms, and in her bed that night. On the same day I had stood up to my father, returned to the place I'd experienced the most traumatising moments of my life, I also opened myself up completely to someone new.

We met on Easter Sunday 1994, the day I arrived in Ireland to work on *Circle of Friends*, and stayed friends after the film wrapped until one day, many months later, we weren't just friends any more. It's not unusual, indeed it's pretty cliché, for a man who has recently departed a marriage to quickly fall into an intense relationship with a much younger woman. But what was unusual, at least for me, was a relationship of any kind in which the other wanted or needed nothing from me aside from my presence. For so long I felt it incumbent to change, originally self-induced to ensure I would please and conform, but latterly to make sense of the havoc I was causing to those around me. Now this newborn version of myself was allowed to bloom; she did not want to change me. That night I returned from Scotland was the beginning of her leading me out of my darkness, showing me I could love and be loved again.

A quarter of a century on, we both know we can pick up the phone at any time, day or night, and we will be there for each other. And is there a more successful marker of a relationship than to know you will always be present, and matter, in another's life?

———

By the time I boarded the plane for my first Hollywood junket and premiere—another Virgin Atlantic flight that mercifully charted an uneventful course to LA—I was completely and utterly in love. But it was not only my personal life that was unrecognisable from my first American foray. My working life was completely transformed, too.

I was in the middle of shooting the James Bond film *Goldeneye*, in which I was playing a really fun baddie, a Russian computer geek named Boris Grishenko, whose catchphrase "I am invincible" or to be precise "I em ecnVEENceebul!" is still regularly shouted at me to this day.

I had auditioned for the part the summer before on one of the darkest days in my personal fog. The day, in fact, when the shadow of suicide had entered my mental periphery. I was probably in the room about half an hour, chatting with the director, Martin Campbell, and one of the producers, Barbara Broccoli, but my feigning of enthusiasm, lucidity, and, especially, emotional balance in those thirty minutes may rank as one of my greatest performances ever. The fact that I didn't want to let anyone down by postponing or cancelling the meeting says a lot about how little I valued myself at the time. Before, immediately afterwards, and, indeed, during, I was a zombie. After I left the meeting on Piccadilly, I wandered aimlessly for hours, and to this day, I don't recall what I did that afternoon, or how I got home. It's the only time in my life that I've had what amounts to a sober blackout.

But I got the part. I was now involved in the longest-running film franchise in movie history, and not only that, a franchise attempting to reinvent itself in a post-Cold War era. In the six years since the previous film, *License to Kill*, the Berlin Wall had fallen and the Soviet Union collapsed, and in addition, the Bond movies' inherent sexism and imperialism—which had perhaps outstayed their welcome due to an affectionate nostalgia for Ian Fleming's original books and the earlier films—now seemed way out of sync with the prevailing cultural attitudes. What *Goldeneye* did was to embrace all those issues head-on, with Judi Dench playing a female M, Bond's boss, calling 007 a "sexist, misogynist dinosaur" and a "relic of the Cold War". The other female characters were no longer just Bond girl arm candy but Bond's partners and equals, and I joked that my character represented for the first time the existence of a Bond *boy*. It was incredibly exciting, more than a little overwhelming—especially as I shot on the very first day of production and had to learn a trick of absentmindedly manoeuvring an explosive pen around my fingers, which was the whole crux of the movie's last reel. I am not the most coordinated person in the world and the enormity of this task gave me actual nightmares before I buckled down and engaged the help of my old friend Jason Isaacs, who taught me how to do it with the precision and calmness of the magician he could so easily have become had the whole acting thing not taken off for him.

Unbeknownst to me at the time, of course, I would become part of video game history, too, when Nintendo released the *Goldeneye 007* game a few years later. I found out about the game's existence when I was at a friend's house and their young son shyly pointed at me and said, "I always choose to be you!" I thought perhaps this was another American idiom I didn't understand, but he was being literal, and later he gave me the great honour of letting me play myself(?!) when my curiosity got the better of me and I asked him to show me the game. The next day I spoke to my assistant at the time, Landon, and told him, very excitedly, that I was in a video game.

"Oh, I know. I own it," he deadpanned. "If you piss me off, I go home and shoot you in the balls!"

The High Life, the sitcom I wrote and starred in with my drama school chum Forbes Masson, had premiered on the BBC a month before *Circle of Friends* was to be released and immediately became a bit of a cult classic, especially in my homeland of Scotland. However, writing and starring in a show about flight attendants changed air travel for me for many years afterwards. Often as I walked down a jetway I would be greeted with the salutation "Fat bum!" by the staff welcoming passengers on board, echoing our characters' lines in the show. I also learned to be stealthy with my in-flight bathroom visits, as those were the occasions, due to the crew galley proximity, that I'd most likely be cornered and teased, offered new plot lines for future episodes, and best of all, told that the show was an incredibly realistic and a true-to-life depiction of life aboard the Scotland-to-London air shuttle service. Please bear in mind that the exploits we got up to on *The High Life* included removing senior citizens' false teeth, freezing them, microwaving them, and reinserting the steaming gnashers into said seniors' mouths using tongs; and getting mixed up in the kidnapping of a Scottish professor who had discovered the perfect ratio of sugar to condensed milk in tablet, the beloved Scottish snack, by a biscuit mogul whose henchman had left a floppy disk with the much-vaunted formula in one of our airplane's seatback pockets. Or an onboard hijack attempt by the (nonexistent) Scottish Liberation Front, in which a Scottish laird's freshly caught salmon is used as a weapon to quell the hijacker—all captured by a film crew headed by a lecherous director shooting the airline's next in-flight video. And don't even get me started on the episode in which we enter the *Song for Europe* competition. Verité it was not!

While I was away in LA, a BBC film I had made at the end of the previous year, *The Chemistry Lesson*, would air. It was written and directed by the playwright Terry Johnson, and I starred opposite Samantha Bond (who was also making her debut as Moneypenny in *Goldeneye*). I played a chemistry teacher whose unrequited love for a fellow teacher makes him enlist the white witch skills of one of his students to help things along. What could possibly go wrong?! The original script had lots of sex—with Samantha and me getting it on in a taxi, in the school photocopier room, anywhere we could, really—and I could hardly believe the BBC would produce something so explicit. Well, I was right to be sceptical, as come the broadcast, most of the sex had been cut. It was the first time, but alas not my last, of feeling annoyed at having got naked, done all the embarrassing and vulnerable sex stuff on camera, only to have it taken out of the final product. Once you've gone to the bother of shooting those scenes, it's the ultimate coitus interruptus (both artistic and personal) to have them cut, let me tell you. There was one full frontal moment left in, when I darted out naked from behind a standing stone carrying my own poop (it was one of the ingredients for the spell, why do you ask?), which was shot on a freezing November night. I was aided in my quest to look vaguely normal in the underpants department by a hot water bottle pressed against my man parts until the very last second, when action was called, and I emerged from behind the stone. The stand-ing stones, incidentally, were fake, and I kept one as a memento in the attic of my flat until I came to my senses and questioned what I'd ever actually do with a Styrofoam rock so left it behind when I moved out. I sometimes wonder if it's still there.

I'd also recently filmed a Dickensian spoof for Comic Relief. *Oliver 2: Let's Twist Again* was written by the great Richard Curtis, who had recently had a huge success with *Four Weddings and a Funeral* and would later write and direct *Love, Actually.* Previously he had written *Bernard and the Genie*, a Christmas film for the BBC in which I starred with Rowan Atkinson and Lenny Henry, who with Richard was a founder of Comic Relief.

On the last day of filming at Pinewood Studios in February 1995, I was acting opposite the late, great Oliver Reed, he of the naked wrestling in *Women in Love* and the hard-drinking, hell-raising reputation during the heady days of the British New Wave. In the week of filming I'd sparred with a cornucopia of rather intimidating British acting heavyweights, among them Jeremy Irons and Diana Rigg. The part of Fagin was played by Ron Moody, who'd played the same role in the 1968 musical film adaptation, *Oliver!* But none were

more intimidating, or drunk, and therefore unpredictable and a little scary than Oliver Reed, who, in this Dickensian mash-up, played a sort of Magwitch character—the convict on the lam from *Great Expectations* who later becomes Pip's anonymous benefactor. Here we are modelling the regulation face wear on Red Nose Day.

Oliver's tenuous grasp on the lines was all the more anxiety-inducing as I was itching to be finished early that night so I could attend the royal premiere of *Black Beauty*. As soon as we wrapped, I bade Oliver farewell, jumped in a car, and sped to the West End, hopping out to run the last few blocks to avoid the perils of the one-way system and the huge crowds that had gathered around Leicester Square. I didn't want to be late for my first royal premiere, after all.

But there was something else that propelled me through the streets so quickly that night, or someone else: my new love was waiting for me outside the cinema, and I had our tickets. I could hear her on the end of my nearly as new mobile phone, jammed to my ear, as she tried to reason with a police officer who was asking her to move along.

"But you have to let me in," she said imploringly. "My boy-friend's the horse!"

I arrived in LA and was driven to the Four Seasons hotel, where, as soon as I discovered everything was paid for by the studio, I began to decant the array of snacks in the minibar into my suitcase. This was my first of many junkets and promotional trips paid for by studios, but I couldn't know that then. Then, I was like the little shepherd girl Heidi, who, when she was taken from the Alps to live in splendour in the big city, would steal a bread roll from the dinner table every night and hide it in her wardrobe, a gift for her beloved grandfather back in the mountains. I was stashing jars of cashew nuts and chocolate almonds so they would be there for me when this week of opulence was over and I was dispatched back to my normal life in rainy London.

I was joined on the junket by my *Circle of Friends* co-stars Chris O'Donnell and Minnie Driver, and the director, Pat O'Connor. There was great excitement in the air: the film was "tracking well" and I was receiving accolades for my excess of onscreen sliminess. But I quickly discovered that junkets, as exciting and glamorous as they may appear from the outside, are profoundly dull experiences. This is due to several factors. First is that the interviews last an absolute maximum of five minutes, and the journalist has a minute or so on either side to enter the hotel room, sit opposite you, say hello, get miked, and then say good-bye, get de-miked, and make their way to the next hotel room to do the same thing all over again with the next actor. That way you can do dozens and dozens and dozens of these interviews a day. And second, because of the time constraints involved, the dozens and dozens of interviews tend to be inherently superficial and banal in tone and worse, utterly repetitive. You are almost certainly asked exactly the same questions in every single one. And that is not hyperbole. It is actually mind-numbingly, maddeningly boring.

Occasionally there were respites, and I'd go to one of the hotel meeting rooms to do "roundtables", where print journalists were sitting round, yes, tables, and their Dictaphones (remember, this was 1995!) were placed in a mound in front of the empty place meant for me. Those interviews were a little more fun as there were more people to engage with and the reporters were writing articles for newspapers and magazines, rather than creating TV sound bites. The possibility of getting a question you hadn't answered forty times already that day was marginally higher. But only marginally.

At one point on the second day of the junket, I was taken down to a larger room where I was told I was to be interviewed by the Hollywood Foreign Press Association. This was a collection of journalists based in Hollywood who wrote for publications around the globe. I was told that the people I was about to be interviewed by also ran the Golden Globe Awards and my blank expression at this information led to me being quickly made aware of how big a deal this actually was. The door was opened for me and I walked in, took one look at the assembled gathering, turned on my heel, and walked out again. The gaggle of publicists and minders assigned to me were understandably a little shocked to see me back in the lobby mere seconds after I had left them.

"Alan, what are you doing?" asked one.

"It's not the right room," I replied. "That's some sort of lunch for senior citizens, it's not the Hollywood foreign—"

Before I could even finish the sentence, the gaggle began shrieking with laughter. It had long been an industry joke that the HFPA members were aged and, in some cases, not even compos mentis, but I didn't know this. I was just calling a spade a spade. I had seen a room full of tables of elderly people eating and chatting and genuinely thought I had walked into a seniors' gathering, or perhaps a tour group from the American equivalent of Saga Holidays. Never in a million years did I imagine that ocean of white hair, that array of hunched, munching figures, the sheer abundance of visors, could possibly be the collection of international entertainment journalists I had expected, let alone the group that controlled the outcome of the second-largest showbiz awards ceremony on the planet—and which often influenced the outcome of the first.

So just as my reaction to what I thought I'd seen had many resonances, the shrieks I was surrounded by were multilayered, too— hilarity mingled with horror, and a sliver of terror. My naïveté was funny, my honesty was horribly accurate, but my action could also be perceived as horribly rude and possibly ruin my or the film's chances of future gongs. I was quickly told this was indeed the right room and pushed back in.

Had I not been disabused of my theory, nothing that happened in the next half hour would have changed my opinion. The questions were idiosyncratic to say the least: my opinion of the Irish Republican Army was solicited, for example, which I felt was the equivalent of asking someone who shot a film in California today what they thought of the Black Panthers. Often the same question would be asked by a different senior, sometimes immediately after I'd finished answering the question the first time. On more than one occasion I began my responses with "Well, as I just said . . ." and I had to speak through a constant drone of very loud bickering, clinking of tableware, and the occasional piercing, high-pitched whine of an errant hearing aid. It was like a raucous children's birthday party set in a rest home. But actually its oddness and utter lack of polish made me feel strangely comfortable next to the sea of slickness that oozed from LA's pores.

Alas, before too long the criticism—that elderly members clung on to their memberships years after they had penned their final article for some magazine you'd never heard of from somewhere you'd never been, solely to retain their access to movie stars—to say nothing of the free food and swag plied by canny studio marketing departments—began to stick, and the group's demographics have begun to skew younger and a little less eccentric, and more recently has begun to address its shocking lack of diversity in terms of people of colour.

The Monday after the junket weekend was the film's premiere. I had never done a red carpet, sadly having missed the event for *Black Beauty* in London, and so I was a little intimidated. Of course, they're not brain surgery: you just walk along a carpet (usually indeed red), get photographed a lot, and then get filmed speaking to people who are separated from you by a velvet rope. It's sort of like the line for a club you're trying to get into, with lots of bouncers and doormen who are incredibly chatty and nosy. The publicist from the film whispered to me who and where each new person was from, but it didn't really matter as I didn't know any of them, and I was game to talk to anyone. That was what I was there for, after all.

After one fun interview I was asked to do an "ident"—which is basically a free commercial for their channel. You've seen them, maybe you've even seen me do them. "Hello, I'm Alan Cumming and you're watching blah on the blah blah channel." That night it felt fun and an honour. Now it feels a bit cheesy and exploitative, and someone usually dives into the frame and tells the journalist I can't do it when I'm asked. All was going smoothly until the lady who had interviewed me told me what she'd like me to say to the camera, which was "I'm Alan Cumming and I'm on E!," which of course referred to E! Entertainment Television, the network dedicated unapologetically to showbiz gossip and which, in later years, spawned the Kardashian Kronikles. However, I had never heard of this channel, and for me, being "on E" meant having imbibed an Ecstasy pill and being totally off my tits. Suddenly my Hollywood idyll of kind, smiley people genuinely interested in me and what I thought turned into a scene of ensnarement where I confessed to being on Class A drugs on national television.

"What? I can't say that," I gasped at the request.

"Why not?" both the reporter and the publicist retorted, hoping this bright-eyed and bushy-tailed Scottish newbie was not turning into a demanding diva before their very eyes.

"Seriously? You want me to say I'm on E?" I spluttered.

"Yes!"

"I can't do that! First of all, I'm not, and also my mum might see this!"

When I was informed that no, they did not think I was high and only wanted me to endorse their television channel, I calmed down and did it, though I was still a little suspicious.

I returned to London, my suitcase bulging with minibar swag, feeling very differently about the city than I had after my first trip. Indeed, because of those few halcyon days on my first junket, the City of Angels has always been my city equivalent of heroin. You know the trope that every heroin user is always trying to re-create the bliss of their first hit? Well, I've always been chasing the feelings about Los Angeles that I had after that second trip. Of course, as with heroin (I can only speculate, as I have never taken it, though if I live to be eighty, I have pledged to try it), the newness and the adventure of my first true Hollywood immersion has never been fully re-created. I have had many amazing times there, but never the same as that week, when I felt like I was in a movie version of my life, the movie with the happy ending, where the guy gets the girl and his life falls into place.

Sometimes I'm asked, especially by acting students, what it was like as a struggling actor. I tell it like it is. I have never struggled as an actor. I've never been out of work. Before I'd even left drama school, I had made my professional television, theatre, and film debuts. My first job in London was a show in the West End. My first job in New York was starring in a Broadway musical, and my first job in Hollywood was as one of the leads in a studio picture.

I am lucky, and I know it. My father knew it, too. He used to say that if I fell out of a window, I'd fall up. He made it sound like another of my failings.

Luck is only the fickle confluence of chance and positivity, but it can radically alter your circumstances. So, looking at it another way, circumstances are just a structure that enables luck to happen. So yes, I am lucky, but I've also made my own circumstances, and always strived to change them when I didn't feel so lucky any more.

domesticity

7

It was the summer of 1995 that I discovered I loved yellow.

I had bought a flat in Islington, my first ever home alone, and had every wall painted a beautiful golden yellow that transformed magically each day as the sun moved west across the London sky.

I was thirty years old and for the first time I had to consider my own taste. It seemed I had left all that to others until then, perhaps another holdover symptom of the need for absence and neutrality around my father as a child, never daring to take up space with an opinion, especially one so dangerous as a colour preference.

Unlike my school friends, my brother and I were forbidden to put up anything on the walls of our large, spartan bedroom. Expression of personality was deemed much less important than the risk of wallpaper soiled by tape marks in my father's house. And he was definitely *not* a yellow man.

The much-prized Farrah Fawcett red swimsuit poster that I had acquired by collecting tokens from a tabloid newspaper that one day would turn its prurient gaze on me was not brandished above my adolescent bed but secreted in a drawer. But although the constancy of Farrah's gaze was forbidden to stare down at me, my father's authoritarianism inadvertently gave me a lesson in sexuality: being in control of when you choose to experience something can sometimes be better than it being available to you all the time.

In adulthood, in my marriage, I continued this pattern of abstention. In those days any particular fondness for my surroundings I allowed to be subsumed into my wife's predilections.

I now love to be surrounded by brightness, happiness, and positivity, and by objects that reflect the experience I have gained, so it's not hard to imagine that my youthful psyche might have suppressed this aesthetic—which indeed many have described as childlike—and deemed it too risky, too subversive. Up and away it went, packed deep inside the box in my mental attic, to await the day my circumstances would have altered so radically that I would need to voice these opinions, make these decisions—and when this eventually happened, in the summer of 1995, I did so on a completely gut level, and yellow, long suppressed within my colour matrix, suddenly burst out onto every vertical surface I encountered.

For the first time, my flat was a true nest, because all the metaphorical twigs and feathers I decided to surround myself with were chosen by me. And the concept of home was made more urgent by the fact that my work began to take me farther away and more often. Travelling so much made me appreciate the idea of having somewhere to return to, a centre, somewhere that was me and was mine. For the first time in my life I was happy closing the front door and being alone. For the first time in my life I was happy with myself.

Of course, I also had the benefit of being in love. And for the first time in my life, it was a love untainted by my past. I was living anew and so I loved anew, with ferocity and passion. I'd never experienced love like this, but I also knew how fickle it could be. It was also a love of great compulsion and sexual chemistry. Several times during our two years together she and I were admonished for being too physical in public, once even over the loudspeaker of Palm Springs airport. But this adolescent lustiness is not surprising when you consider I was basically starting my life over, reconnecting with myself after the revelation that I had been living as the construct of other people—a father whose fury froze any growth that was not palatable to or controlled by him, and a wife whom I similarly—tacitly—allowed to control me, because that felt comfortable. Now I found myself open and free in a way that I hadn't ever before, and although I never felt denied, perhaps my very obliviousness for so long of this jangling, intoxicating, and, yes, dangerous vitality made me dive into life with this woman all the more deeply and urgently.

If it all sounds like a recipe for disaster, it of course was. But what a beautiful disaster, a natural disaster that quickly realigned into something else equally beautiful but far calmer.

Soon after I moved into my flat, I left for Dorset to begin filming the feature film *Emma*, in which I played Mr. Elton, the vicar, who had the hots for Gwyneth Paltrow's titular heroine. I spent my summer dashing up and down to London from various country homes and quaint locales across the south of England, thoroughly enjoying my time and making some new friends, like Toni Colette, who on the first day we shot together told me she had never had a martini. I saw it as a personal challenge that this lack must be filled at once, and so we had a very boozy dinner that culminated in me stealing a butter dish from the dining room of the hotel where we had eaten. I returned to London with a woolly head but no cares in the world, until a couple of days later when Toni called me in utter panic with the news that the owner of that hotel was indeed a collector of antique butter dishes, and the one I had swiped was no common or garden-variety butter dish used by the staff to distribute Dorset's plenty, but part of his prized collection! And worse, he was so angry at my drunken pilferage he was threatening to evict Gwyneth and her then beau Brad Pitt, who were staying at that hotel! I couldn't believe my martini-induced moment of hotel crockery redistribution could lead to the sexiest man alive (according to that year's *People* magazine) and his lady love being ousted from their love nest! Tragedy was averted after I called the hotel where I'd been staying, and after a thorough search of my room the offending—and offended—butter dish was discovered at the back of the wardrobe. (Where else would you stash butter dishes you drunkenly discover in your pockets as you undress?) The precious item was returned, I wrote a very remorseful letter of apology, and Brad and Gwyneth's tenure remained unbroken.

I also remember the day in early October when at wrap we all huddled around a portable radio in the dining tent and, like the rest of the world, gasped as the verdict of the O. J. Simpson trial was announced. Though unlike the rest of the world, we were dressed in our fine Regency attire.

Another indignity that occurred around *Emma* and one that I brought upon myself had to do with my hair. I had, and still have actually, a ritual I think is hilarious whenever I sit in the makeup chair for the first time to discuss the look of a new character. When the hair and makeup people politely ask if I have any ideas or suggestions I always reply, "Oh, you know, just a natural look: blush, blue eye shadow, orange lips," or "I think I'd like to go blond and have a perm."

This time, though, my bluff was called when the hair designer said to me, "Well, we were actually thinking of a light curl and taking you down a tone or two!"

My hair at the time, as it is often, was long on top and cropped at the back and sides. The stylists dyed the top part red, gave it one of those perms that go acceptably wavy if you blow-dry and tease it; but if, like me, you don't own a hair dryer and are a wash-'n'-go kind of guy, then you find your locks, on exiting the shower, transform into tight old lady curls that have an uncanny resemblance to pubes. And in my case, ginger pubes.

Please note I have nothing against gingers, or ginger pubes. Far from it, actually. I just don't want them on my head.

They then stuck matching red curly hairpieces to the sides and back of my head using little springs that were supposed to clamp onto what little hair I had in those areas but instead just gripped my flesh very painfully, making me appear slightly startled at all times if I didn't concentrate not to be. I am a martyr in that movie. Every facial movement evoked a myriad of pinpricks to my temples.

In November I was back in London for the royal premiere of *Goldeneye*. It was the biggest, most glamorously showbizzy event I'd ever encountered. And also, it being a royal premiere due to the presence of Prince Charles, there was an added level of excitement and drama. How that manifested itself to me was a couple of faxed pages of very detailed royal etiquette. Like some how-to dance manual, there was an elabourate description of the precise method ladies should employ when curtsying to Prince Charles, and also the correct way men should bow. The exact language was "men should bow from the neck forwards", which struck me as rather strange because have you ever tried to bow from the neck backwards?!

The fax went on to detail the correct verbiage needed to address the prince ("Your Royal Highness" at first, and from then on, "Sir").

Like many people I have a complicated relationship with the notion of royalty. I believe we all deserve the same respect and opportunities. Kindness and compassion are the traits I believe should be vaunted most in our society. The idea that someone must be treated more reverentially than anyone else because of their ancestry and birth line, or indeed wealth, is anathema to everything I stand for. I treat everyone equally until they do something that, in my opinion, merits less of my respect and tolerance. So, bowing, actually making myself lower and subservient to someone else, and then literally placing them on a pedestal by referring to them as "highness" is just never going to be part of my human engagement lexicon.

Of course, the British royal family no longer has any political power. They are effectively civil servants, paid for by the public's taxes to be a living tourist attraction—a constant, archaic construct so comforting to the people who pay for its services that it is allowed to rumble on relatively unhindered. Even the odd constitutional wobble (Diana, Megxit) only brings more press, more attention, and more commerce. Its demise would be too disruptive for the nation's psyche, but also, we need the cash they bring in. All the ritual—the weekly audience the prime minister has with the queen, Black Rod banging on the Commons door at the Opening of Parliament, the Changing of the Guard—is aristocratic showbiz that sells tea towels and coffee mugs and keeps our tourist industry stable.

When I was offered an OBE (Officer of the British Empire) in the Queen's Honours List of 2009, I did initially worry if I was being hypocritical in accepting it. Perhaps, especially as a Scotsman, I bristle at the inherent class connotations the royal family embodies. But I do understand its value—especially in times of crisis—as an arbiter of public morality, and I admire some of the sociopolitical stances some of its members have taken. But although the OBE is officially an honour from the queen, I was under no illusion that Elizabeth herself had sat up in bed with a cup of cocoa and bounced ideas off Prince Philip before finally plumping on me. The list is instead made up by government representatives, and is reflective of the government's attitudes. So when I was told my citation was not just for my work but also for "activism for equal rights for the gay and lesbian community", I felt the OBE was not just a pat on the back, but an opportunity to show how such activism is valued and also to shame those who stood in its way.

This is the statement I made at the time:

> I am really shocked and delighted to receive this honour. I am especially happy to be honoured for my activism as much as for my work.
>
> The fight for equality for the LGBT community in the US is something I am very passionate about, and I see this honour as encouragement to go on fighting for what I believe is right and for what I take for granted as a UK citizen. Thank you to the Queen and those who make up her Birthday honours list for bringing attention to the inaction of the US government on this issue. It makes me very proud to be British, and galvanised as an American.

All that was a very long-winded way of saying I was not going to be doing any bowing or scraping to Prince Charles at the *Goldeneye* premiere. I didn't even wear the requisite black tie, opting instead for a red velvet Mao suit made for me by the Scottish designer Lex McFadyen. When eventually it was my turn to be greeted by the prince, I stuck out my hand and said, "Hello, I'm Alan!"

I was next to Judi Dench in the lineup. And as we waited for Charles to reach our place in line, we were whispering like naughty children.

"I'm not going to bow, are you?" I asked.

"I'm a dame," said Judi. "I rather have to bow."

Then I told her about the fax and how funny I thought it was about bowing from the neck forward. She too found this hilarious and we both attempted to bow from the neck back, which, of course, involves jerking your head backwards as though you're trying to swallow a very big pill. We were caught on camera by one of the news channels covering the event, giggling and doing our weird spasmodic dance, and it was the source of several calls from bewildered friends the next morning.

I remember being backstage waiting to be announced before the film started and discovering I was sandwiched in between Judi and Tina Turner, who had sung the movie's theme song, also titled *Goldeneye*, written by U2's Bono and the Edge. I was very starstruck by Tina and all I could think to say to her was that I liked the colour of her toenail varnish.

"Oh, you noticed!" she said, delighted. "I've got golden toes," she said, and then batted her eyes to allow me to see the colour of her eye shadow, "and golden eyes!"

The party was incredible. My brother and I were entranced by the 007 ice sculpture into which you could stick your head and have vodka slide down an icy tunnel into your mouth! At one point I looked over and saw my mum in a little huddle with two other women. They were all clutching plates they'd just filled from the buffet, complete with those funny little clips attached to them to hold your wineglass. What made me stop in my tracks was that the women my little mum was chatting to were Judi Dench and Tina Turner! It just didn't compute.

But then, they were all women of around the same age, they were all at the same party, and it made total sense they had found each other.

Actually, that party was a turning point for my mum. It was by far the biggest event she had joined me for, and prior to this, although I knew she was proud to be with me at these kinds of evenings, I could tell their unfamiliar glamour slightly scared her. I worried she felt out of place. In a way I thought she enjoyed them more in retrospect, telling her friends about them from the safety of her own domain. That night, that moment even, as she sipped her wine and shot the breeze with Judi and Tina, marked a change in my mum's confidence. It was as though she realised she too had a rightful place at the table at these sorts of events, and before long she looked forward to them. Our self-worth has grown concurrently, and now I can take her to the swankiest of showbiz bashes and she just takes off and works the room, charming one and all, making friends and meeting up with old pals, happy in the knowledge that she completely belongs and being the darling that she is.

Shortly after *Emma* wrapped, I went to LA for another slew of meetings with casting people and studio execs that is the rite of passage for anyone who is fresh blood in the Hollywood meat market. Most of these encounters have blended into a blur of smiling, manically studying *The Thomas Guide* to Los Angeles *while* driving (this was way before Google Maps), reading snatches of the next script I was going to discuss or audition for at every stoplight, laughing every time a receptionist behind a desk asked me if I needed validation (who doesn't?), and sometimes actually crying in frustration and despair as I wandered up and down level upon level of massive underground garages vainly pressing my car's key fob because I'd forgotten to take note of where I had parked, and all the cars looked the same. "Welcome to LA," my friends said, laughing when I shared my tales of woe.

One meeting I do remember particularly well. I was due to meet a studio bigwig who was obviously running late, and so I was palmed off to an underling who turned out to be really nice. We had a lovely chat.

Suddenly the door burst open and bigwig came in, barely acknowledging me as she snatched my CV from the underling and began to scour it.

"Alan was just telling me he recently played Hamlet," said the underling kindly, a little embarrassed at her boss's brusqueness.

"Hamlet?" said bigwig, suddenly interested. "Kenneth Branagh's *Hamlet?*" referring to the movie version that was soon to be released and was, as we say in Scotland, the talk of the steamie. Side note: she also pronounced Branagh as Bran-AH.

"No," I replied gamely, and with a little bit of biting wit added, "Alan Cumming's *Hamlet!*"

Crickets.

"What else have you been doing?" she said, wearying of me already.

"Well," I began—I'd been doing a lot of these meetings and was by now surrounded by an invisible force field that made me impervious to the vagaries of bored (and boring) studio execs.

"I've just finished shooting a movie of Jane Austen's *Emma*. I played Mr. Elton, who is in love with Emma, but she thinks he is in love with Harri—"

Before I could even get to the last syllable of "Harriet", bigwig, without looking up, said, "Yeah, yeah, I know the plot. I saw *Clueless.*"

That was the beginning of my thinking, *LA is not going to be my town after all*. I love visiting and I have many dear friends who I love seeing there, but I admit to harbouring an ambivalence about the city—though it's more about its being a work town than any actual animosity for the place itself. I just think it's unhealthy to live somewhere where everyone works in the same industry. I have always equated living in Los Angeles with living in Hershey, Pennsylvania, a town created purely to manufacture the famous chocolate bars, just as LA was constructed to churn out movies. I imagine the conversation in Hershey is dominated by chocolate, just as chat in LA is about showbiz.

It is more than just a cliché that every Uber driver in LA has written a screenplay they'd like you to read, or that every bartender is a budding actor. One Sunday many years ago, I was at lunch in a restaurant there when the server turned to me to take my order and said, "Congratulations, Alan!"

Like Martha Stewart when she was questioned about her insider trading scandal during a TV cooking spot, I just wanted to focus on my salad.

"What for?" I mumbled, rather sideswiped.

"Your new movie made twenty-five million dollars at the box office this weekend!"

What shocked me most about this statement was that if I didn't know (or care) how much the film in question had made in its opening, how and why did my waiter?

Another time I was having lunch with a director I had worked with and our server complimented me on my performance in the movie we'd made together.

"Oh, you liked that film? Well, guess what? This man I'm having lunch with is its director!" I said, lobbing the love over the table to my friend.

"You're a director?" our young cinephile gasped.

"Yes," said my chum, rather shyly.

"That's amazing! Our bus boy is a director!"

One of the first scripts I read when I started my Hollywood dog-and-pony show was Robin Schiff's *Romy and Michele's High School Reunion*, which stood head and shoulders above the rest of what I was being sent in terms of its wit and idiosyncrasy. Even the description of the character Sandy Frink—the lovelorn geek who returns triumphant to the reunion in his helicopter having made a fortune inventing a kind of rubber used in every tennis shoe in North America—made me want to play him, and when I discovered there would also be a dream sequence in which he would appear with a new face, I was totally sold! That, coupled with the overall message of the film, that the geeks will inherit the earth, made me want this part very badly.

Landing the role was not easy, however. I had many, many

auditions and meetings, going higher and higher up the Disney hierarchy with each one. Eventually, at the eleventh hour, as I was poised to be offered what would be a huge coup for me and my career, I was slapped down in the most brutal way.

"They want you to be cuter, honey," my agent told me. *Ouch.* So in I went one more time and gave them a total onslaught of cute, and the role was mine!

I still can't actually believe I was cast. Aside from Hal Carter (a young vagabond) at drama school, and the paper boy Blanche Dubois kisses in *A Streetcar Named Desire* at the Royal Lyceum in Edinburgh ten years prior, I had never even played an American, and certainly not one who was effectively the leading man in a Hollywood movie!

One day during filming as we were sitting around between takes I had an epiphany, and turned to Robin and said, "I'm the girl in this film, aren't I?"

She looked at me for a moment and I could tell she got what I meant.

"Yes, Alan, I suppose you are!"

In most Hollywood films, then as now, it is extremely rare for the two leading roles to be women. It was more likely to be two men, with a woman serving as the side character who comes in and out of the story but who supplies the happy ending (sometimes literally) with one of them in the final reel. That is exactly the role, in both senses, I played in *Romy and Michele*. And, when you consider I was nearly turned down for it because an executive (who was a man) needed me to be cuter, I think I also got a little taste of what women in Hollywood are subjected to day in and day out.

The two leads were, of course, Mira Sorvino and Lisa Kudrow. Both of them came to the movie on the crest of big career waves: Mira had recently won the Oscar for her hilarious turn in Woody Allen's *Mighty Aphrodite*, Lisa was fresh from the incredible success of the first season of *Friends*. And it was fascinating to see their different approaches and indeed comfort levels with the material and tone of the film: Mira approaching from a more Method acting perspective, Lisa more versed in improv and sketch comedy.

One of my favourite memories during that time was when Lisa invited me to join her onstage for an evening at the Groundlings, the improv school and theatre she had attended on Melrose Avenue. I think, had I known what was in store, I would have run a mile, because I had no real background in improvisation as performance. But that night was a baptism by fire, with the audience shouting out ideas for plot and character that the other actors and I would immediately have to inhabit. The second half was an entire improvised play! What I learned most from the experience was that improv is not only about brilliant, quick performances but more about brilliant, quick minds. And I don't think there is a more brilliant, quick mind than Lisa's. We worked together again in *Web Therapy* about ten years later, a show—first online and then on television—that was improvised around a written structure, which I found more suited to my strengths. But I will be forever grateful to her for giving me that shot in the arm at the Groundlings. I look back on that night as a seminal episode in the journey to my being confident enough to do my own concert and cabaret shows today.

In the recent tradition in my life of Hollywood calling and dictating where I would be—or in this case remain— in the world, on the same day that the offer for *Romy and Michele* finally came through, I also was offered another movie that Columbia, Jim Henson Pictures, and American Zoetrope were producing together. Talk about a Hollywood trifecta!

My new friend and *Black Beauty* director Caroline Thompson had written and was set to direct *Buddy*, based on the true story of an eccentric 1930s Long Island socialite, Trudy Lintz, who kept a veritable menagerie and eventually reared a baby gorilla as her own child. Rene Russo was set to play Trudy, and Caroline asked me to play her assistant, Dick, which would mean working with a variety of animals, including a quartet of chimpanzees.

I was a little trepidatious about this, for I didn't have a good track record when it came to working with animals. The summer before, I had shot a short film, *Bathtime*, in which I played a man who was in love with his goldfish, and Julie Walters played his amorous neighbour. One of the scenes involved me running through the house, naked, with my beloved goldfish—who was named Diana—flapping in my cupped hands, lit only by shafts of lightning coming through the windows. There was a goldfish minder on set whose job it was to place Diana into my hands, then run behind the set to manage the waiting bucket of water into which I had to fling her once I had rounded the corner and was off camera.

I was very anxious about this scene. Any embarrassment about my nudity was obfuscated by my utter concern for Diana's well-being and my spiralling anxiety about how good my aim was in getting her safely into the bucket of water as soon as I had careened around the corner of the set. On the last take, I think the confluence of all these

concerns resulted in my throwing Diana a little too vigorously. There was a dull thudding sound as she hit the side of the bucket before plopping into the water below.

"Oh, I hurt her," I gasped, coming closer and peering into the bucket, where several Dianas were swimming—the recently on-camera one as well as her array of stand-ins and understudies. (Sorry to burst your bubble.)

"And that's lunch," shouted the first AD.

"Is she okay?" I asked the goldfish handler.

He swirled the water with his hand, perhaps aerating it for the Dianas, perhaps making it more difficult for me to see the fate of that particular fish.

"I think I hurt Diana," I gasped. "I think she banged against the side of the bucket!"

"She's fine," said the goldfish man without even looking, his hand swishing about, almost as if he was trying to animate all the Dianas to appease me.

"She's fine," said the costumer holding aloft a robe for me to put on, averting her eyes from my still-naked body.

"I think Diana's swimming on her side. She looks all wonky!" I said, panic rising in my voice.

"That's lunch!" shouted the first AD again, a bit louder.

He gestured rather violently to the costumer, who threw the robe over me, and in a blur of terry towelling I came to and remembered I was naked in front of the entire crew, bent over a bucket, worrying if I had murdered a goldfish.

In the brief few moments it took for the robe to be tied and normal service to be resumed, the goldfish man and the bucket disappeared and I was whisked off to lunch, where too many people, unsolicited, came up and told me I had not killed one of the Dianas, which obviously meant I had.

After lunch when we resumed shooting the sequence, I sidled up to the bucket in between takes and counted the Dianas. I knew there was one less than before. I had only wanted her to get back to safety sooner, but my overzealousness had been both our downfalls. To this day the dull clunk of that goldfish hitting the side of the bucket haunts me.

———

I got on a plane to London to pack up my yellow flat and prepare to return to LA to start shooting two studio pictures and make a life for myself and my fiancée in the City of Angels.

Yes, fiancée. I suppose I should have led with that.

I had made a grand plan to propose on the flight back to Los Angeles as we began our new life together, but at the last minute work commitments forced her to stay on in London for a few days, leaving me to fly off into the sunset alone. But then on March 19, 1996, the night before I left, she came to my flat and presented me with a red rose. Then, she got down on one knee and asked me to marry her. I said yes. Who wouldn't? It was one of the loveliest things anyone has ever done for me. It was also a terrible idea and marked the beginning of the end of the relationship, though not of our love for each other, which remains strong even now.

I'm one of those people who have no regrets because I believe if you have arrived at a place of contentment in life then everything on the journey, no matter how awful, is a part of the happiness of the present. So how could you wish to change anything? I wish some things hadn't happened, of course. I wish my father hadn't abused me. I wish I hadn't married so early. I wish I hadn't entered into another abusive relationship in my thirties. But I cannot regret. All these things taught me lessons, showed me patterns—some I still struggle to stop repeating—and all have brought me to where and who I am now.

So, suddenly I was engaged, living in a strange city, and working on two consecutive Hollywood films. Perhaps as a consequence of all these things being new and slightly scary, my fiancée and I settled into a life of calm and domesticity, in a little apartment off Fairfax. LA is a quiet city, it closes early, people retire to their homes and nest, and we easily fell into that pattern, too.

But the domestic idyll was short-lived. Everything about our time there had a feeling of uncertainty and impermanence. For some reason we rented an unfurnished flat and then proceeded to rent furniture to put in it. I had never heard of renting furniture before, but it seemed a common thing in a city that traffics in the transitory and the temporary. The furniture, like the apartment, was bland and not at all to our taste, but we put up with it because we didn't know how long we wanted to commit—to the apartment, to the city, and ultimately to each other. Becoming engaged the night before a new chapter in our lives began was incredibly romantic but more so a marker of the intensity of our love, a declaration of constancy in a time of turbulence. We genuinely did want to spend the rest of our lives together—but our lives as they were then in that beautiful moment. And as the song goes, we both had a lot of living to do.

We both missed home. My core group of friends had become incredibly important to me after my divorce and the LA/London time difference made it very difficult to stay connected with them. That summer of 1996 I got an email address and the digital singsongy white noise of signing on to AOL via dial-up became a constant in my life. I was so worried I would lose touch with my pack back in London, that out of sight would be out of mind, as if good friendship was something that succeeded depending on the number of hours of effort you put in. But friendship is not like training for a marathon or becoming a psychologist. More hours spent doing it do not make you better. I understood that the first time I returned home to Britain after many months away and met up with some chums. It was as though I had seen them only a few days before. That's what true friendship is and that's what love is. A connection that can span continents and time and does not diminish, only evolves.

One of the best things about being an actor is that you have lots and lots of intense, intimate, and short-lived relationships. I notice when I work with young actors that when a project comes to an end, they say things like "I can't believe it's nearly over," to which I want to reply, "Why not, didn't you read the contract?!" But the truth is, I understand and remember my own youthful self, lamenting the idea of breaking up the magical circle of camaraderie I had created. As I've grown older, I have come to appreciate the knowledge that the feelings and connections that created that intimacy will never go away; they will just hibernate until the next time you are able to reignite them. Life is, hopefully, long. You will see the people you love again and the spark you had will still be there. Or it won't, and that's good to know, too.

Just as home is not just a house, yellow walls or no, friends or lovers are not possessions: holding on to them does not guarantee you'll always have them.

primatology

8

I found the perfect glasses one day on Venice Beach during that summer of 1996, though, to this untrained eye, it was always summer in LA. I am told there are indeed different seasons in Los Angeles, but they don't really change, they glide into one another, effortlessly, nigh invisible to all but the most hardened Angeleno, who, almost as imperceptibly as the seasons' changing, will introduce fleece to their wardrobe at the first metaphorical leaf drop.

I say metaphorical because fall, in most other parts of the world, is indeed signalled by falling leaves. In LA, it would appear the leaves fall all year round, for why else would I have been awakened nearly every morning I have spent in that city by LA's white noise—the dull yet omnipresent drone of leaf blowers, strapped to the backs of gardeners?

If there really are seasons in LA, why don't the leaves fall in autumn, like everywhere else? And if they do fall in autumn, why do we hear the leaf blowers all year round? And if they fall all the year round, why don't they just rake up their leaves quietly as in every other city in the world, and let us sleep in peace?

I wasn't even looking for glasses. I had lunched with a group of friends and was waiting for them to gather on the boardwalk outside the restaurant before heading down onto the beach. I was idly browsing a sunglasses stall in that way you do when you don't really want or need anything, but you're open to the possibility of finding something magical. Kind of a nonchalant alertness. The instant I saw them I knew I had found my look. The frames were black and round, *Where's Wally* meets European arthouse director or avant-garde musician. Geeky but sexy, which had kind of become my thing at the time. They weren't really sunglasses at all, as their lenses were clear and they were obviously hanging on the rack for novelty value, to attract the dorks like me not enthused by the shiny, the mirrored, or the sporty. They were ten dollars—the best ten dollars I ever spent because they gave me my look. And as Maria Callas said—or at least as Terrence McNally in his play *Master Class* imagined she might have said—"You must have a look!"

Soon after, I flew to Melbourne to visit my fiancée, who was there shooting a movie. One day I took a walk down Toorak Road in the South Yarra district of Melbourne and walked into an optometrist's office. A short—in all senses—saleslady looked up at me over the rims of her bifocals, which were attached to a very elegant chain, and gave me the once-over.

"Yeis?" she asked.

"Hello," I said cheerily.

Crickets.

"I wonder if you can help me? I have these frames . . ." I pulled from my pocket the recently acquired wonder specs. The lady glanced at them noncommittally.

". . . and I have this prescription for my lenses."

Another glance from behind the bifocals, another wave of condescension washed over me.

"And so, I was wondering if you could put my lenses into these frames . . ."

She said nothing, but if there were a language of eyebrows, she would have clearly signalled the word "duh" by the ever so slight, yet withering, raise of her left one. I struggled on, knowing I still held my trump card.

"But I am only in Australia for the next five days. Do you think you can make it happen in time?"

There was a silence as she sized me up, reassessing me in the light of this revelation. I could tell she felt she had been wrong to dismiss me as a dopey foreigner so quickly. Our eyes met. I held her gaze. Finally, she looked away, and almost under her breath, in a languorous Aussie drawl, replied, "Shouldn't be a drama!"

And thus, I learned my favourite Australian phrase, which sits alongside several others, including "Not my circus, not my monkeys" (Poland) and "You eat a ton of shite before you die" (Scotland).

Because it *shouldn't* be a drama, should it?! Not much should, to be honest. And it wasn't. I went back the day before I left and picked up my new, perfect, drama-free glasses, and seriously my life has been better ever since.

Now, more than a quarter of a century later, I still wear those glasses—or a vastly more expensive version of those ten-dollar originals. I feel I have an identity when I wear them. They are *on brand*, as we are so bluntly led to describe anything that is of our essence these days. I still prefer the Callas/McNally version: those glasses became my *look*.

I returned to Los Angeles and began shooting the film *Buddy*, the reason I'd gone to California in the first place. I had begun to train with the chimps for the previous month, on my days off from *Romy and Michele*, though when I say "train" I really mean drive out to their training facility in the desert and let the chimps get used to me, climb all over me, let me hold them, cuddle them, and see me as a friend.

There were five chimps I had to interact with, most importantly the two who played Maggie and Joe in the film, but also their understudies/doubles if they were tired or just not feeling like being movie stars, and one extra floating chimp (I guess the correct showbiz term would be a "swing") who was slightly smaller than all the others and just seemed to enjoy being along for the ride.

The chimp who played Joe was, in real life, named Tonka, and we

fell in love. There is no other way to describe it. We just got each other, the way you do with certain animals, that indefinable combo of a crush, a bestie, and a soul mate that I have only experienced with beings I have either had torrid affairs with, married, or been an owner to. Tonka and I were a thing. Each morning as I walked on set, I would see him sitting in his little plastic chair, keeping focus on his trainer but his eyes darting around the set, looking for me. Once he'd spotted me, he would try to contain his glee as he waited for the trainer's signal that would allow him to leap from his chair and bound into my arms. It was, without a doubt, the most heartwarming experience I've ever had on a job.

There was a scene in the film where I was drunk and the two of us shared a glass of whisky, pushing it back and forth across a table. The trainers were worried it wouldn't work because chimps don't like to share their food, so the table between us was constructed to be just a little longer than the length of Tonka's arm, in case he lunged for me as I sipped his drink. Tonka never did. He let me share his food off camera, too, to the amazement of the chimp minders. I had been chosen by Tonka. He became desperate to groom me, and on my very last day on the movie, fittingly just outside the Natural History Museum, the trainers let him.

AUTHOR'S PERSONAL COLLECTION

Most days I'd be holding Tonka between takes and he would begin to take sneaky looks inside my ears or up my nose or run his fingers through my scalp and the trainers would intervene, but on that final day, they let him continue. It was the strangest sensation having an animal picking through my hair—for nits or bugs presumably—and begin to make a series of lip smacks and raspberry noises as he did so. I wasn't in costume but wearing shorts and a vest, so he went to town on my hairy legs and armpits, too. The trainers were careful not to let it go further when he obviously wanted to have a look inside my shorts, and when Tonka began taking my hand in his and slapping it on his head that's when our bonding ritual was over because Tonka clearly wanted to play more aggressively and things could get dangerous. Basically, Tonka thought of me as another chimp, and I could not have been more flattered. I felt it was the ultimate compliment, to be accepted by another creature, even across the interspecies divide. Even when I caught chimp flu from him, I wore it as a badge of honour.

A year later I went back to Los Angeles for the *Buddy* premiere and press junket. It was lovely to catch up with Caroline again, and I found it incredibly thrilling that I was in a colouring book as part of the film's merchandise campaign. Like seeing myself on a bus stop or on the side of a popcorn bag at the cinema or being a question on *Jeopardy!*

or a clue in the *New York Times* crossword puzzle, those things never get old for me. I was also looking forward to seeing Tonka, as I'd been told he would be with me for a publicity photo shoot. I actually worried he wouldn't remember me.

I brought my friend Sue with me on the press trip and we had such fun frolicking around town. Somehow or other one of the PR people thought Sue was my assistant and so we pretended she was and of course the more we carried on the joke the more complicated and twisted our deceit became. As Sue was lounging by the Four Seasons pool having a pina colada, a phone would be brought to her by a waiter and it would be a press person letting her know an interview of mine had been pushed by fifteen minutes.

"I'll let him know," she'd respond gaily and get back to sunbathing.

We went out to the training facility in the desert and had a cuddle with the chimps, but there was no sign of Tonka. Someone told me they thought he was working on another show, and so I needed to get familiar with these new, younger chimps instead. The story of our special connection was brought up in practically every interview during the junket as it was included in the film's press releases, and I began to suspect they were going to surprise me with a special Tonka reunion at the premiere. But no, one of the baby chimps we'd cuddled was wheeled out and walked, or rather hugged, the red carpet with me.

It wasn't until the week after, when I was promoting the film on a live daytime talk show called *Crook and Chase*, that I discovered the sordid truth about Tonka. A producer bounced into my dressing room to go over the questions I'd be answering on-air, and during the chat he casually dropped the line, "It's such a shame about Tonka, isn't it?"

I felt sick to my stomach.

"What do you mean?" I began, feeling a little wobbly. "Is he . . . did he die?"

"Oh God, no," scoffed the producer. "Didn't they tell you? We wanted to reunite you two live on-air! But you know, he's gotten a little older—haven't we all?!—and so he's gotten a little sexually, you know, aggressive, and what with him being in love with you and all, the trainers worried that if he saw you, he might try to . . ." He nodded at me knowingly as I tried desperately to process this shocking new information.

"And that wouldn't go down well in the flyover states, now would it? Ha! I mean a monkey trying to rape you live on-air?!" he giggled.

I was stunned.

"He's a . . . chimp," was all I could manage in response.

"What?" said the man, rustling his papers and fiddling with his headset, ready to move on to the next dressing room and brief the next guest.

"He's a chimp, not a monkey."

"Oh, right. Sound will be in to mike you in a few. Have fun!" And he was off.

I sat for a moment and contemplated the conspiracy of silence I'd unwittingly been a victim of. The reason I hadn't seen Tonka was that my presence, my very being, was too dangerous for him. He would still see me as a chimp, a peer, something to desire and be jealous of— as he had been during the shoot when he once swiped at my makeup artist's brush as she powdered my face—and I might send him into a frenzy of primal, carnal desire that would end up, well, I think we all get it.

Now, when I'm having one of those not-so-great days, when I'm feeling a bit old or unattractive, I cheer myself up by remembering I am a sex symbol in the primate world.

I asked around and the story was confirmed. Tonka was now six, sexually aggressive, and no longer able to be trusted to work. He was now retired and living in Palm Springs. Over the years I have taken many trips to Palm Springs and I've fancied I might run into him. I've always loved that town, seeming, as it does to me, to be populated almost entirely by old people and gay people (or a combination of the two), most of them connected somehow to the business of show. How perfect that Tonka should end up there. For he was in showbiz, now old, and all the signs seemed to point to him being gay, too. Or at least a bi-curious George.

Nowadays, I feel very differently about wild animals being trained for movies, and even wild animals being housed in zoos. It isn't so much the treatment of the chimps on set—they were cared for well and very loved, but it's what happens to them afterwards. For Tonka is not, as I used to imagine, lying in a hammock in Palm Springs being cared for by some rich and benevolent primate fancier. Perhaps he was to begin with, but then his owner died, and he was sold and that is where his story takes a terrible turn. The regulations in the United States for buying and selling wild animals are woefully lax and do not have the animals' health or dignity as a priority. Basically, anyone can buy a tiger or a chimp and keep these animals in whatever conditions they choose. Sadly, that is what has happened to Tonka. I saw a picture of him recently languishing in squalour and his own mess in a tiny indoor cage at a so-called sanctuary in Missouri. I have been working with PETA to get him and the other primates there released to a facility in Florida that would re-socialise them and let them roam wild on a man-made island. The fight has been mired in the courts for several years, but I have not given up hope. I feel I owe it to my little friend. I hope I get to see him happy again one day.

———

My relationship was over, certainly the engagement part of it, but neither of us had the courage to finally commit to ripping off the Band-Aid and setting each other free. We were still negotiating ways to be in each other's lives, and beds, but what we really needed was some time apart.

I was offered the movie *For My Baby*, written and directed by the Dutch filmmaker Rudolf van den Berg, and I jumped at the chance. I had almost worked with Rudolf a couple of years before on a movie based on *The Oresteia* that was going to shoot in Tunisia, but it fell apart at the last minute as these things are prone to do, leaving a half-built Greek fort in the middle of the North African desert.

For My Baby was, if anything, more intense than *The Oresteia*. I was to play Daniel Orgelbrand, an Austrian Jewish stand-up comedian whose sister was killed in the concentration camps before he was born, and whose ghost returns to haunt him. I left for Hungary soon after *Buddy* wrapped, via a pit stop in Amsterdam for costume fittings. It all came together incredibly quickly, and I soon found myself in the Hotel Astoria in Budapest, which had been the Nazi headquarters during the World War II occupation. The vibe there was as if not much had changed in the intervening decades, and in the bar after a few glasses of wine, if I squinted my eyes and listened to the accents around me, I could imagine I was back in those days.

It's not the best thing to be alone and lovelorn in a foreign city. I spent far too much time in my hotel room deconstructing the previous six months and self-flagellating, convinced that the two major breakups I'd had in the past three years were to become the template for my life.

I made some bad choices: I had an ill-judged affair. I drank a lot. The hotel was strange and echoey and rattled with history. The doors to the rooms opened out into the corridor, as if we were on board a cruise ship that we couldn't get off. I look back on my time in Hungary as a bizarre fever dream, the narrative of the film ebbing and flowing with the reality of my circumstances, the character's haunting commingling with my state of despondency about the crumbling mass that was my life.

One day off, I decided I needed to make some sort of gesture for myself to prove I had truly cut the cord. I carried a picture of my fiancée in my wallet, and in a dramatic fit of anguish I ripped it into shreds and threw the pieces out the window of my hotel room, watching them dance in the breeze down the avenue towards the River Danube, crying softly to myself. (I may have also been drinking.) As grandiose a gesture as it was, it was still cathartic, and it helped.

A few days later, my bag was stolen from my trailer and in it was my wallet. My wallet held my wedding ring, which I had held on to, not knowing what to do with this symbol of my old life. Now I had been relieved of that burden, too. I took it as a sign.

But then I realised that along with this lightness came a darker, more troubling loss: my perfect specs! Yes, after that day in Budapest my ten-dollar frames from Venice Beach, brought to optic life in Melbourne, would see no more. Even worse, I had lost my look.

I searched for the positive. I was about to embark on another new phase of my life: single again, moving back to London, and taking some time off. Maybe it was good I didn't have a look to hide behind. Maybe I should find a new one. Or maybe I didn't need a look at all.

I spoke to my friend Caroline back in LA, sharing with her how I had broken up with my fiancée, was living in a Nazi hotel, and had lost my favourite glasses. I joked that even the art on my hotel room walls was depressing. A few weeks later a package arrived from California and inside was a painting, a colourful abstract that cheered me immensely. The piece had been a prop in *Buddy*, painted by my old friend Tonka. Up it went on that dowdy wall, and my mood lightened whenever I walked into the room.

Just over a year later, I walked into a swanky optometrist's on Fifth Avenue in New York City with an envelope full of photographs under my arm. During the filming of *Romy and Michele's High School Reunion* I had done a shoot with my friend Andrew Macpherson. We'd spent a day in the valley, me cavorting around as he snapped away. Luckily, in many of the images I was wearing those perfect glasses. I had decided in the intervening year that, although I didn't *need* a look, my instinct had been right, and I liked the look those glasses gave me. I had been without them for a year and I missed it. And now I was ready, able, and willing to part with the many, many times more money than the ten dollars they had originally cost, to bring those specs back into my life. I was seeing everything more clearly.

I'm wearing them right now.

debauchery

9

I couldn't wait for 1996 to be over.

I'd spent nearly the whole year away from my home in London and my core group of friends, and I so needed to be back there and among them to usher the new year in.

But my Hogmanay (as we Scots call New Year's Eve) didn't start well: I woke up in the Nazi hotel in Budapest, hungover from the previous night's *For My Baby* wrap party, having slept through my alarm, my car to the airport, and my flight home. I managed to book a later flight that connected through Prague, but there was a tight connection. The possibility of starting 1997 alone in some dowdy Czech airport hotel room was looming.

Hogmanay is a big celebration for the Scottish. I always say our two favourite pastimes are oversentimentality and drinking, and Hogmanay allows us to flex both those muscles with abandon. The reason it features so heavily in our national psyche (aside from oversentimentality and drinking) is that after the Reformation in 1560, when Scotland separated from the Catholic Church, celebrations of Christmas became more and more frowned upon, until eventually in 1640 they were banned altogether by an act of the Scottish Parliament that was not repealed till 1712. By then it was too late: Hogmanay was our thing.

There are many rituals associated with the holiday: we open the front door to let the new year in and open the back door to let the old one out. We also must have a "first foot", someone who is the first person to cross our threshold and bring us symbolic gifts to ensure we have a good and prosperous year. This usually includes some sort of fuel like a log or coal (to warm us), some bread or cake (to feed us), and some booze, just because. Most important, the first foot should be a tall, dark-haired stranger. I have made many an unsuspecting guest at one of my New Year's Eve parties (usually one of my friends' new plus-ones—to fulfil the stranger criteria) go outside at 11:55 p.m. laden with logs and whisky and cake with strict instructions to only knock on the door when they hear that the bells have rung and the new year has arrived. Of course, what usually happens is that in the ensuing mêlée of kissing and singing and weeping, their knocks go unheard for several minutes until I suddenly remember and open the door to find them numb with cold and very confused about this tradition, my country, and me.

I made it back in time to drop my bags at home then head off to a friend's flat for a really lovely, quiet gathering to await the bells. It was one of my calmest New Year's ever, but very necessarily so. I was completely exhausted. The hectic schedule, both at work and after hours, on *For My Baby*—compounded by a post-breakup fatigue as well as a healthy dose of travel—made my body cry out for rest. I was world-weary in every way.

As I flew across Europe on my way home, I began the ritual spiritual assessment of the previous twelve months and was saddened by the pattern that was emerging: yet again a great time professionally was undermined and overshadowed by decay in my personal life. I'd started the year deeply in love, about to embark on a new adventure of working in Hollywood. I was ending it single(ish) and disillusioned— with both relationships and Tinseltown. As much as I'd enjoyed making *Romy and Michele* and *Buddy*, neither of them nor in fact any of the films I had made over the past couple of years had really challenged me as an actor. I felt very ambivalent about the idea of making films at all. I also needed to get out of Hollywood because I associated my relationship's demise with being there—the two somehow became fused together in my mind, and LA gets a bad enough rap without me blaming it for our breakup. And if the city had been to blame, then, if anything, I should thank it. We were not meant to be, she and I, at least not as a couple.

But I asked the universe and the universe provided. On my return to London I would begin a rare but much-needed spell of not working. The cause of this magical hiatus was Stanley Kubrick. Over the past year I had auditioned on tape four or five times for his new film *Eyes Wide Shut*. It was for a role that appeared in only one scene, with only a few minutes' time. Finally, I was offered the part, or actually, asked were I to be offered it, would I be available. And were I available, would I accept the role? I said yes I was and yes I would, and so I did. But the filming dates were in flux. I was told they had no real idea of when my scene would shoot. It could be in a week, or in three months. I knew I had to go to America for the *Buddy* press tour in the middle of May, and so I decided to just wait. Not only did I need a break, some me time, but this was Stanley Kubrick. The genius, though not exactly prolific genius: his previous film, *Full Metal Jacket*, had been released a decade before, and it was generally acknowledged that *Eyes Wide Shut* would be his swan song. I couldn't pass up the chance to work with such a legend.

Stanley's inability or lack of interest in scheduling a film with the usual military efficiency turned out to be a great gift. I needed some time. I needed to listen to my body. I needed to let go of a relationship and move on in my life. I needed to have some fun. Now at the beginning of 1997 I suddenly had the time to do all of the above *and* get to be in a Stanley Kubrick film and a part of cinema history.

So for the next few months I slept late, met friends for lunches and drinks and dinners, kissed strangers, stayed out late, fell in love, went on vacations, had massages and acupuncture, saw my family, got stoned, took swimming lessons and had my front crawl corrected, went to parties, stole more butter dishes from hotels, tried things once, saw concerts and plays and films, read books, played games, took pills, kissed more strangers and told them they couldn't fall in love with me, lay in the bath for very long periods of time, sometimes reading books and playing games, took spontaneous trips, danced and danced and danced and had lots of sex. (Actually, there was some crossover in the latter two activities, thanks to my old chum Matthew Bourne's stunning production of *Swan Lake*.)

In short, it was a magical time, and all the more magical because I knew it was finite—the summons from Stanley would signal my return to the normal confines of life: alarm clocks and going to bed alone sometimes and at a reasonable hour, and schedules and remembering to go to the supermarket and having to make decisions, in advance, and write them down—but till then I let myself go.

I have a game I play when travelling with friends where you aren't allowed to refuse anything. If it's on a swanky flight somewhere that means having as much wine and warm nuts and ice cream sundaes and hot towels and pillows and snacks as you're offered (dietary and other health exemptions aside, of course). Part of the fun is realising how much we are conditioned to restrain our desires. The joy is never saying no to them. That's how I lived my life that winter and spring of 1997.

Over the years my life has become more and more diverse and complicated and, I suppose as a necessary consequence, very regimented and planned. But I still manage to let go, to experience abandon even now. And just as the knell that signalled my return from Neverland back then was Stanley Kubrick, today I ensure I still can be a bit of a Peter Pan by similarly structuring a deadline for my debauchery. You see, I am all about fun. I think fun is very important. But it just has to be scheduled.

———

Finally the day came, and I found myself on the set of *Eyes Wide Shut*. It's always awkward on your first day in any new job, not knowing who's who and how everything works. By then, the film had been shooting for over a year, and would eventually hold the Guinness World Record for the world's longest continuous film shoot, coming in at four hundred days! So, things were pretty well into their stride by the time I rolled up as new boy.

I was called for rehearsal and walked onto the set to find Tom Cruise and Stanley Kubrick standing before me. I had met Tom briefly when he had come to see *Cabaret* in London, but this was my first ever encounter with Stanley, who was peering at me over his glasses.

"Hey, Stanley, I'm Alan," I said, proffering my hand to this old man, who, on first glance, reminded me of a Hobbit version of Salman Rushdie.

"You're not American!" he retorted gruffly.

I had heard tales of Stanley being formidable and demanding, so I was slightly on guard already.

"I know," I said, still rather taken aback. "I'm Scottish!"

"You were American on the tapes," he continued.

Something in me snapped, or maybe I just took an objective look at the situation—I had been waiting for months to shoot this scene after auditioning for it many times, on several continents.

Fuck you, old man, I thought to myself. *I know I was American on the tapes.*

But I actually said, "Yeah, that's because I'm an actor, Stanley."

Nothing was said for a moment. Tom cleared his throat a little awkwardly. But I thought I caught the hint of a smile beneath Stanley's bushy beard.

"Let's run the lines," he replied.

Like many people who are perceived as bullies, Stanley, I can imagine, could fulfil that prophecy if those around him were cowed or fearful, their anxiety about working with him too obvious. I can see him taking the most familiar path in those situations. We all adjust our behaviour according to what we deduce is expected of us. It's like people pleasing, just without the pleasing.

But I had stood up to Stanley, and I could tell he liked it, found me intriguing because of it, and we went on to develop a strong bond, have great chats, and share many laughs.

It's well-known that Stanley did many, many takes of scenes, and I had girded my loins to be ready to repeat and regurgitate my performance ad nauseam.

In the past, when the number of the take announced by the clapper loader went higher and higher, I'd known that anxious shame that I somehow wasn't getting it right and was wasting everyone's time. But on Stanley's set, the clapper loader made no announcement, and instead the sound recordist in the corner of the set murmured the take number details into his mic, unintelligible to the actors, and therefore that pressure was gone. And even better, although we did many, many takes on every angle we shot for the scene—and for the version that Stanley abandoned after two full days—I knew exactly what was required of me each time we went for the next one. Stanley would take me to the monitor, and we'd watch each previous take and discuss the most detailed intonations, facial movements, or gestures and he'd give me incredibly precise direction on all before we tried again. Every time we went for a new take, I knew exactly why, and I can't begin to tell you how rare that is for an actor working in film. There is nothing more annoying to me than hearing, repeatedly, a director cry at the end of a scene, "Perfect! One more!" I always think, *If it was perfect, and perfect again, why are we doing another?!*

My scene involves me, as a hotel clerk, being questioned by Tom Cruise as he tries to find out information about a missing man. And I think part of the reason it is so memorable, aside from it being the only funny scene in the entire movie, is that I am basically cruising Tom. The clerk is incredibly flirty, and I remember voicing my worry to Stanley that perhaps I had gone a little too far in how enamoured

I was and how full-on my seduction seemed (and remember, that was *me* saying this!). Stanley would have none of it.

"No!" he encouraged me. "Keep going! It can go up another notch!"

Of course, the fact that I was a queer man flirting so brazenly with Tom Cruise only added to the sensation around the scene. Indeed, the entire film was engulfed in a frenzy of sexual innuendo building up to its release that led many people to assume they were going to see Tom Cruise and his wife, Nicole Kidman, actually have sex. I was even asked on a couple of red carpets if I would be having sex with Tom in the film!

Of course, when the film came out this assumption led to many being disappointed. And although sex sells, in this case perhaps it was a bad idea to encourage a perception of the film that was so inaccurate. The film is about jealousy, not sex. Despite his intentions to the contrary, Tom's character does nothing during the wild night he embarks upon in response and retaliation to his wife's frank confession of a sexual fantasy about another man that could be construed, in that straight relationship lingo, as out-and-out "cheating". Yet, as Nicole's character says in the final scene, no one night is ever the whole truth of a relationship.

To which Tom replies, "And no dream is ever just a dream."

I worked only a week on *Eyes Wide Shut*, yet perhaps a reason why my time on this film is so entrenched in my mind is that it was an experience that completely confounded my expectations. All the stories I'd heard before starting were that Stanley was a despot and Tom some sort of sacred Hollywood cow that we mere mortals must not gaze upon. Nothing could have been further from the truth. Tom was sweet and approachable and talked lovingly of his wife, and no, nothing registered on my gaydar. Stanley was hilarious, interested, and interesting, and we had great chats about Kafka and Chekhov, and he made fun of me for showing pictures of Tonka the chimp.

I did see quick flashes of the other, darker, fabled Kubrick, though. The makeup artist, a lovely Scottish man named Robert McCann, had told me Stanley was not a fan of makeup, which rather horrified me as I did not want to go down in cinema history as that hotel clerk with the blotchy face. (My months of partying and abandon did have some dermatological downsides!) So Robert very discreetly made my complexion a little smoother, and that was our little secret. One day on set, I was getting a little sweaty with all the lights and the cramped confines, so Robert waited till Stanley was preoccupied and then snuck towards me brandishing a powder puff. Suddenly Stanley turned to us and barked, "What are you doing?!"

Robert leapt in the air, terrified. "I was just . . ." he stammered.

"NO makeup!" said Stanley as though he were at a protest.

I felt I had to intervene. "Stanley, it's just, well . . ." I gestured to my forehead. "It's the shining, Stanley!"

In that moment I realised what an incredibly goofy, yet a propos, thing to say to the man who had terrified us all with his movie of the same title. Stanley smiled, the crew began to giggle, and soon we were all guffawing at my ditziness.

We were shooting at Pinewood Studios at the same time as the Bond film *Tomorrow Never Dies* was in production on the Albert R. Broccoli 007 Stage next door. One day, during the filming of a close-up on me, there were a series of very loud explosions coming from the Bond set that made it impossible for us to continue, so it was decided we'd have a little break to wait for them to finish. The first AD, an old-school stalwart of British films who had worked with Stanley several times before and with whom he had a very funny, slightly snippy, old-married-couple type of relationship, asked us actors if we wanted anything while we waited. Tom said he'd like a cup of tea. I was in need of a little energy and so said, "Could I have a banana, please?"

The first AD looked a little taken aback at this request.

"A banana?" he repeated rather scoffingly, in the mould of Lady Bracknell's "A handbag?" from *The Importance of Being Earnest*.

"Yes," I reiterated, feeling a little unfairly put upon for my snack choice. "I'd like a banana, if that's okay."

He raised his eyebrows once more, then turned away and said into his walkie-talkie, "All right, can I have a cup of tea for Tom, and Alan will have . . ." and with such scorn that made me feel like I'd asked for a bowl of only red M&Ms, continued, "a *banana!*"

I found it at once amusing and bewildering to be so fruit-shamed. But it also rankled me in other, deeper ways. Ways that made me feel I was being challenged about my very worthiness to be in the room.

"Actually . . ." I called out as he was almost out of earshot but not quite. "I've changed my mind."

"Yes?" he sighed.

"I'd like two bananas, please!"

He turned away and mumbled the extra-banana order into his walkie-talkie. I felt a little hot under the collar at the sudden chill of our exchange, and then through a gap in a collection of lighting stands and screens, I saw Stanley, sitting in the corner laughing quietly to himself. Our eyes met. I smiled and blushed, and he gave me a nod of approval.

As expected, at the end of the week, Stanley asked me to stay on and shoot the scene again. I told him I would like nothing more, but I had to leave for LA and the *Buddy* junket. He understood and told me it was because he was having such fun and wanted to keep on exploring, rather than having any problem with what we had shot. We hugged good-bye and I thanked him truly, for being such an inspiration. For I genuinely believe that had I not worked with Stanley Kubrick, had I not auditioned more times than I have ever auditioned for any role ever, had I not decided to take some time off and hold out to be free to experience that week with him, I might not still be an actor today.

I was feeling very ambivalent about acting in general at the time. The theatre seemed too terrifying, exhausting, and unsure and I had no desire to pursue new stage projects, and after my initial Hollywood sojourn the prospect of film acting felt unchallenging and pedestrian. But Stanley changed all that.

The detail and precision with which he encouraged me to imbue every second I was onscreen truly reignited my interest in acting. I felt more excited by those few days of work, and those few minutes onscreen, than I had by anything in years. If *Eyes Wide Shut* had been a normal film or TV project, my scene would have been shot in a morning and I'd have been sent home before lunch. But there is that saying that there are no small parts, only small actors, and Stanley revealed to me how much of a truism that can be.

So, thank you, Stanley Kubrick.

———

There are very few actors who can say they made back-to-back films with Stanley Kubrick and the Spice Girls. In fact, I know there is only one, and that is me!

On my return to Britain at the beginning of 1997, I had a crash course in the Spice phenomenon. While Britain was succumbing to their all-conquering wiles, America had yet to be so lucky, and to me the Spice Girls had barely registered on my cultural radar.

Those were the days before music was dropped worldwide at the exact same moment. Those were the days, in fact, when music was not *dropped* at all. It was released, on CD predominantly, before the revival of vinyl and after the demise of tape (though I still have the cassette copy of the first Spice Girls album in pride of place on my shelves!).

"Darling, I have a rather weird one for you," said the voice on the other end of the line one morning after the night before, deep in the midst of my Don Juan gap year. It was my London agent.

"Uh-huh." I remember being preoccupied with something (actually someone) at that exact moment.

"Have you heard of the Spice Girls?"

"I'm currently alive, so yes!" I quipped.

"Well, they're making a movie and they want you to be in it!"

"What??!!"

It turned out that Geri, aka Ginger Spice, had come to see me in *Hamlet* on a college group outing just days after her own father had died. Seeing me in the throes of lachrymose mourning about my character's father's loss connected with her in her recently bereaved and vulnerable state. Four years later, she insisted I was the natural choice to play Piers, a documentarian chronicling the band's every move in *Spice World: The Movie!* I have always wanted a T-shirt with *Ginger Spice Saw My Hamlet!* emblazoned across it.

I am eclectic in all manner of ways. Some might see it as flighty or ADD-ish or trying to cover all my bases. But truly I am excited by many things and I keep my mind and my heart open to everything. My lack of desire to be restrained in any form is central to my very being, my taste certainly, my output definitely, but also my sexuality, and even my hair.

When I do concerts, I will sing a Kurt Weill song followed by a Miley Cyrus one. I am as engaged by Beckett as I am by Bananarama.

And this is nothing new. From the beginning of my career I have careened from genre to genre, up and down the ladder of cultural taste. In my first few years out of drama school I went from a soap opera to a play that posited the idea that nuclear weapons are illegal according to international law; from a campy surreal comedy double act to a bleak German tale of unemployed youths who reenact Roald Amundsen's journey to Antarctica. More recently I have been as enthused at writing, directing, and acting in a musical condom commercial (co-starring Ricki Lake) as recording a CD of Shakespeare speeches, having Chekhov revealed to me by working with a Russian director, duetting with a jazz band, designing shoes or wallpaper or T-shirts, or working with a new writer on a play that pushes the envelope on interracial, intergenerational queer relationships and involves much nudity and a lot of swimming!

So, the consecutive culture clash of Stanley to Spicey was very me, and the experience of shooting the film only augmented the already glorious summer of love I was having in my real life. The Spice Girls' music and their ethos of girl power—which is essentially equality and empowerment combined with an unabashed and jubilant embrace of fun—vibed completely and became the soundtrack to my Dionysian season of discovery (albeit their version was a tad more PG-rated).

They were that rare thing, a band that was popular with kids and grannies, their music catchy and fun enough to top the charts and their sociopolitical phenomenon revelatory enough to be the subject of the culture and opinion pages of even the loftiest tomes. They were young, humble, irreverent, and talented, and on the ascension. Ahead of them, of course—after world domination—would be the descent, the resentment, the tabloid-led schadenfreude, the ennui. And later still, the return, the nostalgic reimagining, and a place forever in our hearts. But that moment I spent with them working on the film was their time, their innocence, when everything they did was charming and powerful at once.

I am often asked my favourite of all the films I have made, and I always answer *Spice World*. I do it partly to confound any intellectual snobbery, but also to point out that for me, the experience of making a film is far, far more important than how it turns out, or is perceived, or *performs* at the box office, in the ratings or reviews.

I have done films that had amazing scripts with great casts, and I had great fun making them, and they have turned out to be terrible. And I have had the most miserable working experiences of my life, jobs where I literally counted the minutes for them to be over, turn out to be something I am really proud to have been a part of. The point is, there are so many extenuating circumstances in the making of a film, so many things that are out of your control, that all you can do is your best and try to have as good a time as possible while you're doing it. Hopefully the gods will smile and you will be proud of how the final product turns out—as God knows, you will be reminded enough about it for the rest of your life. But we can't live in the future, or let others' opinions be the sole judge of the worthiness of our existence. Know that the fun you've had, the people you've met, the friendships you'll maintain, the places you've gone, the things you've learned and experienced, the life you've tasted are what matters.

So, that summer running around London, laughing, and frolicking with five girls who were at the very zenith of their pop princess potency, being taught the dance moves of the Spice Girls' songs by the Spice Girls themselves, was golden for me. I felt at home, I felt happy, I was carefree. Every day was an adventure, and anything seemed possible, and that's how I want all my life to be.

On my last day the girls called me into their trailer. Yes, the five of them shared one trailer, often with their mums in tow, while Richard E. Grant (who played their manager and who Melanie C recently quipped to me is the only manager they've never fired!) and I each had equally as big trailers just for ourselves. Mine even had a bath. I still wonder who is ever going to have a bath in their trailer?! A quick shower I can understand, at the end of a long day, or perhaps to wash off makeup or blood or some other occupational hazard. But to stay at work and lounge in a bath in what is essentially a camper van, probably parked on a public street? No thank you.

I was presented with a card full of messages of thanks for agreeing to be in their film. Yes, they were that nice. But best of all, the message from Emma called me a "Special Spice boy".

Drop the mic. Thank you, good night. That card, along with Polaroids of me with each Spice on my last day of filming, is framed and has pride of place in my study.

In the autumn of 1997, I returned to the Czech Republic. I had made my feature film debut there six years earlier, in Ian Sellar's *Prague*, opposite Bruno Ganz, the legend of German cinema and theatre (though he was actually Swiss), and the French movie star Sandrine Bonnaire.

In *Prague* I played a Jewish Scot (my first European Jew, but far from my last!) who goes to Prague to search for a piece of film

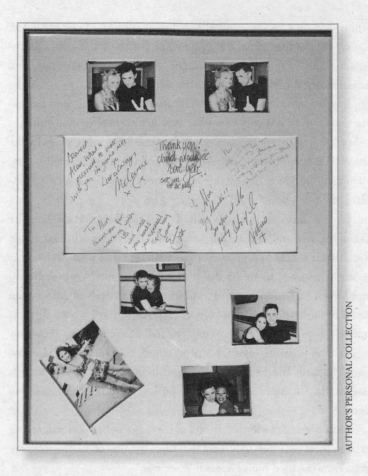

showing his grandparents being taken away by the Nazis during the war, and of course finding more than he bargained for. I arrived in Prague barely fifteen months after the Velvet Revolution, and the spectre of the communist occupation and its lingering bureaucracy was still very vivid. A dinner reservation would have to be made a week in advance, yet often upon arriving at the restaurant we would be the only customers. I remember a sort of savoury whipped cream featuring heavily atop most dishes. Vegetables were scarce. Salad usually meant a side bowl with a soup of sugary water and some slices of lettuce floating on top. Once, after many such evenings, I looked into my salad bowl and shrieked to my dinner mates, "I have a slice of tomato!!" and when they were all as equally excited, I knew we had turned a corner.

We shot at Barrandov Studios, which, during World War II, had been taken over by the Nazis and made to churn out Goebbels's propaganda films. Now they were being invaded again, but by Hollywood. Indeed, the West's slow takeover was palpable on a daily basis everywhere during that spring of 1991. Practically every day I would see some new lurid sign being hung above a store as that even more potent invader took hold: commerce. In the few months I was there, many Western chains opened their gaudy doors, making the neighbouring Czech stores still hanging on by the skin of their postperestroikan teeth look drab and dull in comparison.

But on my return in 1997, all the old stores were gone. Where Prague had seemed exotic and literally Kafkaesque in the postcommunist no-man's-land I had found in 1991, now, in 1997, it felt like any other quaint European city, just more quaint than most, as it had been Hitler's favourite of all the capitals he had invaded and so he was careful to ensure it not be bombed.

The film that heralded my return was *Plunkett & Macleane*, an eighteenth-century highwaymen romp with Jonny Lee Miller and Robert Carlyle playing the titular roles. Bobby had been in the year below me at drama school, and I had once played his dad in a play despite him being several years older. We'd also acted together in the first two parts of John Byrne's Slab Boys trilogy at Dundee Rep a decade before. It was good to see him again. It was also good to be able to celebrate with a fellow Scot, as during filming the vote for Scottish devolution happened, resulting ultimately in the reformation of the Scottish Parliament. Another great Scot, Ken Stott, was Chance the dastardly Thief Taker; Michael Gambon played Lord Gibson, whose

daughter, the object of Macleane's desire, was played by the lovely Liv Tyler.

I played Lord Rochester and he was my favourite kind of part: one that doesn't work very often but is talked about often by other characters, so it feels like he is in the film more than he actually is. I had a hoot playing him. From the top of his Philip Treacy hat to his buckled shoes he was pure theatrical dandy with the best lines. But he was also a dandy with a heart and a conscience, and he saved the day in the final reel. He is right up there in my gallery of uber-sexualised antiheroes.

The first time we are introduced to Liv's character in the film is at a gambling party, and my character says of her: "Very choice, very choosy. Wouldn't fuck me, must be a lesbian!"

Alas, only the "Very choice, very choosy" part made it into the finished film, but the original line was the very epitome of Lord Rochester, the real-life seventeenth-century rakish aristocrat and libertine poet that I portrayed. He had a great entrance, a peacock of vivid colour in stark contrast to the monochrome Hogarthian setting where hordes of men were literally hanging from the rafters to watch two cockerels tearing each other apart.

"Don't you just love a juicy cockfight?" he purrs.

"Still swinging both ways, Rochester?" Jonny's Macleane asks him.

"Jamie," he replies. "I swing *every* way!"

discovery

10

I fell in love with New York the second I saw it. The first time I visited was in 1996 for the premiere of *Emma*, and even from the plane, looking down at the streets below, I said to myself, "I'm going to live there!"

I had never known a city that made me feel giddy. I was also quite literally giddy the night of the premiere, as the movie's director, Doug McGrath, had invited us to his apartment to pregame with champagne cocktails, the kind that include a sugar cube doused in bitters and then drowned in a combo of brandy and champagne. I'd never had them before and they were delicious, and strong, especially on an empty stomach. Suffice to say I was pretty squiffy as I walked the red carpet and had to cling to my much taller fiancée's arm to stay steady.

The after-party for the *Emma* premiere was held at the Boathouse in Central Park and it was a truly magical night. I was surrounded by a bunch of friends as well as the person I loved more than anyone in the world, and—just when I thought I could not be more entranced by this place—I saw fireflies for the first time! We don't have them in Scotland, or anywhere in Britain, in fact. They seemed then, and still are, otherworldly to me, like being surrounded by some Disney attraction. As I write this, I can see them outside of the window of my house in the Catskill Mountains, twinkling away through the darkness in the meadow. They still remind me of the promise and the magic of

AUTHOR'S PERSONAL COLLECTION

my first days in New York, and when I found out that the reason they flash their bioluminescent glow is that they are looking for their mate, the firefly with the matching signal, the light that will bring them home, I felt even more bewitched by them. For isn't that what we all do? I've just stumbled through life, showing my light to others, hoping I'd eventually find another who recognises mine and can shine theirs back. Eventually, after showing my light to so many, I found my human firefly.

Sometimes, though, a firefly will imitate the light of another species, and once it has lured the stranger next to them will eat him alive! That's happened to me, too, but that's another story for another time.

New York City bewitched me, and I wanted, nay needed, more. Luckily it looked like that was going to happen. This time, not Hollywood, but Broadway, called.

Ever since it had closed in London, there had been rumblings that the production of *Cabaret* I'd appeared in at the Donmar Ware-house immediately following *Hamlet* would come to New York. Now the rumblings were becoming a reality. We were scheduled to open *Cabaret* on Broadway in early 1997, with Natasha Richardson set to play Sally Bowles opposite me.

So that evening at the after-party, my publicist was selling me as one of the stars of *Emma* who would also soon be making his Broad-way debut. I remember her sense of achievement when she told me I was to be introduced to Liz Smith, the legendary gossip columnist of the *New York Post*. I didn't know anything about the *Post*, or Liz, or indeed Broadway, for that matter, but by the reaction our interaction garnered from those around us, as I listened to her question me in her lovely Texan drawl, I could intuit that all three were pretty big cheese.

The London production of *Cabaret* had been incredibly intimate (the theatre only holds 250 people) and the seats in the stalls had been removed and replaced with cabaret tables and chairs so that the audi-ence felt they were actually in the Kit Kat Club in Berlin, where Sally Bowles is the star and the Emcee rules the roost. Although now it is fairly common for theatre to be deemed an "experience" rather than just something to be viewed, in those days it was pretty revolutionary, and this production of *Cabaret* was part of the vanguard of what we now call immersive theatre.

But *Cabaret* was revelatory in another way, too, in that there was no normal orchestra. All of the cast played instruments—some more than one—as well as acted, sang, and danced. Nowadays it is de rigueur for aspiring musical theatre actors to be able to play an instru-ment or two, but back in 1993 when we opened in London, actors playing onstage had never happened before.

The reason for both these innovations was the concept the direc-tor Sam Mendes had for the original production, and indeed the rea-son why I overcame my initial reluctance to be a part of the show. Sam had first asked me to play the Master of Ceremonies in London, early in 1993. I said no. I think I actually used the phrase "I don't do musicals!" I was about to play *Hamlet*, remember! In retrospect I was being a little grand, but truly musicals were not, and to a certain extent still are not, my thing.

I worry that musicals, with their packaging of material into bite-sized songs and the various inherent glossy tropes, can potentially demean or diminish the material being discussed. This is not a revolutionary idea—the whole premise of Mel Brooks's *The Producers* and the reason it is so bellyachingly funny is this very idea.

Sam persisted. He took me out for lunch. I explained my concerns. I told him I had actually already been in a production of *Cabaret* at the Brunton Theatre in Musselburgh, just outside Edinburgh, in 1987. I had played Cliff, and while the director then had allowed me to insert passages from Christopher Isherwood's original novels to beef up the drama of Cliff's opening and closing monologues, I still couldn't reconcile the razzamatazz of the showbiz scenes with the awful historical facts of the book scenes. I also found I couldn't do that thing that I so admire musical actors' ability to do: to one minute be delivering dialogue quite normally, and in the next to be siiiiinnnnnnnggggiiinnng!!

Playing Cliff as he experienced both the personal and political maelstrom of Weimar Berlin had been a very emotional, cathartic thing to do, and I'd enjoyed the experience of that *Cabaret*, but I wasn't in a hurry to repeat it. Also, the Master of Ceremonies seemed to me a flimsy role, a turn, a mere device to carry the story along, almost puppetlike. But the net covering all of this was my worry of showbiz, artifice, and step ball-changes masking the worst of humanity. I felt that if I was going to play the Master of Ceremonies of a dingy cabaret club during one of the most dangerous times in history, the production should have that feel: dingy, seedy, debauched, dangerous. Not spruce and perky and sanitised.

It turned out that Sam and I were completely on the same page. He wanted the Kit Kat Club to be grimy and real, Sally Bowles to be flawed and broken. He told me Jane Horrocks was to play Sally and I was immediately drawn in. Jane is an amazing actor, who completely flings herself into a role. She would be the perfect brittle, damaged waif that Sally is in the Isherwood books, a character whose vulnerability and rawness is often lost by having the role played by a Broadway belter— again, perhaps, because of the expectations of the musical form. It is the central conundrum of the casting of *Cabaret*: the leading lady of the show isn't supposed to be a very good performer. If she were, why would she have ended up in a grubby old hole like the Kit Kat Club? But, of course, you can't have someone who can't sing as the lead in a big Broadway musical, can you?! If Sally is too proficient and secure in her craft, she loses the fragility she needs for the rest of the story. Jane would be able to nail both the delicate performer and the brittle offstage persona. She and I had met the year before on a film we shot in Wales, *Second Best*, directed by Chris Menges, with William Hurt playing a postmaster who adopts a troubled child. Jane played William Hurt's social worker and I played the boy's, and we got on really well.

I had read *Goodbye to Berlin* and *Mr. Norris Changes Trains*, the two books by Christopher Isherwood that spawned the John Van Druten play *I Am a Camera* and later Kander and Ebb and Joe Masteroff's *Cabaret*, but what struck me more and was fuel to the fire of my initial reticence to do the show was Isherwood's memoir, *Christopher and His Kind*. Here I found the real, unsanitised version of his time in Berlin. The romantic notion that he and his literary chums W. H. Auden and Stephen Spender moved to Berlin to chronicle the rise of fascism is completely destroyed by the frankness of this book. Isherwood, Auden, and Spender actually went to Berlin for cock! They were posh, queer English chaps who hightailed it to Berlin, where sex was cheap and anonymous and the shame of sexuality from the repressed, upper-class English society that spawned them was a lifetime away. But too soon their bacchanalian idyll was shattered by the chokehold of Nazism. *That* was the story and the sensibility that I felt we should be telling in our production of *Cabaret*.

And luckily, that was also the story Sam wanted to tell. Not only that, he wanted the Emcee character to be much more involved in the whole narrative, to act as a commentator, a conscience and guide for the audience throughout the whole show. He was to be omnipresent and ultimately a literal representation of the decay and degeneration of the time. At the moment, it just felt obvious and logical and right, but I now realise how rare it is for a director and an actor to come to a project so completely united.

I was now hooked, though also very anxious, as I was already daunted by the prospect of *Hamlet*. Here I was, agreeing to take on one of the greatest roles in musical theatre immediately after playing the Gloomy Dane. Not for the first time, I felt a bit of a fraud. And that feeling was only exacerbated when, as I feared, there was griping and discontent among the London musical crowd, or "West End Wendys", as they were known, that it was a disgrace that this plum and coveted musical role should have gone to (gasp!) a "straight" actor.

I should point out, in case you don't know, that *straight* here is not referring to my, or anyone else's, sexuality. No, for some reason I have still to fathom, "straight" has come to mean anything nonmusical in the theatre. So at the time I was perceived as—ironically when you consider my sexuality—a straight actor. Nowadays it is not unheard-of in some quarters for me to be referred to as a musical actor, but considering I have only ever done two musicals on the stage—*Cabaret* and *The Threepenny Opera* (I have a niche and I'm sticking to it!)—it would seem that isn't really accurate, either.

Of course, calling anything in the theatre "straight" can be a bit of a stretch, and actually what Sam and I were about to do with our joined intent for *Cabaret* was to infuse a musical role with the sensibility and critical thinking of a straight performance. Equally, I have seen some actors mostly known for doing musicals bring an energy and a performative layer to certain roles such that it would be impossible to imagine a straight actor bettering. As Edith Wharton said in *The Age of Innocence*, "Everything may be labelled, but everybody is not." That production of *Cabaret*—which utterly and completely changed my life—was a product of my ignoring the boundaries and constraints of what was expected or accepted and going with my gut. It was to be the start of me doing that in my real life, too.

As the *Emma* premiere party ended, my friend Camryn Man-heim asked us back to her place in the East Village for a nightcap. Camryn and I had bonded on the set of *Romy and Michele's High School Reunion* after I told her she had some food in her teeth.

"Thank you, Alan," I remember her saying. "No one ever does that!"

She had come to the premiere on her motorcycle and offered me a ride back to hers on the bike. With my fiancée and some chums following in my designated limo, Camryn and I sped off on her Harley, taking Fifth Avenue all the way downtown, with me riding pillion, literally laughing with glee inside my helmet. It was the perfect evening: celebrating a new piece of work surrounded by people I love, experiencing the ethereal magic of fireflies for the first time, and now an exhilarating joyride down one of the most iconic streets in the world. I had never been happier than I was that night. Only in New York, kids. Only in New York!

agony

11

I used to dread weekends. Especially in the autumn once October came around. That was when the pheasant-shooting season would begin, and every Saturday I'd find myself in a line of young men walking slowly through the woods of the country estate I grew up in, shouting and banging trees with a stick, encouraging the birds to flee the safety of their nests or roosts and fly towards a row of rich, older, and usually slightly drunk men (simply referred to as "the guns") who would do their best to shoot them dead. It's actually defined as a sport.

What I had to do was called beating, and I hated it. First of all it meant being out in the freezing cold or rain or snow all day, except for the short respites when I and the other beaters would be bounced to the next location of carnage in the back of a clanky old Land Rover that smelled of sweat and wet dog and animal blood, to await the assembly of the rich old men and begin the process all over again.

Being out all day in that peculiarly Scottish damp cold meant having no feeling in my fingers or my toes. I remember one Christmas getting a present of a pocket warmer, in which a stick of charcoal could be burned slowly inside a red-velvet-covered metal case, and it honestly felt like the best gift I had ever received.

At lunch we would be driven back to the stables, the only part of the old estate that remained after it had been blown up to avoid taxes in 1955, aside from the adjoining chapel, which was where the guns would have a sit-down lunch, while us boys walked around in circles banging our boots on the cobbles to try and regain the feeling in our frozen feet, munching on meat pies delivered from the local baker in the back of the same Land Rover we'd been in and out of all morning. The biggest thrill for me was getting a can of cola or some other fizzy drink to wash down my pie. We never got fizzy drinks at home. We were a strictly orange squash household.

The guns would drink lager and whisky. It topped up the nips they took all day from the silver flasks they secreted inside their Barbour jackets.

At the end of the day, we'd stand in a circle in the stables' courtyard, our hands outstretched, and one of the gamekeepers would press a few pound notes into each of them. When I got home, I'd sit by the fire and begin to thaw. Taking a bath would be an almost too painful pleasure as the tingling of the chilblains in my feet reacted to the hot water. I hated everything about beating. I hated the cold, I hated the smells, I hated the blood on my hands from having to carry the bleeding birds. I hated the constant barrage of the rifles, I hated the piercing whistle that was blown to signal the boys to start walking, I hated the rich, fat men to whom I was an invisible serf, and I hated the obsequious behaviour of the gamekeepers who praised their sozzled masters each time they blew the head off another poor creature that had been reared specifically for them to do so, and then loaded more cartridges into their barrels so they could do it all over again.

One rainy Saturday we were progressing in our customary line down a long, thin strip of woods that was abutted on both sides by arable land. Birds screamed in panic before us as they fled blindly into the guns' line of fire. Everything was as it should be. But then, word came along the line that there was a deer up ahead. When I caught my first sight of the creature, even from a distance, I felt unease. It looked panicked, no doubt alarmed by both the gunshots emanating from the clearing up ahead and the oncoming line of young men shouting and clacking their sticks against any bit of nature in their path. It was pacing back and forth, snorts of fear making steamy deposits from its nostrils in the freezing air.

"Why doesn't it just jump the fence and go into the field?" a boy near me cried out. It was true, the beast could easily escape its present dead end, but I'm sure it always connected open spaces with danger and was overwhelmed that this sliver of forest, its usual cover, was now a hotbed of threat.

As we made our way closer and closer to the end of the canopy of trees and the waiting lines of guns, I could see the deer become more and more agitated. I felt scared because I could tell something terrible was going to happen, but I couldn't take my eyes off its beauty. It was after mating season, so its antlers had been shed. This turned out to be in my favour, given what happened next. I wondered at what point the deer would make its decision to flee, and which direction it would take. I saw it look along the line of approaching boys and stop when it came to me.

Oh God, I thought, *I am the weakest link.*

Suddenly the deer bellowed and began running towards me. Other boys scattered as it approached, voices crying out in fear as its huge bulk thundered forward. But I froze. It was no use. There was nothing I could do but experience the inexorability of it all. I could smell it now, the sweat that glistened on its back and the mucus around its snout. I could feel its heat. Our eyes met and I saw that I was to be his sacrifice. A couple of metres away from me it left the ground and my gaze followed its flight. At the apex of its arc it towered above me like a mythical being. Then it came lower, and closer, and I felt its spit hit my face. At the last minute my body turned away in survival mode, and just then it made contact. Its skull against my hip and ribs. The terrified grunting and clattering of hooves as it regained its footing was deafening. I was propelled into the air, then everything went black. I share this story as it is the moment in my life that most closely chronicles what it felt like opening *Cabaret* on Broadway in 1998. Just like the deer racing towards me, the first night was a collision that I was helpless to avoid and would knock me sideways.

The opening was set for March 19, 1998, and I looked forward to it in some way heralding an easing of the pressure I had begun to feel during the previews. I was the new boy in town, the Scottish weirdo who had come out of nowhere and was fast becoming the toast of the Great White Way. The word on the street was the show was going to be a big hit and I was going to become a Broadway star.

"Your life's going to change," people would say when they came backstage after a preview, and they meant it as a positive thing. But having just recently begun to like my life again, I felt their words more as a harbinger than a blessing. *How* was my life going to change? And did it really *have* to? I was on my own in a new city having what I didn't realise at the time was a once-in-a-lifetime experience. It was thrilling, but also overwhelming and confusing. Every night after the show I would go into the shower and burst into tears. I wasn't sad. It was just a way to let everything out, to expunge the waves of excitement and fear that washed over me in equal measure.

One night, early on, the stage manager banged on that shower door to tell me that Whoopi Goldberg was there, and she wanted to meet me. I shouted I'd be out soon and went back to my sobbing. Then I heard Whoopi herself banging on the door. "What's he doing in there! I want to meet this guy!"

Another night after my shower I came bounding down the stairs and was stopped in my tracks by a vision. Waiting patiently outside my dressing room was Lauren Bacall. I was still on the half landing above her, my skinny pale frame draped only in a towel. She turned and looked up at me, her arm outstretched, her finger jabbing with each word: "You!" she began, "are a sensation and a killer!"

Every night felt like some surreal showbiz dream. Once I opened my dressing room door to find the opera diva Jessye Norman towering above me. "I have one of your records!" is all I could manage to say.

There was a part in the show at the beginning of the second act when I would go into the audience and take a woman and then a man up onstage for a little dance. It was all completely improvised both in my choice of who I'd pick and what I or they would say as we had our little waltzy chat. One night before the show, Natasha Richardson, who was playing Sally Bowles, came into my room and told me that Mikhail Baryshnikov was in the audience that night and suggested I choose him to dance with. And so I did. Of course, the crowd went wild, especially when I said things like "You should do this professionally." But I realised that night that it was a mistake to bring up someone famous. That moment in the show worked because I was in control and the audience members were being played with. That night with Misha, I was the one desperately trying to maintain control of the onstage dynamic while at the same time totally freaking out at how magical it was to dance with Baryshnikov. One minute I was downstage right doing my usual opening gambit with a man of "No, no, I lead" (which he wasn't having any of), and the next I was way upstage left and truly it felt like I hadn't touched the ground once. So, to say I was swept off my feet would be accurate on every level. It took all I had to get this dancing witch back to his seat and continue with the show. When he came to my dressing room afterwards, after the initial laughter recalling what had been the highlight of the evening for everyone, I made another of my now increasingly common goofy comments: "You're a really good dancer," I said earnestly.

"Thank you, Alan," replied Mikhail Baryshnikov. "So are you!"

This was the longest preview period I'd ever been a part of—over a month of performances before the official opening—and I just wished it would happen already.

As exciting as it was to feel the show was going to be a success, and my interpretation of this iconic role was being lauded in the home of modern musical theatre, at the same time the feeling and the vocalising coming from all sides that *something big was going to happen* was triggering for me. Not so long ago, a similar phrase had been a constant refrain in my life. But then the word "bad" had been in the place of "big".

For a long time after that summer four years before when my life had gone off the rails, when divorce loomed and breakdown beckoned and the reality of my father's abuse came flooding back, *something bad is going to happen* was like an evil mantra embedded in my psyche. For a long time, I associated change with pain. And big change would mean big pain. Of course, no part of what people thought was going to happen to me after the opening of *Cabaret* involved pain—in fact quite the opposite—but nonetheless, I knew that my anxiety was more than just normal first-night nerves.

I've always appreciated knowing what other people think of me, good or bad, and certainly that goes back to my childhood, where I knew exactly my parents' views of me, though their opinions were radically opposed. My father told me I was worthless, my mother told me I was precious. They couldn't both be right, and so I learned early how necessary it is to make up my own mind about myself, as well as how important it is to understand where and how you are placed in others' minds. As a performer, one of the things I crave with the opening of a play is getting to know how the show and my performance are to be perceived in the world. It's truly not about needing affirmation—though of course it's always much nicer to be in a hit than not—but to know if my opinions of the piece correspond with the outside world's. I am someone who has strong opinions about my work and the work of others. I don't like everything I see so I don't expect everyone to like what I do. Also, I feel it is entirely possible and indeed important to be able to separate your opinion of the piece you are doing (and indeed your work in it) from the commitment and energy you use to serve the writer and the production every night. To put it another way: I have been in shows I think are complete stinkers, but that never stops me from going out every night and giving it my best shot.

The opening night finally arrived. I had never known anything like it. I could barely get into my dressing room for the sheer mass of bouquets and gifts and balloons that were spilling out onto the landing and down the edges of the staircase to the stage. The goodwill I felt from both the company and from New York City was palpable.

The great thing about a Broadway opening night is that there are no critics in the audience. They are brought in over the last few previews and the reviews are held until the opening night is over. Nowadays, however, due to the glories of the internet, that no longer means reading the papers' first editions at the opening night party over a celebratory (or commiserating) cocktail. At my last New York play opening I had read most of the notices by the time I got out of the car to enter the opening night party. I had even read a couple before the curtain had come down! There aren't even any real, money-paying punters in the first night audience, either. The tickets for every Broadway opening night are blocked off to the public and the whole thing is dedicated to celebrating the birth of a new piece of theatre, ushered into the world surrounded by friends and family and the theatre community.

By contrast, the first nights I had known before, latterly in London and in Scotland before that, were utterly terrifying. There, *all* of the critics attend en masse. This makes the evening less of a celebration and more of an ordeal, something to be got through rather than a chance to enjoy performing the work you have made to your loved ones and peers before the scrutiny and judgement of it becomes public. What makes it worse is that from the stage you can actually sometimes see the critics, and hear them, scratching away on their notepads! It is one of the most self-conscious experiences I think anyone could imagine. Of course, the awful thing is that if you have a bad night, if something goes wrong, then that is the version of the show that will forever be considered. And so, the desperation to get everything right, for it to be perfect, is what makes a British opening—actually it is named quite frankly and accurately "press night"—not a celebration but a test. So when Erin, the show's press representative, with whom I had spent a *lot* of time over the previous few months, told me that *The New Yorker* wanted to send a photographer to capture me coming offstage after my triumphant Broadway debut, I told her unequivocally that my answer was *no*. I felt I had done more than my fair share of publicity to promote the show already, and backstage is a hallowed place for me, not a place for a press photographer and certainly not *during* the performance (they wanted to set up the camera in my dressing room while the show was still going on) and definitely not on opening night!!

Just the logistics of fitting a photographer into my minuscule room, let alone any equipment, with me racing in and out, performing the regimented quick changes with my dresser before racing back down the stairs again for the next scene, was way too stressful. My dressing room was tiny—so tiny that I could lie on my chaise longue and wash my hands in the sink at the same time. It was more a large closet with a sink than a dressing room.

And also, I knew this night was going to be hard for me. Even with my nightly weepy releases in the shower I still often had bouts of panic and anxiety that brought on a racing heart and shallow breathing. The publicity team pushed. I said no again. "She is Diane Arbus's daughter," they crowed. I didn't care. The producers chimed in. "This was a big moment in my life and Broadway history," they pleaded, little understanding how wrong that psychology was. I finally buckled when I realised I was probably inducing more stress for myself by continuing to refuse their pleas than I would by actually allowing it to happen. And I also thought of the great Charles Bukowski line, "If you're going to try, go all the way. Otherwise don't even start." I was opening a huge musical on Broadway, after all; maybe this is just what they do? There's a theory that the adrenaline rush an actor experiences on an opening night is the equivalent of having a minor car crash. Well, I was in the car crash now, it was going to happen, maybe I should just take my foot off the brake and go with it?

The first thing Amy Arbus said to me as I ran into my room to do a quick change and saw her perched on my chaise longue, her camera clasped close to her chest, trying to take up as little room as possible, was: "I know you don't want to do this."

"Oh," I stammered. "Well. I didn't but, you know, you're here now, and it's fine."

"I promise I won't get in your way," she said as I disappeared back down the stairs to make my final entrance.

When I walked back into my room again ten minutes later, it was actually nice to have a stranger there in order to force myself to hold it together. Almost immediately guests started to arrive, and the room was packed. Backed into the standing space between the sink, the window, and the chaise, I lit up a cigarette and slugged from a bottle of wine. Amy caught the moment, my agent's hand holding aloft a plastic cup of wine coming into the shot, perfectly capturing the celebration and oddness of that instant. I was feted but alone, the toast of the town but a little distant and more than a little scared.

I am so glad I acquiesced to Amy coming and taking that picture. It really is like looking inside a time capsule when I study it now. There on the ceiling above me is the cardboard cutout of the Spice Girls I had pinched from the special screening of *Spice World* I had taken the *Cabaret* cast to one Saturday morning before rehearsals;

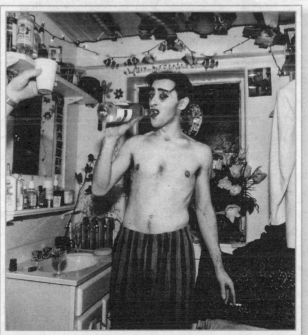

there are the flowers I'd painted on the wall, and the words "Wilkommen, bienvenu, welcome" above the window.

I stayed in touch with Amy, the photographer, and over the years we became good friends. Sixteen years later when I went back to the role of the Master of Ceremonies for the third time—the revival of the revival, again in New York City in 2014–15, she again came and took my picture on opening night—this time with my full and willing cooperation. She shot me in the same position, swigging a bottle of wine—no cigarette this time!—and it's fascinating to see the difference in the two images: in my body, my openness to her lens, my comfort, and my happiness.

Our theatre on West Forty-Third Street, rechristened the Kit Kat Klub after the name of the fictitious venue in *Cabaret* itself, had until very recently been used as a nightclub, Club Expo. (In fact, at weekends it was *still* used as a nightclub, and I used to come down the stairs after having drinks in my dressing room and dance on the very stage I'd been singing on less than an hour before.) The whole place was falling to bits, and backstage was pretty disgusting. We all went to town with fairy lights, and a fresh coat of paint was slapped on everywhere, which meant that the single mottled glass window in my room wouldn't open. When I finally managed to pull it up that first time during the tech rehearsal to see what lay beneath, I found a slightly raked roof entirely encased by walls from the surrounding buildings, a sort of wonky outdoor room with the sky as its ceiling. There were syringes and old condoms strewn across the floor. It was the epitome of grotty, but to me it was perfect. I could see its potential. When spring came, I had it cleaned up and some plants and a couple of trees delivered. With the addition of some rugs, pillows, and sparkly lights it became the most vaunted roof terrace in town, where I'd entertain postshow guests under the stars. Sometimes I entertained postshow stars under the stars! That summer the garden became my sanctuary. I'd go out before the show and have a little time to myself, water my plants at the intermission. I even showered alfresco after the show via a hose attached to the sink tap inside, and of course on the nights when the theatre was transformed into a nightclub there was much pregaming before descending to the revelry below. It was like having your own private room at a club, somewhere to escape to avoid prying eyes when naughtiness began.

The only problem was that the only way into the garden was through the stiff, rickety single-hung window that my guests had to crawl through. I remember the night Christy Turlington came backstage with her granny, and as I watched both of them clamber through the window I realised something had to give.

Luckily, around that time, my contract was up for renewal and my agent had asked if there was anything else I wanted in addition to the hike in salary. What did I request but a new dressing-room window! One that made it easier for everyone—even a supermodel's granny—to make the pilgrimage to my magical garden and share a drink with me. Lo and behold, within days my wish was granted.

That first opening night, I took forever to get to the party. I wanted to savour the quiet time with my friends who'd come over from London. Tasha Richardson popped her head in on her way out.

"It's very poor form to let your leading lady arrive at the party before you, Alan!" she quipped. So, I got into my suit, a sparkly tuxedo that had been given to me for the occasion by Hugo Boss—rather ironically considering the revelation years later that the actual Hugo Boss had designed uniforms for the Hitler Youth and the SS—and off I went.

After the obligatory press line as I entered the party, I turned to Erin the publicist and thanked her for having guided me through the last few months. I told her that I'd be sorry not to be seeing her every day now that the show had opened. She looked at me rather strangely, as though she were talking to a slow child.

"But Alan," she said, "we're going to be seeing lots of each other. Award season is about to begin!"

"What?"

All those people were right: my life did change. The show was a sensation, I did become a big Broadway star, and I did see a lot of Erin as I was nominated for all the awards. Every day there were receptions and photo shoots and press calls. The pressure didn't ease, it just changed. It now wasn't about whether the show would be a hit, it was whether I would win a Tony. It was of course incredibly flattering, and initially fun—I joked about my name seemingly having been changed because every time I was introduced now, I would hear "Please welcome Tony Nominee." But at every turn there was some new and unexpected reason to feel anxiety. I was told I had won Outstanding Actor in a Musical at the Outer Critics Circle awards, the first of the season. I liked the fact they told you ahead of time. It made the evening of the actual ceremony more of a celebration, devoid of the worry about whether or not you'd be getting up onstage and having to make a speech and trying to hold it together.

I think a lot of people assume that actors are really comfortable with the notion of leaping to their feet and expounding extemporaneously. Some are, but they are the minority. We are more used to playing other people than ourselves, and add to that the lethal combination of alcohol and surprise that many award ceremonies involve, is it any wonder more actors don't burst into tears while clutching their newly acquired gongs?! So, for the Outer Critics Circle awards at least I was expecting a relatively stress-free evening, aside from the public speaking bit, until Erin dropped her bombshell.

"They want you to suggest someone to present the award to you," she said nonchalantly one day in the car going to some photo shoot.

"You mean, like one of my chums from the show?" I asked. Erin gave me the slow-child look again.

"Well, no, they really prefer someone famous. So, if there's anyone you'd like to ask . . ."

It will probably make people who know me well laugh like drains when I say that I didn't know anyone famous in New York back then. I had only been in the city a few months. In fact, I only knew a couple of people outside of the *Cabaret* company. For a week I racked my brain in vain. Every celeb who came backstage was a potential candidate, but I knew it would be too odd and disingenuous to ask a stranger, and

I'd never have the courage anyway. Finally, and rather ashamedly, I told Erin I didn't know anyone appropriate (that is, famous enough) to give me the award.

"Oh, I forgot to tell you," she said. "You don't have to ask anyone. Someone has come forward and offered to present it to you!"

I breathed a huge sigh of relief. What were the chances?!

"Who?" I asked.

"Lauren Bacall," replied Erin with a smile.

And so, my first ever award in America was given to me by an American legend, my new pal, Betty Bacall.

The Tonys were fast approaching and the pressure was mounting. Almost every day it seemed we were performing on *Letterman*, or *The Rosie O'Donnell Show*, or I was taking my clothes off and having guy-liner applied before going in front of some star snapper's lens, or I was being whisked around cocktail parties full of voters where I couldn't even have a drink as I had a show to do that night.

And after every performance, the madness would continue. Everyone came to see *Cabaret*. I actually still can't believe some of the legends I met backstage, especially people so exalted and almost mythological in their connection to another era—and, to this little boy from rural Angus, Scotland—another planet: Arthur Miller, Gregory Peck, Gena Rowlands, Kirk Douglas, Janet Leigh, James Earl Jones, Carol Channing, Lou Reed, Eartha Kitt, Barry Manilow, Paul Newman, and Joanne Woodward. It was an intensive crash course in American cultural royalty.

Perhaps the most monumental guest to attend the show, however, both in terms of star power and connection to the material, was Liza. Liza is one of those people whose surname has ceased to be either important or necessary, so I won't bother to use it here. As with Cher and Madonna (though there will forever be two Madonnas!), Liza had reached the level of single-name recognition.

The theatre was abuzz with the news of her attendance. I thought back to my days at drama school when, in my second year, I was directing a play and was searching for a suitable piece of music to be played as its conclusion. One of my classmates, Marion, suggested I listen to the album *Liza with a* Z, which was the TV special collab-ouration between Liza and Bob Fosse. At the time I was nineteen, and neither Bob Fosse nor Liza had really registered in my late-blooming showbiz lexicon. But I listened to the record and without really under-standing why, I was blown away. Even in my tinny Walkman head-phones as I rode the Glasgow underground home, Liza managed to connect. I decided to use the song "It Was a Party". Its spiralling despair but at the same time desperation to hold on to the optimism and fun of yore struck a chord with me, and totally worked for the denouement of my directorial debut.

As I was marvelling that later that evening I would meet the woman who had so moved me all those years before, I was interrupted from my reverie by Natasha.

"Alan, you know Liza's in this evening and I have to make a speech at the curtain call and invite her to come up onstage?"

"What?" I gasped. This was all news to me. Liza would join us *onstage*?! I'd need a while to process that.

"You mean, she'll come up and . . ." I stuttered.

"Well, you know, she played Sally in the movie, and we have to pay homage to her. It's what they do here," continued Tash, once more helpfully guiding me through the mores of Broadway etiquette.

"So . . ." I began a question.

"So, I think you should go down and get Liza and help her up the steps onto the stage," she said.

"What?" I could feel the anxiety rising in my chest.

"I just think it would be nice for the leading man to do that, don't you?"

How could I argue with that? So instead of focusing on my per-formance that night, all I could think of was how I was going to extri-cate a Broadway and Hollywood legend out of her chair and somehow propel her towards centre stage, possibly against her will. Would I say anything? Should I merely make gestures? And when should I begin this task? Before Tasha started her speech or would that look weird, like I was fleeing? During, or would that be disrespectful?

Of course, I was foolishly putting myself in Liza's position and imagining the horror I would feel if I went to a play in which I had once performed and the person who was now playing my role asked me to join them onstage, and the leading lady came off said stage to drag me up there with them. Because for me that *would* be a total and utter nightmare.

But I did not grow up in the United States—and even now I am desperately trying to catch up with its popular culture and societal mores—and back in 1998 I did not have the slightest grasp on that fusion of homage and schmaltz that engulfs a room when an American entertainment legend is present. And, even more obviously, I am not Liza. Liza, I think, loved the idea of being taken up onstage that night, or at least she made us think she did, and that's what it's all about. It was the first instalment of the showbiz master class she continues to give me to this day.

But there was more. At intermission, as I was nervously practising what I would say to Liza as I made my approach, Tasha came downstairs to my room once again.

"I'm slightly worried that Liza might stay onstage too long and think that we want her to sing or something. So, once she's had her standing ovation and we've hugged her, I think you should sort of gently guide her back to her seat."

So now I was not only dragging a legend onstage but also having to dump her off it again before she could burst into song! My evening was becoming more fraught by the second.

As it turned out, the entire scene played out like a sincere and magical dream. Tasha made a lovely speech about being so nervous performing in front of Liza. Indeed, Liza was sitting so close to the stage she practically *was* in front of us. She was at one of the front tables, sitting on the aisle, and as I walked past her in my character's drugged-out haze having just introduced Sally Bowles to sing the titular swan song, she grabbed my arm and whispered loudly, "Terrific!"

And I needn't have worried about getting her up out of her seat. As I came towards her, she took my hand and I guided her up the steps, the first night of many I would act as her chaperone. The crowd went totally nuts and in lieu of saying anything above the deafening cheering and applause, Liza basked humbly (a difficult combo but the pro that she is, she pulled it off with élan) then spun round towards us, flung her arms open wide in a signature Liza dance move as though propelling all the love the audience was directing to her back onto the *Cabaret* company. It was a thrilling, breathtaking, utterly generous moment, and I was so mesmerised I totally forgot about my getting-her-off-the-stage duties, but a helpful nudge in the ribs from Tasha brought me back to reality and I subtly but firmly guided Liza towards her seat. She kissed me and I clambered back to join my castmates.

"Alan, I want to be your friend forever," Liza trilled as she entered my room shortly after. I had showered quickly that night and I hadn't cried. Meeting her was utterly exciting, of course, but it didn't come with the anxiety and breathlessness of so many of my postshow experiences. Somehow, I felt Liza would understand me, that she probably did her own version of crying in the shower, too, like the screaming under a bridge she did at the end of the film of *Cabaret*. With absolutely nothing to go on beyond the few moments of contact downstairs, I already felt we were connected.

We hugged and chatted and then I turned to say hello to Fred Ebb, the show's lyricist, who had been her date that night. Fred was a wisecracking darling and he and John Kander, the composer, had always been so kind to me. They had come over to see our original production in London at the Donmar Warehouse and were delighted by the earthiness and raciness on display. Afterwards John had said to me, "Has there ever been a time a director has asked you to do something and you said no, I can't do that, I won't go that far?"

I thought for a second. "No," I replied.

"Clearly," deadpanned Fred.

As I turned back to Liza I saw she had moved out of the way to allow Fred through to hug me, but as my room was so tiny, she was now in a really awkward position, squashed against the wall with her face literally *in* my recently dampened towel that was hanging on a hook.

"Oh gosh, Liza," I said as I helped her out of her cramped imprisonment. "You're all squashed up against my towel."

"Oh, Alan," she gushed in that wavering, tinkling, soul-revealing voice like a hot spring bubbling out of the earth, "I'd squash up against anything for you!"

A few weeks later, Joel Grey came to see the show and it was my turn to make the speech and invite him up onstage for an ovation. Since I had come to do the role of the Emcee in New York I'd been quizzed constantly in interviews about Joel and his iconic performance in the stage and movie versions of *Cabaret*. Everyone seemed to want to know if my interpretation was rooted in some sort of contrarian desire to be the antithesis to his. I always replied no, I really hadn't thought of him at all when I was preparing or rehearsing. I'd seen the film, of course, and loved it and him, but as the stage show is quite different from the film in plot as well as obviously in medium, I truly never felt any desire to do anything other than play the part how I thought it should be played, in the moment that I was doing it. In one interview I rather exasperatedly said I had never been asked more questions about someone I had never met. Soon after a note was delivered to me at the theatre from the man himself, stating, "You think that's bad? I come home every night and my answerphone is full of people telling me how great you are!"

On the evening Joel attended I was incredibly nervous, but actually more about meeting him and the speech I would have to make afterwards than about performing in front of him.

I think it must have been strange for Joel, having been associated— and rightly lauded—for a performance both on stage and film, only to have some Scottish scamp come along and be endlessly compared to and contrasted with you. This is how I look at it: great roles are ones that can be reinterpreted over and over again. When you play Hamlet, many, many different actors, who can be referenced in relation to you, have put their own individual stamp on that part. Each version has something unique and idiosyncratic and each one is very much affected by not only the production but the circumstances and time in which it is performed. There is no one definitive performance of Hamlet, but a compendium of them throughout the ages.

The Master of Ceremonies in *Cabaret* is one of those great roles that invite vastly different and equally iconic interpretations, but I suppose that since the show was only written in 1965 (the year of my birth, coincidentally), and there have only been four Broadway productions of it (Joel appearing in the first two and me in the others), *and* that maybe the musical is a form that tends to take fewer risks in terms of reinterpreting its classics than "straight" theatre does, there have only really been two very well-known versions of that character—Joel's and mine. My hope is that before too long there will be a young actor (of any gender) who is starring in a new Broadway or West End version of the show and their Emcee will be ranked alongside ours in terms of its total reinvention.

Awards season was now in full swing. In addition to the Critics Circle, I won the Drama Desk, Theatre World, and New York Press awards. I was honoured by the Drama League, named one of the 100 Most Creative People in Entertainment (!) in *Entertainment Weekly*'s It List, and given a special award at city hall by the New York City public advocate both for my performance and for "exemplary leadership, commitment and advocacy on behalf of the gay and lesbian community and all New Yorkers". The best part of this last honour was being driven back uptown to the theatre in one of those special, unmarked police cars. Traffic was a little heavy and I was starting to worry I'd be late to start my preparations for that night's performance when suddenly a siren started blaring. I looked around to see where it was coming from and realised *it was coming from inside the car*! The vehicles in front of us immediately began to peel away towards the sidewalks and magically an empty lane appeared. We sped off, running red lights with abandon and me squealing with glee. I felt like a combination of a criminal, an invalid, and a member of the royal family. It was deafening and utterly thrilling, and I got to the theatre on time.

But lurking in my future, the final hurdle in this great marathon of laurels, was the Tonys, broadcast live on television and in front of six thousand people in New York's iconic Radio City Music Hall. I would be performing "Wilkommen" with the Kit Kat boys and girls and rehearsals for the number were a source of great stress. What I didn't realise beforehand was that awards ceremonies showed truncated versions of all the Broadway numbers. The version of "Wilkommen" I opened the theatre show with every night was seven and a half minutes long. On Tony night I would sing live but over a pre-recorded track that was at a faster speed than the live band I was used to; the music and choreography were cut and pasted into a version that captured the feel and sensibility of the actual show, but trimmed down to a bite-sized and palatable three-minute chunk that could slot in before the next commercial break.

To some this may sound fairly simple and easy to pull off, but to someone who is not a quick study in dance and who was already in a perpetual state of anxiety about this new altered-reality life, it totally freaked me out. The Tonys were the final part of an exhausting, glittering, jittery odyssey, and represented the gateway to what I hoped would be a return to some semblance of normality, when I could just go to work and do the show and go for drinks afterwards. Rinse and repeat. Don't get me wrong: I was incredibly grateful for this experience, so fulfiled that my work in the show was connecting and being revered, but the level of attention and the pressure I felt carrying the production was something I hadn't experienced on such a sustained and intense level before.

One thing that helped ease the tension was yet another awards ceremony: the FANYs. Yes, that's right. The Friends of New York Theatre, which technically should have spawned the acronym FONY—but perhaps not wanting to sound inauthentic or, more likely, recognising a good gag when they saw one—decided instead to plump for FANY. The evening was relaxed and funny, a gathering of young theatre nerds who wanted to celebrate the Broadway season and not take things too seriously. I found it hard not to considering the differing meanings of the word "fanny" in the United Kingdom and the United States. I remember one of my first nights in New York, having a saucy laugh with some chums and one of them saying, "Oh, Alan, I'm going to smack your fanny." I was stopped in my tracks. Accepting my Best Actor in a Musical award I said, "Ever since I heard about these awards, I have craved FANY. And tonight, I finally have my hands on a FANY!"

The weekend before the big night saw a bumper crop of legends drop by after the show. On Friday, I was dumbstruck when Sean Connery walked into my dressing room. For those of you who are not Scottish I feel I should give you some context to try to convey the magnitude of this encounter. Sean Connery was the King of Scotland. But a sort of virile, benevolent, vital, and present king, not some old bloke in a cloak. So, to see him before me, arms outstretched, repeating only the words "Alan, Alan, Alan" and pulling me into an embrace was at once a comfort, an honour, and a destiny.

But he was wearing a white cardigan, and all I remember thinking as we went in for the hug was that I was going to smear great wads of my still very present makeup all over the King of Scotland's virginal apparel. He didn't mind, however.

The next evening, the Saturday, Angela Lansbury was in our audience. Both Sean and Angela were in town for the Tonys, Angela to present and Sean because he was nominated as one of the producers of the Yasmina Reza play *Art*.

Seven years before, I had won an Olivier award for my performance in *Accidental Death of an Anarchist* at the National Theatre in London and Angela had presented it to me. Now, here she was again. Perhaps Angela Lansbury was my lucky theatre award talisman?

My date for the Tonys was Camryn Manheim, my *Romy and Michele's High School Reunion* co-star. Two years previously, when we had been shooting that film, Camryn had a Tonys viewing party at her house in LA. She was a New York transplant and many of her friends were there that night. I remember arriving late, and everyone being very excited about a musical written by one of their friends that seemed to be doing quite well. Not knowing any of the shows or the actors they were cheering for, I felt more excited by the sushi Camryn had made. It turned out the show they were cheering for was *Rent*, and their friend its late author, Jonathan Larson.

"You'll probably be performing on the Tonys next year, Alan," Camryn said to me that night. (At that point *Cabaret* was slated to be in the upcoming 1997 Broadway season, before the original venue fell through.)

"Hardly," I scoffed. "What are the Tonys even like?" I asked between munches.

"I've never been," she replied rather sadly. "I've always dreamt of going."

"Well, if I get invited next year, I'll ask you to be my date!" I promised.

It took a little longer than either of us expected but I am a man of my word, and Camryn strolled down the red carpet with me in 1998. I also had my besties from London, Susie and Andrew, come along, too. We walked in together, my little pack of comfort to keep the rising showbiz anxiety at bay. We were all in our finery. Camryn especially had gone to town in a gown that put the *d* in "décolletage"! I was casual, though again bursting with historical irony, in a black T-shirt and black leather suit by Hugo Boss. My dyed black hair was flopping over my eyes and on my feet were black platform sneakers, an homage to the Spice Girls! I looked how I suppose I was perceived—a skinny, slightly subversive, European oddball.

We took our seats. Sue and Andrew were farther back, and somewhere else in the mêlée were two other London chums, Sebastian and Peter. It felt good to know I had bestie backup, no matter what happened—should I win and have to get up and make a speech, lose and be showered with pity, or royally screw up my performance in front of millions of people.

At the early morning dress rehearsal in Radio City before going on to our theatre to do our matinee (no wonder I was exhausted!), I was delighted to discover that photographs of presenters and other celebrity guests were stuck to the seats where they would be sitting that evening so the camera people could practise where to look for reaction shots. I had been told that Annette Bening would be presenting my award, so I posed for a photo with her picture. I joked that it would probably be the closest I'd get to her all night.

In the first part of the telecast, as I watched from the audience, I heard the cheers emanate around Radio City when my image appeared onscreen and I was referred to as the "sensational new star of *Cabaret*."

The out-of-body experience was heightened by the fact I was seeing myself onscreen arriving at the very awards ceremony I was now sitting watching! It was a pretty apt symbol for the way my life had felt

COURTESY OF RIVKA KATVAN

for the past six months: a strange loop of glamour and celebrity that I was both at the centre of and outside looking in to all at the same time.

Soon I was whisked away to Radio City's labyrinthian backstage and reunited with the *Cabaret* ensemble. I had little time to chat, though, as I had to be poured into my costume and have the pale body makeup applied along with the requisite bruises, track marks, and red glitter to my nipples.

Before long we were escorted down in a massive elevator to the stage level. *The Lion King* had just performed and as the elevator doors opened, we saw a large group of actors dressed as gazelles, zebras, and lions being herded off stage left. Publicists in ball gowns and headphones were ushering presenters and winners to the press room. The whole scene was Fellini-esque. We were walked to our marks, a stage manager casually told me to stand by, and then magically from somewhere I heard Rosie O'Donnell introduce us, followed by loud cheering and the opening notes of our song. I started to curl my index finger in a come-hither manner, a spotlight fell on it and glided up my body to my face. I hoped I was four bars in because I started singing, "Wilkommen. . . ."

Three minutes later it was all over. I watched it again recently and I was a little taken aback. I don't think the Tonys had ever before seen an androgynous-looking man touching himself and both sexes of his equally scantily clad castmates. By that point both we in the show and Broadway in general were fairly used to the risqué and groundbreaking nature of the production. Now we were beaming it into living rooms across America and the scandal was reignited on a national level.

"*Cabaret!* The show that requires no Viagra," quipped Rosie as we took our bows.

As soon as we came offstage, the ensemble members were whisked to a waiting bus to take them back to the theatre and I was rushed back upstairs to be de-sleazed and made to look like a respectable, proper actor once more. As I was being led back down through the corridors to my seat in the auditorium, I bumped into Tasha Richardson, who had just come offstage after winning Best Actress in a Musical. I gave her a congratulatory hug and she began to weep in my arms. She explained that her tears were for her late father, the director Tony Richardson, to whom she'd just dedicated her win saying, "This is for you, Papa. It is a Tony, after all."

A photographer asked us to pose for a picture, someone in a headset apologised but said they *had* to take me away, and that little moment of intimacy was over. Now it was a race against the clock to get me to my seat.

The show was running long. I manoeuvred that always awkward social interaction of telling the hired person who was in my seat (they are actually called, rather bluntly, seat fillers) that I was now back and they could go. I could hear Rosie O'Donnell address the audience and say that the show was running way over time and we were in danger of being cut off before the last award of the night, Best Musical, was announced. The remaining presenters were going to cut to the chase and immediately announce the nominations, and anyone who was nominated for one of the last few awards was asked to cut their speech down to a bare minimum if they won. I marvelled that this night could actually get more stressful.

"Sixty seconds to air," some disembodied voice announced, as I mumbled frantically to myself, editing my prepared speech in my head. As the countdown continued, I decided that should I win, I would begin with, "I want to thank everyone Natasha Richardson thanked." That way I'd save so much time. But then I thought, is that weird? She also thanked her husband. So, I decided I'd add, "Except Liam Neeson."

There, that would be better. But wait, was that even weirder?

My reverie was broken by "And we're back in five, four . . ."

Suddenly Annette Bening was onstage. Time was indeed tight as she began announcing the nominations almost before her applause had died, and they didn't cut away to the nominees, as is usual, but stayed on Annette, presumably to save even more time.

"And the American Theatre Wing's Tony goes to . . ."

In the couple of seconds before the winner's name was called, I experienced a strange sense of calm. It felt just like that moment many years before when the terrified deer had lunged at me, seeing me as his most likely chance of survival. And just as with the deer, tonight I was in this position because of who and what I truly was.

authenticity 12

It's hard to be your authentic self when you don't know who you really are.

To truly be whole as a person you need to be aware of everything that's happened to you, and for a long time I was running half-empty in that department. If large and painful swaths of your childhood are not accessible to you, you can hardly hope to become an evolved adult. So, for a big chunk of my life I was a chameleon, becoming whichever version of me was required by whomever. Not a bad skill for an actor to have, you might imagine—though not too healthy when you aren't able to stop.

Of course, like life, acting benefits from authenticity. I now understand that the best kind of acting—of art in general in fact—is what comes from within, not what we display. Making peace with what lies within is how we live authentically, too.

I'm fascinated by the concept of star quality. It is a much-overused and -misused term, most often erroneously defined by someone's achievements. If someone is paid millions of dollars per movie, they are generally perceived to be a star. But they might not have star quality. Merely being famous maketh you not a star, in my book at least. Just being on a screen or stage is not the measure here. What interests me is why we are drawn to look at someone up on that screen or stage more than someone else. You know it happens. Certain performers just draw you in. Of course, sometimes it is because they have the flashy roles, or because they are loud or weird or pulling focus on purpose, but sometimes it is because we simply prefer to look at what they are doing, how they are reacting. They draw us towards them because they are more fascinating.

Being a performer is not the only arena in which you can be a star, however—my kind of star at least. Some of the brightest stars I have ever encountered have been waiting staff or bartenders or drivers. Star quality is about being prepared to be, or simply just being, vulnerable and open. It is the energy a person exudes that allows us to see into their very soul, to their most authentic self.

I know a farmer who is a huge star. And I have a friend who works in the field of LGBTQ+ rights who is, to me, one of the brightest in the firmament. They both shimmer, inviting my curiosity. And that of everyone who meets them.

I used to think that acting was all about putting layers on top of yourself: accents, costumes, physicality. Of course, it is a lot to do with that, but these should only be augmentations to what is at the core of a performance, and that is the performer themself. I think of myself as an interpreter of the words I say, not just a vessel to carry them to an audience's ears and eyes. I think an audience should see my characters and hear their words through a prism that is me—my experience, my sense of humour, and even my beliefs and opinions.

I remember the moment exactly when I realised what acting was all about. You'd perhaps hope this happened when I was a child, or during a class at drama school, but no. It occurred while I was actually onstage, in the middle of a performance at the Royal Lyceum Theatre in Edinburgh in 1986. The play was *Mr. Government* by Stuart Paterson. It was a bleak story of a man's struggle to reconnect with his rural Ayrshire community after World War I. I played Donal, a boy with learning difficulties, who turned out to be the son of the returning antihero. There was a scene in which I had to get very upset and I was working myself up in all sorts of ways to try to fake this emotion. One day I did nothing. I listened. I said the lines, got lost in the scene, and simply let myself feel what my character was feeling, what indeed had been written for him. I was authentic. I lost my self-consciousness. I stopped trying to put layers on top and let a bit of myself come through. And that night, the scene was more moving and arresting than it had ever been. *Oh,* I remember thinking to myself as I walked back to my dressing room. *So that's what acting is all about!*

And I think it's no accident that I was playing someone child like when this epiphany occurred. I often cite that we should look to children to remind us of what acting should be. Actors used to be called players, and that is simply all it is: playacting, pretending to be someone (or something) and meaning it. If a kid comes up to you and declares they are a dragon, and you say, "Yes, wow, your breath is so fiery, I can feel the heat from here," then they are a dragon. That is really all acting is about.

So, I hereby apologise profusely to all the audiences who—before I had this momentous epiphany—paid good money to see me in *Macbeth* and *Macbeth Possessed,* at the Tron Theatre in Glasgow. Or in *Trumpets and Raspberries* and *The Ugly Duckling* for Borderline Theatre Company, *Tartuffe* and *A Streetcar Named Desire* at the Royal Lyceum, Edinburgh, the episode of *Travelling Man* on Granada TV, and the film *Passing Glory.* It's not that I was bad in these, it's just that I could easily have been better, and it irks me to this day that I wasn't.

I had graduated from drama school a year earlier, in 1985, but hadn't found my voice there, either literally or metaphorically. But you can't really blame me—I'd actually never been asked to use it.

In the three years of my studies I wasn't asked to use my natural Scottish accent, my authentic voice, once. The plays we studied were varied—Chekhov, Shakespeare, the Greeks—but modern Scottish playwrights were completely ignored and the most contemporary piece I performed was Alan Bennett's farce *Habeas Corpus,* in which I played a fifty-something doctor from Hove in the south of England!

Yes, we sometimes talked in Scots in the odd verse class, where Robert Burns or other Scottish poetry luminaries would be read aloud, but for every play we did, in every acting class, the expectation was that we would speak in RP, or Received Pronunciation—also known as Standard English, the Queen's English, BBC English. Also known as talking posh, and according to Dr. Catherine Sangster, the head of pronunciations at the Oxford English Dictionary:

It's identified not so much with a particular region as with a particular social group, although it has connections with the accent of Southern England. RP is associated with educated speakers and formal speech. It has connotations of prestige and authority, but also of privilege and arrogance. Some people even think that the name "Received Pronunciation" is a problem—if only some accents or pronunciations are "received", then the implication is that others should be rejected or refused.

My Scottish voice and, by extension, a major aspect of my authentic self, was not a priority in my training. And so, I grew to view that voice as unimportant.

I went to drama school at the end of an era. I suppose one of the potential problems of attending a conservatoire or an arts institution of any kind is that the staff's practical experience of the career they are training you for stopped the day they started to teach full-time. And alas for me (but also thank the gods!) the world of acting had changed quite radically since the days my teachers and their teachings were guiding me towards, which at times felt more like the 1950s or '60s. A couple of lecturers were veterans of what was known as weekly rep—where you'd literally rehearse a play for a week, put it up for a week, and while it was running be rehearsing the next play for the following week—and one of the main criteria of being an employable actor was owning your own dinner suit! They came from a time where sounding like me was not acceptable. Scottishness, to them, was seen as a problem, a barrier to becoming successful, and so too, almost by osmosis, I began to see my nationality as an impediment to my success.

I graduated and, as a young Scottish man starting out in the business, I began to get roles that were, well, young Scottish men, but I was ill-prepared for them. I could swan around a drawing room spouting bon mots in an English accent with the best of them, but here I was, pleading my innocence in the interrogation room of Maryhill police station in Scottish Television's *Taggart*, and I had never played anyone contemporary, let alone Scottish!

Of course, RP classes were also very useful. Not only did we learn to speak in the accent that was, and indeed still is, the prevalent one used in the majority of British drama, but more important, our ears were trained to listen for the idiosyncrasies and musicality of *any* accent. The residual gain throughout my career has been to use the skills I was taught to eradicate my own accent when it's required and discover many more.

But in all three years of drama school, the only time I didn't talk posh when performing—aside from our first-year play which was an American one, William Inge's *Picnic*—was in our final year theatre-in-education class, when we performed a programme of scenes from *Macbeth* in local high schools. In one of them, the sleepwalking scene, I was cast as Lady Macbeth. I worried that the spotty youths of Glasgow might have enough of a problem dealing with a man, nay, a boy, playing a woman, let alone his sounding like he came from Kent, and especially when he was supposed to be the queen of Scotland. So, I decided to play her using my own Scottish voice. It was a revelation for me. Suddenly I wasn't just concentrating on vowel sounds and diphthongs. I wasn't just trying to *sound* right. I was trying to connect, to make sense of the text as myself—or as the me interpreting a mad queen. (Please feel free to insert your own jokes here.) Thus began my passion for performing Shakespeare, and especially for performing him in my natural Scottish voice. I played Romeo at the National

Theatre Studio in London in 1991, and Hamlet for the English Touring Theatre in 1993, both times using my own accent.

Playing Hamlet—the greatest role in the English-speaking world for an actor—in my own voice was seen as very radical at the time. It was also seen as offensive. One of the articles about the production when it arrived in London included the line that there ought to be a sign outside the Donmar Warehouse warning patrons they might not understand all of Shakespeare's lines, as Hamlet was being performed with a Scottish accent. An accompanying cartoon had me holding the skull and saying, "Alas Poor Yorick, see you Jimmy!" The allusion was clear: to the cartoonist, and by extension the newspaper's readership, a Scottish voice meant ill-educated, ill-mannered, and unintelligible.

But my interpretation of the gloomy Dane was considered rather outré for other reasons. The production was a hybrid of modern and classical design. I appeared originally in traditional doublet and hose, but for my first soliloquy, to the strain of an electric guitar chord, the doublet was unzipped and discarded and I strode downstage to address the audience looking extremely contemporary in the long-sleeved black T-shirt and matching leggings I had on underneath. A Sunday newspaper heralded the next Hamlet to tread the London boards after me—Ralph Fiennes—with a description of each of the previous incumbents of the part, graded and encapsulated in three words. Mine were "quick, mercurial, cycling shorts"!!

The message I took from the reviews of my Hamlet—every single one of which mentioned my Scottish "choice"—was that even though Hamlet was Danish, he should sound English. It's the same with Jesus: he may have been an Arabic Jew, but he should appear white and sound American. The dominating culture dictates how history sounds. And England dominates Scotland.

I have used Received Pronunciation for some Shakespearean roles, for example in the two films I made with the director Julie Taymor, *Titus* and *The Tempest*. Both decisions were based on the characters' class: Saturninus in *Titus* is the impetuous and spoiled emperor of Rome, Sebastian in *The Tempest* the slightly vacuous brother of the king of Naples. I rest my case. But when I don't have to place someone in that way via an accent, I feel the guttural and elongated qualities of the Scottish accent augment the passion and the visceral qualities of Shakespeare's poetry.

At college it didn't seem to be enough to be able to lose my accent, to have flawless RP. While we weren't actively encouraged to lose our own accents in real life, we certainly weren't *dis*couraged from it, either.

One Saturday in my second year I flew down to London to audition for a big Hollywood movie, *Young Sherlock Holmes*, to be directed by Barry Levinson. My Scottish agent, who had taken me on after I'd landed a much-vaunted Equity card from performing cabaret, had warned me that as soon as I walked into the room, I would have to pretend to be English. No matter how well I read, no matter how good my audition was, I wouldn't get the part if I walked in as me. There was no negotiation. So, I did as I was instructed. From the second I walked through the door I pretended I was English. I felt like an absolute fraud—because I was one. I was a husk. I had no authenticity, no connection, no personality. I was just an accent with no backstory. I didn't know who I was. I didn't get the part. I never did it again.

There were so few role models back then of successful Scots who didn't succumb to the Anglo-fication factor and become, as a very dear old Scottish actress once scoffed as though it were the worst insult she could muster, "practically English". One shining exception in my childhood was Billy Connolly. The Big Yin, as he is known in Scotland, is a comedian and singer who toned down neither his material nor his presentation of its utter Scottishness when he ventured south to London. It was incredibly inspiring, if not a little confusing, to see an out-and-proud Scot be accepted and loved for the very thing we'd been encouraged to believe could be his downfall. I used to marvel at why we Scots have such an inferiority complex, why we think we're not good enough, we won't translate, people won't get us. And then I remembered that we were constantly told all those things.

I met Billy in the early 2000s when I was hosting the Britannia Awards in LA, and I was completely overwhelmed. He is a god to me.

"Billy!" I gurgled. "You know how in one of your shows you tell that story about how you lost your virginity in a tent in Arbroath?"

"Uh-huh," said the Big Yin, curious at where this was going.

"Well," I continued, beginning to glean the story was going to be very humiliating, but gamely ploughing through. "I passed my driving test in Arbroath!"

Many years later, Billy was doing a run of his show in New York City, but I couldn't see him because I was on the exact same schedule in *The Threepenny Opera* on Broadway. One night I was having drinks in a bar in the East Village called Eastern Bloc (which just so happens to now be called Club Cumming!!) and I met two Scottish guys who said they had been to see Billy's show that night. I told them how I would've loved to have gone.

"He actually mentioned you," said one of the Scots.

"What?!" My heart stopped for a second.

"Yes," said the other boy. "Something about you meeting him in LA and telling him you'd passed your driving test in Arbroath!" Can you imagine the honour to know that the legend that is Billy Connolly was telling the story of me gushing to him at that awards show in his act?!! He apparently regaled the crowd with my goofy "You lost your virginity/I passed my driving test" and finished it off with, "I think I got the better deal!"

Many years later I was asked to present Billy with the Great Scot Award, given annually by the National Trust for Scotland Foundation USA. That night I was able to tell the man himself just how important it had been to me to see him never compromise his own voice and authenticity, but instead brandish it as a badge of honour. It was his example that led me to understand that communicating with people from other cultures has little to do with clarity of accent or any self-imposed parochialism of material. No, humour is a universal language. Emotion is a universal language, too, and the stronger a person's spirit the deeper and more profoundly they connect with an audience, no matter who or where it is.

At the end of my speech I welcomed Billy to the stage and watched him weave his way through the tables of standing, adoring fans. He went up to the mic and slayed for the next ten minutes.

Billy had Parkinson's disease by then, and as we manoeuvred our way through the ecstatic throng, trying to get back to our table, I reached my hand out for his. For a moment time stopped, and we were just two wee Scottish boys holding on to each other, trying to navigate our way home. I'll never forget it.

In the car afterwards, the reality of what had happened began to seep in. I had been able to explain to and thank someone who had

been such an inspiration to me and a huge influence on my life. You don't get to do that often. It was a little overwhelming, and I found myself weeping. Big, splashy tears of happiness and collective Scottish sentiment. Tears from way deep inside. Authentic tears.

———

In the early days my alma mater was named the RSAMD (Royal Scottish Academy of Music and Drama) and housed in a town house annex in Glasgow's West End for the first-year drama students, and a sprawling building and beautiful old theatre in the city centre for everyone else. A few years after I graduated it moved to a swanky, new building up the road, and then, when the services it offered expanded to more than merely music and drama, it became known as the Royal Conservatoire of Scotland, or "the 'Toire", as I was horrified to learn some years ago. You know you're old when your place of learning changes both its location *and* its name!

There was a tradition that the first-year drama students put on an evening of cabaret for the rest of the school at the end of the first term. I had made friends with a boy in my class named Forbes Robertson, and we decided we would do something together. Of course we left the planning until the last minute, but one evening after classes we went into a rehearsal room and made up two characters named Victor and Barry, two Dapper Dans from Glasgow's West End and the founding members of the Kelvinside Young People's Amateur Dramatic Arts Society (or KYPADAS for short; think about it). As they said in what was to become their well-worn opening gambit, "Kelvinside is a district in Glasgow, Glasgow is a city in Scotland, and Scotland is a country to the north of England and to the left of Mrs. Thatcher."

Little did we know that within a few years Victor and Barry would become national treasures. They had their own TV and radio shows and sellout runs at the Edinburgh Fringe Festival and across the country. They played the Sydney Opera House and toured Australia, and they performed before royalty, though not entirely successfully. Our gag about Princess Margaret munching chocolate liqueurs made

Forbes Masson *are* Alan Cumming
Victor and Barry

her—according to a friend who was seated near her at the Scottish Ballet gala—"visibly stiffen!"

Margaret Thatcher's radical right-wing policies in eighties Britain engendered an explosion of political satire and ushered in the era of the stand-up comedian as political pundit rather than raconteur. Victor and Barry were an anomaly in this world, a harking back to the old days of variety and music halls, and perhaps that is why they thrived: two slightly surreal, genteel characters whose politics, though no less biting, were definitely with a small *p*. They sang songs about Marks and Spencer's, the joys of buying fish from a van and their hometown of Glasgow:

> *It's a cultured city and we don't mean penicillin*
> *The people have names like Senga, Shug and Lloyd*
> *Some of them aren't quite the full shilling*
> *You'd be the same if you were unemployed*

In 1988, after being the toast of the Edinburgh Fringe Festival, Victor and Barry were invited to perform in London as part of the Perrier Pick of the Fringe Season at the Donmar Warehouse. This marked both Forbes's (who was now Forbes Masson, due to Equity name clashes) and my West End debuts, though a few weeks later I would open at the Royal Court Theatre in another show from that year's Edinburgh festival: *The Conquest of the South Pole*—a German play by Manfred Karge that introduced me to the director of my future *Hamlet*, Stephen Unwin, as well as the assistant director, none other than Tilda Swinton.

Going to London for the first time with a homegrown Scottish comedy act was a big deal, and Scottish Television, for whom we were practically the in-house mascots by that point, decided to cover this auspicious debut in a documentary called *Victor and Barry Take the High Road* (a nod to both the famous song and the long-running Scottish soap opera in which I had recently appeared).

The big question, though, and really the point of the documentary was whether Victor and Barry, and their sense of humour, would "travel". It was taken as read that a modicum of success in Scotland necessitated a move south to London, but I remember at the time being genuinely worried about whether we would be actually understood—not just appreciated—when we got there to the capital.

I think being constantly reminded of your difference can in some ways define you. So, when I realised that Victor and Barry could indeed be understood—and with a few tweaks to the script, our Glasgow-centric banter could find allusion and commonality anywhere—it made me want to hold on even more fiercely to what had made the act work in the first place, and that was our voices: our views on the world, what made us laugh, what we knew would connect with people. For the first time I understood the joy of writing: when an audience not only enjoys what you have written but understands your perspective and intent in having done so. Although Victor and Barry had greased-back hair and wore cravats and monogrammed blazers, we were letting our authentic selves come through as we created them, our Scottish selves, and that I believe is why they were such a success.

A few years later Victor and Barry transmogrified into a BBC2 sitcom we wrote, *The High Life*, set aboard a sad Scottish airline, Air

Scotia, with Forbes and me playing flight attendants Steve McCracken (him) and Sebastian Flight (me—and yes, that is an intentional reference to the character from *Brideshead Revisited*) battling with our inflight purser, Shona Spurtle—aka Hitler in tights, Pol Pot in pantyhose, Mussolini in micromesh—played by the great Siobhan Redmond, and our dopey captain, whom we innocently named Hilary Duff, played by Patrick Ryecart. We made only six episodes, but it is the thing that most people come up to me and talk about when I go back home, out of all the films and plays and TV shows I have made over the past four decades. The reason for that is because as totally irreverent and surreal as our escapades were, once again our authentic voices came through. We connected.

In playing and writing those roles, I began to understand the concept of authenticity more fully. It's not about sounding or looking like yourself. It's about letting an audience see who you are no matter what disguise you are wearing.

———

I think Americans and Europeans have very different ideas when it comes to acting. America, the home of the movie, is also the logical domain of the movie star. And American movie stars tend to have personalities that are very identifiable, so that when we hear "a Tom Cruise movie" or a "Jennifer Aniston movie", we generally know what that means. These people have an identity they bring to each role, which we recognise, and the roles they play tend to embody that identity. We know what we're getting, and we come to rely on their giving us what we know. Unless they're Meryl Streep, we don't really want our American movie stars to disappear into a character. We don't want Julia Roberts to be an evil blonde Russian. We want her to be Julia Roberts, or the version of her we know and love.

With European actors, it's a different game of boules. I wanted to become an actor so I could continually become different people. Being a version of myself didn't enter into the equation—another reason why I found playing a young Scottish man so taxing, I suppose! I think in Europe we prize an actor disappearing into a role, or perhaps confusing our expectations, especially when we've known them as something or someone else. That's what we think acting is. It's not just being a better-groomed version of ourselves.

———

Performing in cabaret—the form, not the show—has also been an incredible way to feel utterly vulnerable but also connected with an audience. Cabaret has always been a part of my life, in so many ways. But I had always done it in character, never as myself. When you're an actor, the character serves as a veil between you and the audience, and it's a very different thing to be up onstage talking about my own life and singing out of context, as me. I'd always hoped that one day I would have the courage to do a whole show on my own, as I had seen others do. On the rare occasions when I had overcome my terror and actually sung as me, I felt a visceral connection with an audience that surpassed anything I'd felt playing a character. It also felt terrifying and unsafe, so in some way I suppose I was drawn to the familiar. I hoped that one day I could make it a regular part of my performing life.

So when the Lincoln Center for the Performing Arts in New York City asked me to create an evening of songs and stories as part of their American Songbook series, I was filled with both possibility and dread. On paper this was the perfect structure to make real something I had been dancing around for a very long time. But I would actually have to do it. Finally commit.

When this happened, I was rehearsing a play in Glasgow—*The Bacchae* by Euripides, for the National Theatre of Scotland—and just by chance the very next day my old chum Liza Minnelli came to town to do her first-ever show in Scotland!

I had dinner with Liza at her hotel and told her about the offer and how much I wanted to take this risk, but also how much I was shaken by the prospect. She asked me what my biggest fear was, and I told her I didn't feel I was a singer. I was an actor who sings.

"Me too!" she exclaimed.

No, *Liza*, I thought to myself. *You're both a singer and an actor!*

But she went on to tell me that every time she got a new song, she thought of it as a play. She's a character in the tune and she has a journey through it. It has a three-act structure and then it ends. It sounds simple, because it is, but it completely changed my attitude towards singing.

"I always think, who is this woman?" Liza expounded. "Where does she come from? What kind of fridge magnets does she have?"

I thought that was a little unnecessarily detailed, but, hey, it clearly works for her.

We talked a lot about how to structure a show, the songs I might sing and why I would want to sing them, how to be a showman, but at the same time how to retain my authenticity. I will forever be grateful to Liza.

It was another master class from the mistress. There is no one who walks the tightrope of fragility and pizzazz like her. I have felt an audience really worry for her at the start of a show, and watched her take that worry, that energy and use it as fuel to propel herself into a realm of utter bravado and triumph. The transformation is magical to watch. But of course, as we also discussed that night in Glasgow, you have to be able to do it again and again, night after night. An actor's skill is to invoke, or re-create, or fake someone else's emotions night after night. A cabaret artist's is to do the same with their own authenticity.

The next night was her show, *Liza's at the Palace*!

It was part a concert of Liza's greatest hits, part homage to her godmother, Kay Thompson, the author of the *Eloise* books, musical arranger for many MGM musicals, and star of *Funny Face*, in which she brought the house down with her big number, "Think Pink!"

Liza told several hilarious stories about Kay, but one in particular was incredibly touching. She shared that when she was sixteen she got a job in summer stock and landed a role in a musical that had a ten-second dance solo. She was so proud of herself and just desperate for her mom and her godmother to come and see her perform. And so, Judy Garland and Kay Thompson schlepped off to some tent in Massachusetts, sneaking in as the lights were going down to avoid making a fuss, and watched the show. When Liza came on and did her ten-second dance solo, Judy and Kay were so overwhelmed with joy, pride, and love that they both burst into tears. But neither of them had a hanky, so Judy got out her powder puff and dabbed her tears with it, then passed it on to Kay, who dabbed her tears, too. Afterwards, they went backstage to see Liza, who asked, "Was I any good?"

They told her how amazing she had been, and how proud and emotional they had become while watching her. Her mother then told her about using the powder puff as a handkerchief, and she gave it to Liza, still damp with hers and her godmother's tears.

I always say the two favourite pastimes in Scotland are drinking and oversentimentality, so there was many a hanky pulled from a pocket at this detail of that night in Glasgow. But then Liza went in for the kill.

"And I still have that powder puff to this day."

The place erupted in a combination of sentiment, sympathy, and huge love and appreciation of her utter vulnerability. As we say in Scotland, she could bring a tear to a glass eye.

I had taken as my dates my two friends I was working with on *The Bacchae*, the director, John Tiffany, and the associate director and choreographer, Steven Hoggett. We were like three excited schoolboys throughout the show. Liza gave me a shout-out at one point, saying she had learned so much from me (yes, really!), and afterwards John and Steven joined me as we went backstage to greet her.

"Was I any good?" she asked as we entered her dressing room.

We went back to her hotel room and ordered drinks and french fries. Liza was smoking and telling stories and we all basked in her glow. Then we began to talk about the show I would be doing at Lincoln Center the following year, and what songs I might sing and stories I might tell. At one point, apropos of nothing, I had a thought.

"Liza, do you *really* still have that powder puff?"

She turned to me, a little bemused.

"No, darling! None of that ever happened!"

And that, ladies and gentlemen, is show business.

But perhaps my greatest moment of artistic authenticity came when I arrived in New York in 1998 to do *Cabaret.* No assumptions were made about my class or education or intelligence because of how I sounded. In fact, I was celebrated for my voice and my Scottishness and my difference. Sexually I had never felt more confident or adventurous. I felt strong, fearless even. It was a confluence of comfort, openness, and vulnerability in both my person and my working life that could not have made me any more ready or better-equipped to play that role.

ecstasy

13

". . . Alan Cumming for *Cabaret*!"

The first thing that I saw was Camryn's boobs. As soon as my name was read out, she pulled me into an embrace and my head went straight into her décolletage! And then I thought, *Run, Alan, Run!* And so I did. I sprinted to the stage—no mean feat in a pair of platform sneakers—making a quick rolling stop to hug two of my agents in the front row, and I positively bounded up the steps towards Annette. But in my haste I had forgotten to leave my bottle of water at my seat and as she handed me my Tony, I handed her a bottle of Evian and asked if she would hold it for me!

"Oh, gosh, thank you so much. I want to thank everyone Natasha Richardson thanked, except Liam Neeson. . . ."

The next thing I knew I was in the press room, goofing around for photographers and then before a seemingly endless parade of video cameras giving sound bites to outlets from around the world. In the middle of one interview I was blindsided by someone. A hand appeared on my left shoulder; a tall body joined it to my right. For a split second I thought I was being mugged, Tonyjacked if you will, on live TV. But no, I was being beknighted. It was Sir Sean, fresh from his Tony win as one of the producers of *Art*. He hugged me close, then looked down the lens of the camera in front of us and proclaimed, "This is my new son."

That I was even standing next to Sean Connery was a source of such deep and myriad emotions, but to be so lauded by him was verging on a religious experience. At the very least I had now assumed sovereignty. Sean was King, and so now I was a Prince of Scotland! He had made it so.

Winning the Tony felt much more a relief than a triumph. That night I felt a huge weight lift from my shoulders. Just to have some resolution to the months of speculation and agitation was a win in and of itself. And also, the relief that I hadn't disappointed anyone (aside perhaps from the other nominees!).

I took Ecstasy that night I won the Tony. It had become my drug of choice. I'd missed the Second Summer of Love in 1988–89 because I was married. Ours was not a union that embraced really letting go and splashing in the sea of positivity. Don't get me wrong, it was loving, but ordered. It worked for us both that way, but familiarity bred content. And when it was over, I was ready to take some risks and experience what abandon felt like.

It's fascinating how something so seemingly simple as taking a pill has fulfiled so many different, yet appropriate, functions in different phases of my life. The first time I took it it opened me up, daring me to accept that I could relish an experience—and myself—when I was not fully in control of either. Later I used it to explore the me that was hedonistic and sexual and free. I have used it, foolishly, as a shortcut to intimacy, when loved up became the only route to loved in. In New York, in 1998, I used it to rebuff stress. The feeling of coming up on Ecstasy is akin to having a minor panic attack: you experience rushes, you are jingly, twitchy, your breath shallow. It can sometimes feel too much. All that perfectly describes how I often felt during the time of *Cabaret*. Taking an E of an evening after a show induced those similar feelings, but instead of having to keep them at bay, to fight them and regain some control in my life, I could let go and allow them to consume me. Then the pill's wave of benevolence and sensuality would enfold me, and I could truly relax. Ecstasy was my self-prescribed anti-anxiety medication. And it worked.

I remember coming up in a cubicle of the gents' loos at the Marriot Marquis hotel, where the official Tonys after-party was. That was where I'd been told I should make a dutiful appearance before joining my *Cabaret* chums for our party at our favourite postshow hangout, Café 123 on Forty-Third Street. I could hear men discussing and dissecting the evening, the fortunes of the shows, the upsets, the best moments. It was like listening to a radio play in which I became a character as I heard my name being mentioned. But I didn't care. I didn't even care that my pupils were dilated, and I was going to have to engage with those men and bright overhead lighting and mirrors. I was in ecstasy, and all was right with the world.

In my naïveté and fish-out-of-waterness I had no way of gauging if the way I had been embraced and the positivity and goodwill I felt each time I left my apartment, let alone the stage door, was normal, and something that every first-time Brit on Broadway experienced. It wasn't till a few years later, sitting next to a stranger at a dinner that I fully understood—or perhaps was now ready to process—this incredible welcome, and she just happened to be the conduit.

"New York loves you, Alan," this stranger told me.

"And I love New York," I replied. And I do. I feel proud to be thought of as a New Yorker.

But she went on. "You know, in twenty-five years of living in this city I have never seen it open its arms to anyone the way it did to you when you came here to do *Cabaret*."

I have thought long and often about why this happened, and why it happened to me. Part of the reason, I think, is what was going on in America at the time. I remember eating breakfast before I left for rehearsals one morning in late January 1998 in my rented apartment in the Meatpacking District. The TV was on in the background and there was an air of growing hysteria in the hosts' rhetoric. I began to realise something big was happening in Washington. I turned up the volume to learn that President Clinton had been involved in an extramarital affair.

Americans and Europeans have very different attitudes towards their public figures' private lives. I can't remember, or even countenance the idea, of a European politician's extramarital affair completely consuming both the news cycle and the zeitgeist of an entire country, and for so long. Of course, the dawning of the internet compounded the reach and magnitude of each salacious detail of this particular affair. And then there was the central ingredient of any scandal: denial. A perfect storm, if you will.

But more than that, I think Americans and Europeans have very different attitudes to sex in general. America, I now see from my vantage point of having lived here a couple of decades, is riddled with shame about sexuality. And that should come as no surprise when you remember that the first non-native people to set foot on US shores were a boatload of religious zealots who left England because it was not puritanical enough!

There are many ways this puritanism still manifests itself today. Enjoying sex and being open about it is still viewed in some quarters as very déclassé. There is still a pioneer spirit about the notion of sex positivity. Slut shaming is ingrained in the national consciousness, even by those who practise what is being shamed. An abundance of desire—for anything actually, not just sex—is more likely to be seen as a problem first rather than something to be celebrated or encouraged. Letting go, which to me is a positive and necessary part of the human experience, is seen as a lack—of restraint, of decorum, of self-respect—and instead of giving oneself up to an experience, or a feeling, or a desire, it is instead characterised as giving in.

And when we get down to the nitty-gritty, the rough and tumble, the slap and tickle, I feel there is even more telling puritan residue. Some have argued that when President Clinton uttered his immortal line "I did not have sexual relations with that woman, Miss Lewinsky", he was telling the truth. His idea of the truth, that is.

To many, many Americans, "sex" only occurs when vaginal

penetration by the penis takes place. It's unclear if this rule applies exclusively to the vagina or whether anal sex also counts, though I imagine the latter is used as a loophole, too. As it were.

Fellatio, cunnilingus, analingus, mutual masturbation, digital penetration—all of the above fall under the quaint, but very telling American umbrella of "fooling around". It says a lot about a culture when it correlates sexual contact with foolishness, don't you think?

So many Americans can (and do!) state that if they got naked with someone, put their penis in someone's mouth, or had a penis put in theirs, perhaps even ejaculated into that mouth, or received ejaculate into theirs, gave or received oral stimulation to the vagina or anus perhaps to the point of orgasm, put their fingers (or indeed anything other than their penis) into the vagina or anus of another person or had anything other than a penis inserted into their vagina or anus, even if they *both* (or however many were involved in this interaction) orgasmed, they would attest that nothing of what might have occurred would constitute them having had sex. It would just be *fooling around*.

One of the many reasons I find this frustrating is that, by this logic, lesbians never have sex! It also makes it easier to understand why so many Americans I have known could do with a few pointers on their foreplay skills. But if they have grown up being constantly subjected to this sexual existentialism, then is it any wonder they are a little overzealous to get to the verified, clear-cut sexual finish line?

And if something doesn't really exist, then it can't matter. By this hypothesis the value of any pre "sex" sexual interaction between the participants—the vulnerability, the intimacy, the emotion, the connection—is nil. It may as well never have happened if it even did. I suppose the upside is that this postulation also denies the existence of guilt, of cheating, and of responsibility. But it also denies joy. No lasting pleasure can be gained if even one of the participants dismisses what happened between them as unimportant or invisible. All there is, in spades, is shame.

Nineteen ninety-eight was a feeding frenzy for the new puritans as the Clinton scandal unfolded and Americans were forced to contend with issues of sexual politics they longed to keep—and long had kept—hidden. This was the landscape I found myself in as we embarked on our Broadway production of *Cabaret*.

The years of the Weimar Republic saw great sexual liberation and even the first gay rights movement in Berlin. The kind of club the show depicts would certainly have been home to sexual acts and their commerce, and that was very much something at the core of what Sam Mendes and I wanted to project with my character and the whole ambience of the club. Aside from the overt sexuality, bisexuality, and homosexuality depicted in the club scenes, there was also Sally Bowles's abortion for the more prudish audiences to contend with. (The song "Cabaret" is actually sung immediately after she has returned from aborting her and Cliff's child and is more a paean to a life of debauchery and addiction than the uplifting, life-affirming roundelay it is often perceived as.)

Even four years prior in London, the reaction to the openness and shamelessness of the sexuality we presented, mine in particular as the Master of Ceremonies, was remarkable. And now here we were with a bigger and more expanded version of the show we had done in London (the Broadway veteran Rob Marshall was now choreographing and co-directing with Sam). And it wasn't just the production that had expanded. In the previous four years I had become more comfortable with myself and confident in my abilities in the role and so was willing to push the envelope of my character's sexual manifestations even further than I had in London. (I still joke that I am proud to have administered Broadway's first fist fuck!)

The Kit Kat Club became the social utopia Americans could cavort in before returning to the harsh reality of real life, where every night on television the love affair between a young woman and her boss was dissected with prurience, shame, and utter moral superiority. But *Cabaret*'s ending mirrored the present all too clearly: licentiousness and liberation will be quashed. They *are* coming to get us.

The publicity photos for *Cabaret* were everywhere, and in them I was always semi-reclining and semi-naked, with straps around my crotch, my nipples rouged, and one arm slung over my head re-creating one of my dance moves from the show, revealing my hairy armpits. Those armpits and nipples were the talk of the town. Seri-ously, the length and bushiness of the former were actually discussed in gossip columns, and even many years later I had to ask Terry Gross on National Public Radio's *Fresh Air* to stop talking about them and move on to another subject!

As 1998 wore on and the country clutched its collective pearls as more and more salacious details of the presidential infidelity were revealed, I found myself splattered across bus stops, semi-naked and sexually ambivalent. Every photographer I worked with—and there were many—seemed to want me to take my clothes off or cross-dress or a combination of both, and I was happy to oblige. I like being photo-graphed. When it's with someone with verve and vision it feels like a great collabouration between two artists, and the resulting pictures a really satisfying by-product of the commercial necessities of publicity. Around that time I worked with many great photographers like David LaChapelle, who shot me for *Interview* magazine naked on a plastic sofa wearing plastic high heels and only a violin encased in plastic cov-ering my manhood; naked in a bath wearing only a diamond necklace and stockings and suspenders; on a trapeze in a corset and bondage shoes; and in a red flowing dress with my bum showing.

I loved those pictures. I still do. David has very kindly allowed the red dress photo to be used twice as the poster for plays I have appeared in: first for Jean Genet's *Elle*, which I did off Broadway in 2002, and then five years later for the National Theatre of Scotland's production of *The Bacchae*, in which I played Dionysus. When that show opened in London, the image was on billboards in many tube stations, but alas, the London Underground marketing boffins deemed my bare bum to be too potentially disturbing for commuters, and so the red dress was airbrushed over it. So yes, my arse has been censored.

I found it fascinating—and still do—that a man being sexually objectified and projecting loucheness, androgyny, and pansexual-ity was so triggering for so many people. In the context of the show each night it made perfect sense, but out in the world, alone, I was a semiotic mind fuck. There have been many, many women who have been presented and exploited in this way; indeed, our whole culture is underpinned by the selling of the female form and its easy availability to us. But a man being presented or *used* in this way took titillating to a whole new level.

For me, at the centre of this storm, the sexuality I was being asked to project both in my work and the surrounding ancillary publicity felt completely appropriate for *Cabaret* and my role in it. And had I not insisted this be the very crux of the performance and experience I wanted the audience to have when I was struggling with accepting the part in the first place?

What was harder to contend with was that, at thirty-three, I was being objectified in this way for the first time in my life. Previously I got cute, puckish, boyish, impish, and childlike a lot—and I have to say I still do. I'd moved into creepy and oleaginous with *Circle of Friends* and *Emma*, but now here I was as full-blown sex symbol. Geeky, arty, skinny, European, mischievous, slightly dangerous sex symbol, but sex symbol nonetheless.

I quickly assimilated to this public perception in my own life. I did feel sexy, and I was having a lot of sex. I liked my body and I felt comfortable in it. I think that is what makes someone sexy: their own comfort with themselves. It's another form of authenticity. And if you feel desirable and are aware that people desire you, I think you are on a fast track to self-confidence!

I was, however, slightly destabilised by the onslaught of celebrity that came with the success of *Cabaret*, and the ensuing uncertainty of whether people wanted to be my friend, to be in my orbit, to be in my bed because they genuinely connected with me or they were more entranced by the golden shower of celebrity I was drenched in. This was America, after all. Celebrity is its proto-currency. But then, just as the golden sheen of my Broadway experience began to tarnish, Holly-wood called again!

I was offered the part of the emperor Saturninus in *Titus*, Julie

Taymor's film adaptation of Shakespeare's *Titus Andronicus*, with Anthony Hopkins and Jessica Lange and which was due to start shooting in Rome that September. I asked the *Cabaret* producers if I could have some time off and they kindly agreed, as long as I added the time back on to the end of my contracted run. I felt like I needed a change of scene, some time away from the frenzy of my new life, some time to connect and check in with me again.

Just before I left for Rome I was photographed by Annie Leibovitz in my by now iconic armpit-baring pose for the 1998 year-end issue of *Vanity Fair*, in which I was being inducted into the Vanity Fair Hall of Fame, alongside eighteen other men and women (and a peregrine falcon) who "broke records, rules and new ground" and "gave the year its edge".

Alongside Steve Jobs, Jeff Bezos, the falcon, Prudence Bushnell (ambassador to Kenya), the man who invented Beanie Babies, Tom Wolfe, some baseball players, Steven Spielberg and Tom Hanks, a collection of youthful TV stars, an astronaut, Cameron Diaz, Ben Stiller, and Sean "Puffy" Combs, there I was, yet again, semi-clad and androgynous.

But there was one more person, someone who got two —count them!—photos when all the rest of us only got one, someone who was perhaps partly, though inadvertently, responsible for why I was deemed worthy of being included in this list of 1998's finest, or edgiest, and someone who, little known to either of us then, would become one of my dearest friends: Monica Lewinsky. We had both been defined by our sexuality in 1998, yet mine was celebrated while hers was utterly denigrated. The prurience of the patriarchy at work, indeed.

We finally met in New York in early 2000. My friend Glenda Bailey, who was then editor of *Marie Claire*, threw a party for me to celebrate an article I had written for her magazine. I'd been dispatched to the fashion trenches of Paris to witness the bizarre ritual that is the haute couture season, where the world's richest fashion victims gather to shop not off the rack, but off the model. Although the price they pay for these creations could get you a nice apartment in many major cities, several of the women I spoke to told me they might never actually wear their acquisitions, but keep them as things of beauty to gaze upon and admire, and that led me to feel there was a double standard at work. Why should collective sneering at their profligacy for dropping so much on a piece of clothing be condoned, yet a similar amount paid for a painting be unremarkable? Again with the patriarchy, I sense.

Monica had attended the party because *Marie Claire* had recently run a piece about her, and we were sat next to each other at a dinner afterwards. She is the kindest, funniest person and we immediately connected. But the frenzy her presence induced in the room was insane. Strangers were reaching over the banquette we were seated in, trying to touch her. Leaving the restaurant was, quite literally, a mob scene. Nowadays when we go out to dinner, we are interrupted by people saying how much they admire her, or that they loved her TED talk.

I love Monica, and I think the fact she is so well-balanced when at one time she was the most vilified (and wronged) woman in the world *and* the first to ever undergo the now all-too-common and despicable modern construct of internet shaming speaks volumes about her strength of character. That she has risen phoenix-like from the ashes of humiliation and cultural abandonment to use her platform to shed light on the insidious dangers and prevalence of cyber bullying is a further testament to her goodness. I am incredibly proud of her and all she has achieved.

———

By the middle of September, I found myself at Cinecittá studios in Rome, where *La Dolce Vita* and *Cleopatra* and *Romeo and Juliet* had been shot, sitting at a table opposite Anthony Hopkins for the *Titus* read-through. It was another of those moments when I marvelled at the bizarre duality of my life: that on the one hand I was taking a vacation from starring on Broadway to come to Italy and make a film with these great artists, and on the other I was there solely due to a series of happy accidents that had become the signposts for my tumble through life. Of course, like any good duality, both were equally valid and true. And like any good artist, I had a healthy perspective on my place at the table. I understand my own power, but I never assume it to be eternal.

One of the reasons I had been so keen to do this film was the chance to regroup and reboot, to be away on location, a respite far from the madding crowds of my New York City life. But it was not the calm, restorative experience I had hoped. The production was disorganised and chaotic, and we quickly went way over schedule, and were it not for Paul Allen, the Microsoft cofounder, being an executive producer, I wonder if we would have been shut down completely.

The sheer frenzy of making *Titus* is encapsulated best by my journey to set each day. The second I left my apartment in the Prati district, the terror began. Have you ever driven in Rome? You'll know what I mean, then. The gateway to Cinecittá is accessed via a death-defying dash across many lanes of oncoming Italian drivers. So even before I arrived at work I was in a high state of anxiety, and then someone would open the door of the car and it would truly begin. I hadn't appreciated what a shouty culture Italy was. That is the real soundtrack to *Titus* for me: the screaming. I would emerge gingerly from the car, blinking, fingers in my ears, and rush to sit in the makeup chair.

"Alano, would you like a coffee?" the makeup artist would ask me, a little too loud I thought, but perhaps he had to speak at that level in order to be heard. If you can't beat them, join them, I suppose.

I'd nod in affirmation, not wanting to add to the noise pollution.

"Carlo! Carlo! Un café americano por Alano subito! SUBITO!!" he would positively shriek. And so it went.

Some of the screaming was in anger and frustration at the chaotic production, and some of it from myself, on occasions—like when out of the blue the producer told me she would not be paying for my plane ticket back to New York, or when a take was interrupted for the umpteenth time by crew members talking at full volume and I was told the reason for this was that sound was never normally recorded on these *sound* stages, as dialogue in Italian films was usually dubbed later.

"Shouldn't someone tell the crew that we *are* recording sound, then?" I asked.

Incidentally, I met the man who dubs me into Italian, one night at a dinner. I have actually met several of the voice actors who dub me in various languages over the years. It's quite fun to see who represents you aurally in other cultures, and to see if they capture, or at least share, some of your spirit. However, Italian me went way beyond the call of duty. As the evening was winding down, he offered to walk me to a cab, which I thought was very nice of him.

"Alan, I am sorry. I cannot make love to you tonight," he said as we headed down the Via something or other, apropos of nothing. Zero.

"What?" I replied, completely blindsided. (I am usually pretty good at seeing these sorts of things coming, believe you me!)

"I have to get up very early in the morning and so I cannot come home with you and make love," he explained.

I paused, wondering what the correct response was in such a scenario.

I wanted to ask what gave him the idea that I wanted him to make love to me in the first place, and if he really imagined that it was in the cards, why he thought getting up early would be an acceptable excuse not to? I mean, I think I'm worth a little bit of day-after fatigue! But I didn't say any of this.

"Okay," was all I could muster.

Titus had an incredible array of artists on board, from Julie Taymor down. The production designer was Dante Ferretti, who had worked with Pasolini, Fellini, Zeffirelli, Scorsese. The director of photography, Luciano Tovoli, had worked with Tarkovsky and Antonioni. The costumes were designed by Milena Canonero, who had worked with Kubrick, Coppola, Norman Jewison, Warren Beatty.

The cast was equally as accomplished and glittering. Tony and Jessica as Titus and Tamora, the amazing Harry J. Lennix as Aaron, Colm Feore, Matthew Rhys, it went on and on. But I think it fair to say that *Titus* was not a good time had by all. It was a truly epic endeavour, and I think part of the reason we were all so blindsided by the scale of the undertaking—and therefore the scale of its derailment when things went so quickly awry—was that we all thought we were in a small independent Shakespeare film and we quickly realised we were making *Ben Hur*. Tony even said he was retiring from acting after that film, though he obviously caught the bug again quite soon. And although the feeling of being adrift at sea in a typhoon is how I best remember the experience to this day, the actual work, when we were able to shut out the noise and the chaos and just be our characters in that world, was electrifying. I think it is a really great film that I am very proud to have been a part of.

Plus, there were upsides. I did get to spend some much-needed time alone. I did get to take many trips back and forth to London and enjoyed the comfort of the familiar in my life there once again. I even bought a new flat in Chinatown, and a few years later I would see my giant face on a marquee for *Spy Kids* in Leicester Square below as I stood at my kitchen sink doing the dishes. It was one of those "here's an old building that we've gutted, here's the water, here's the electricity and the gas, the rest is up to you" sort of affairs. In other words, a mammoth commitment both financially and time-wise, and that I was to undertake it in London and not my new love New York was surely a sign that I was not yet ready to completely sever my roots and live the American dream.

I also got to make out with Jessica Lange! We were playing husband and wife, after all! She was Queen of the Goths, captured by Titus after ten years of war, the prize for my emperor Saturninus. Jess and I hit it off and buoyed each other immensely when the *Titus* seas grew stormy.

One day we were chatting idly between takes about our bodies, getting older, gravity, that sort of thing. She talked about her boobs getting saggy and understanding the allure of a boob tuck. I replied that my balls had gone south, too.

"I wonder if there's such a thing as a ball tuck," the two-time Academy Award winner pondered.

"Well, there should be!" I retorted, to much laughter.

A few weeks later we were shooting a postcoital nude scene together, me asleep in a foetal position on top of her as she listened to Titus speaking, my hand judiciously placed on top of her right boob. We were both naked, but a little square of gauze had been proffered to us as we disrobed and it was now between our genitals, a micromesh totem of decorum that seemed designed to make everyone feel better about our nudity except us. We were actually having fun. The only weird thing was this itchy piece of gauze that made us feel really self-conscious. When, due to the angle of the crane shot that glided up and away from us, the camera caught a glimpse of the gauze peeping out from between our conjoined bodies, we were actually relieved. Its removal, incredibly tickly and very awkward at one and the same time, released us.

We lay together naked, completely comfortable, waiting for the next take.

"I don't know what you're talking about, Jess," I mused, looking down at her breast that my hand was cupping and harking back to our previous conversation about the effects of gravity on our bodies.

"You have fantastic boobs."

"Oh, honey," she purred. "If your hand wasn't there that thing would be halfway round my back!"

I think Jessica Lange and I are both very sexual beings. We experience life and communicate it—to an audience as well as in our private lives—through our own sensual prisms. I saw in Jess something of a kindred spirit. Like kind-of-could-be-trouble kindred spirit. And I love our naughty, flirty relationship to this day. A few years ago, as we arrived together at a Golden Globes after-party on an unseasonably rainy evening in Los Angeles, she turned to me and said, "Why is this floor so sticky?"

It was sticky. It made a weird, squelching sound each time we lifted our swankily clad feet. Without missing a beat, I replied, "I heard it's because when the young gentlemen here found out you were going to be coming to this party, they all spontaneously ejaculated on this floor!"

Jessica Lange did not baulk; she was maybe not even surprised. She merely rolled her eyes, grinned, and said, "Oh, Alan!"

We entered the event and the party began.

Finally, I returned to New York and the run of *Cabaret*. I was nervous. I had never taken a gap from a theatre show like this before, but luckily muscle memory does exist, and even though my sexy harness was a little tighter after the months of eating in Rome ("Can I just have some vegetables tonight?" I had asked the owner of the restaurant in the Piazza Navona I frequented with the cast. "Why?" he had replied. "Are you sick?"), I still managed to squeeze into it and after a couple of shows it was as though I'd never been away.

But because *Titus* had fallen so behind schedule, I had to keep flying back to Rome, much to the annoyance of the *Cabaret* producers, who had heralded my initial return to the production with a huge ad in the *New York Times*, a picture of me as the Emcee looking bewitchingly over my shoulder and the headline "He's coming back". To placate them, and also fulfil my filming obligations, I twice flew back from Rome and went straight to the theatre for the evening show. Yes, I woke up in Rome and went to bed in New York having flown across Europe and the Atlantic and played the lead in a Broadway show!

Immediately my life outside the show, perhaps because of my absence from the New York scene for a few months, did not just slip back to its pre-*Titus* levels of hysteria; it actually ratcheted up by several notches. In my first week back, in addition to the eight performances of *Cabaret*, I also, on Tuesday, was the opening and closing model in my friend Cynthia Rowley's show at New York Fashion Week. Between shows on Wednesday I had a fitting for the outfit Tommy Hilfiger was making me for the following Monday's Met Ball, then rehearsed with Joel Grey for the upcoming Kennedy Center Honors, in which we would be performing in a salute to Kander and Ebb. On Thursday I shot a day on an independent movie, *Urbania*, playing a man dying of AIDS. On Friday I had to fly down and back to Washington, DC, for further Kennedy Center Honors rehearsals. The night before I had gone to the *Shakespeare in Love* premiere party and had been out on the town late with some of the cast, and very nearly slept through my alarm, and then had the further impediment of boarding a plane going to Seattle, Washington, before I was disabused of my geographical error and then sprinted, hungover, to the DC flight, leapt on just as the doors were closing, and flopped exhaustedly into my seat. Just then I heard a tinkling voice I recognised coming from the seat across the aisle.

"Alan! Darling!" It was Liza.

She was a part of the Kennedy Center Honors tribute, too. The plan was that I would start off by singing "Wilkommen", and halfway through Joel Grey would magically appear behind me and take over. At the end of the number I'd emerge again from behind a gaggle of dancers and we'd finish the number together. Then Bebe Neuwirth, the star of *Chicago* that was currently running on Broadway, would begin singing "All That Jazz", and in the same fashion Chita Rivera, who created the role of Velma, would appear and continue the song. Then things would get really crazy. Liza would enter and begin singing "New York, New York" and the stage would begin to fill with various New York celebrities as well as cabbies, firemen, and a massive choir! Then for the big finish, me, Joel, Bebe, and Chita would sprint back on and join Liza; and that's where things started to go horribly wrong, for me at least.

As I have said, I am a bit of a musicals fraud. At that point I had only been in one musical in my entire life. And here I was, onstage with four of the greatest musical stars of the American theatre and feeling very out of my depth. I could fake it when I was just doing a chunk of what I did every night on Broadway—and my experience of doing the Tonys made me a little less nervous about this TV special format!—but the salute was ending with "New York, New York", a song that I didn't really know, and Liza's iconic dance moves that I just couldn't master. It looks so easy, a sort of stepping forward and pointing up and down affair, a bit like one of John Travolta's moves in *Saturday Night Fever*, but to me it was like rubbing your tummy and your head in opposite directions at the same time.

In rehearsals I was having real trouble and went off into a corner on my own to try to master it. Liza saw me and, bless her, came over to try to help.

"I just can't get the shoulder thing, Liza," I confessed.

"Oh, honey, it's easy," she said. "You just sort of push forward with this leg . . . and kinda point down but your opposite arm points up . . . and your shoulder . . . see?"

I didn't.

I was just about to thank Liza and pretend that I'd got it and then suggest we go and look at the snacks table when Chita came over, too.

"What's going on, babe?" she inquired.

"Alan can't get the shoulder thing at the end of 'New York, New York'," said Liza helpfully.

"Oh, hon, it's like this."

Now any chance of my ever getting it totally evaporated as I began to fully process that both Liza Minnelli and Chita Rivera were trying to teach me a move that any eight-year-old in a Saturday morning dance class could muster in their sleep. I wobbled feebly on, pointed up, Liza and Chita actually taking my various limbs and trying to sculpt my body into recognition.

Eventually, when they could see their efforts were futile, Liza said, "Oh, darling, just make it your own!"

Great advice, actually.

Sunday was the day of the show and the producers insisted I do the Sunday matinee of *Cabaret* at Studio 54 (where the production had moved to while I had been in Italy) then rush to the airport and fly to DC for an 8:00 p.m. curtain at the Kennedy Center. Yes, really.

Traffic was bad, and I missed the plane I was supposed to catch. I became more and more nervous as I remembered that I was actually opening the entire show, so when we finally landed in DC, I made sure I was first in line (to *deplane*) and be able to get to my waiting car and make up for my tardiness. But the FBI had other plans! As the door opened there were two very burly men in black suits and both of them screamed my name at the top of their lungs.

"I'm here! It's me!" I squeaked.

They grabbed me and began sprinting back up the jetway, dragging me behind them like a rag doll.

"FBI! Clear!" they shouted to any hapless travellers unlucky enough to get in our way. At one point we went down an up escalator, all the while me panting and hanging on to one of the burly men's hands. The reason for their haste, and indeed for their appearance at all—as nobody had mentioned to me I'd be getting an FBI escort—was that when the president arrives in a venue the doors are locked for security reasons, so if I didn't get there before him, I'd be locked out, too!

They threw me in the backseat of their car and off we sped. The ride was both nauseating and exhilarating. Cars were literally running into the centre reservation to let us past, all the while the siren blaring and me feverishly trying to remember those pesky shoulder moves of

Liza's. When we got to the theatre, the FBI men leapt out and started high-fiving each other and a bunch of other men, presumably other agents, who were on guard at the stage door. I then tried to open my car door, but found it locked. *The child lock's on*, I thought. But then I remembered this was an FBI car, not a people carrier. The people who normally sat in my seat were probably gang lords or serial killers. They didn't have a *child* lock. The agents had just forgotten both to open the door and that the whole point of their mission was to get me *into* the theatre, not just outside it. I started knocking on the window to get their attention, but they were now chest bumping and shouting at each other triumphantly. Eventually one of their colleagues saw me waving and knocking and alerted them. I have never been pulled out of a car faster.

About fifteen minutes later Walter Cronkite said my name and I was pushed through a mylar curtain and into the president's gaze.

As if I didn't have enough on my plate that evening, I was a little nervous of encountering Walter Cronkite. He had come to see *Cabaret* earlier in the year and during the entr'acte, I had gone out for my usual game of choosing a woman, then a man, and doing a little improvisation with them while we danced. But that night I could not get the man I'd chosen to come up onstage with me. All my usual ironclad lines of encouragement like "You know you want to" didn't wash, and the man in question just wouldn't budge off his seat. The band was playing on, the cue for my exit fast approaching.

I started back, defeated, but at the table just by the steps that led to the stage, I saw the back of an older gentleman's head and thought I'd just grab him and hopefully the band would realise and improvise a little.

"Come on, granddad," I said as I hauled the man towards the foot-lights. Suddenly the place erupted. Cheers, applause, screams. In my naïveté I remember thinking how nice it was that American audiences were so supportive of their elderly. Eventually their cheering ebbed enough for me to say, "And what's your name?"

"Cronkite!" said the elderly gent, rather brusquely.

"What?" I spat, my German accent totally MIA.

"Walter Cronkite!"

By the end of the show in Washington, I was completely elated at having made it through the evening, and especially to have, if not conquered, then at least faked convincingly Liza's shoulder thing (as she suggested, I made it my own). So my guard was down as I entered one of the cavernous rooms at the after-party, still pretty sparsely populated as the audience had yet to arrive. As I strode to the bar, already imagining the first sip of my martini, its sole customer turned around towards me and I saw, to my horror, it was You Know Who. I froze, and as Walter Cronkite's gaze met mine, his cheery demeanour changed, and he began to stride across the empty room towards me. I seriously considered making a run for it. I actually thought I was about to be bitch slapped by an octogenarian cultural legend.

But just as he arrived in front of me, Walter's rather stern visage melted, and his eyes wrinkled into a lovely and benign grin.

"May I have the pleasure of this dance, young man?"

chemistry

14

The message of *Cabaret* is to embrace the different and the decadent, and on my return from Rome until the end of my run I did exactly that. New York stood in for Berlin and, like my character onstage, I gorged myself on all it had to offer me—bodies, minds, booze, drugs, ideas. My every waking minute there was vibrant, and I felt more alive than I ever had, but alive in all ways: in love, in lust, in fear, and in pain. But *Cabaret* also counsels for the need to be vigilant, to speak up when extremist behaviour threatens to infiltrate the mainstream. And that is also what I did, too, though the extremism was of my own making. My relationship with the city was, and still is, a chemical, visceral one. Back then I was fucking it, now I have married it. And my exit in June 1999 ensured, just in the nick of time, that neither of us got killed.

Because then, you guessed it, Hollywood called, again. And just as it had in the past, it took me away from a situation I needed to be removed from and deposited me in a new one that was just the salve I needed—even though at the time I really had no concept that I needed saving or salve.

I could have gone back to London. Perhaps I should have. After all, my swanky new party pad high above Leicester Square was being constructed in that city, and I could have gone there to oversee the creation of it and what was to be the next phase of my life. But I didn't. Going back to London didn't feel right. Going back to London would inevitably mean me falling back into a series of unions that, though toxic for both parties, I could not help constantly returning to.

The only other man I had loved so unconditionally and been so hurt by was my father. As a child I had no choice but to be in that relationship. Now I was a grown man and theoretically free to walk away from these torturous dances but that just wasn't an option for me yet. I still felt I could fix them. I could make them happy.

I used to think that angry people were somehow attracted to me, that—like my father—they could smell my vulnerability, my weakness. But no, I know now that it was me that was drawn to them. But you can't fix an angry person. Their anger is really their hatred of themselves and only they can change that. When you try, the hatred just gets directed onto you. Trust me on this.

It had been just five years since the data dump of my childhood abuse and I was still feeling the fallout, so I suppose I should cut myself some slack for not severing the cord and practising better self-care sooner. But ultimately this intermittent, intense union would be my salvation, for what I learned from it. I learned about the behavioural patterns that make it so easy to rationalise and normalise manipulation and control when you are in love, and I learned, eventually, how to break them. I learned there is no situation that does not benefit from kindness, as difficult as that may be to enact. Until, of course, you finally hit the wall and must confront the fact that the kindest thing to do for yourself is walk away.

So I knew I didn't want to go back to London. I also knew I wanted my next job to be fun, not just the experience of doing it, but the content itself. After the challenges of *Titus* and *Cabaret*, I wanted a break from such intense and dark materials. But be careful what you wish for—I ended up doing three such jobs all at the same time.

I was asked to play an alien in a Flintstones film. I thought it would be fun, and it was. It was also quite a lot of money and the renovations in London had gone way over budget, so there were two good reasons to say yes. Then I was asked by Rob Marshall to play Rooster in the new Disney version of *Annie*. I knew Annie was an orphan and she had red curly hair and a dog, but that was really the extent of my knowledge of the plot—which may have accounted for the countless times during the shoot I referred to Annie's benefactor as Daddy Starbucks. Finally, Robert Downey Jr. had gone to jail and so NBC had to recast his role as the Devil in an animated series called *God, the Devil and Bob*, and you guessed it, they asked me to fill in. All three projects agreed to make the dates work and I thought, well, why not? So I spent the summer of 1999 working three jobs. If it sounds like a Joan Crawford picture, it kind of was.

Indeed, for the next few years I made back-to-back films, traversing the globe, enjoying the peripatetic life. I was on the road so much and for so long I used to bring parts of home with me: photos of loved ones I'd stick on hotel room walls, bits of fabric to cover nasty lampshades, a little rug that made me happy. I even took some arts and crafts supplies so I could make collages whenever I pleased. I had two giant silver trunks, the kind roadies fill with electric cables and lights after gigs, and I wheeled them through many airports and hotel lobbies, once even sleeping on top of them in a terminal at JFK after I missed the late flight to London. The trunks and that missed flight were indicative of the state of my life back then: scattered, impulsive, animalistic, and messy, yet disciplined and structured enough to mostly keep the show on the road. I'd been interviewed in my hotel bar by a magazine reporter and after a couple of martinis the interview adjourned to my hotel room and probing of a different kind ensued—for a little too long! The uncomfortable night of little sleep was worth it, though, even when I woke up in a start to find myself in the middle of a Hasidic Jewish prayer circle after a flight had arrived from Israel.

I went back to New York and moved into a little studio apartment I had bought on Fourteenth Street, which became my first true American home. I had decided I wasn't going to go back and base myself in London for the foreseeable future, and also as an alien of extraordinary ability (which my type of green card was called), I needed to have a proper base in the States. And it was becoming clear to me that if I had any time off, I wanted to spend it in New York. It was my town. It was my spiritual home. Buying what was to become my London dream pad had only been a means to regulate my life, to make me feel I had a foundation and commitment and future somewhere. When I bought it, my life had been very unregulated. Now there was some order. The madness and the glory of *Cabaret* was behind me and I was essentially back to being a jobbing actor again; it was just that my jobs were Hollywood movies.

I was in New York for the night before Thanksgiving, a notoriously big party night. I went with a couple of friends to the Roxy, a huge club in Chelsea, where I had gone almost every Saturday night after a two-show day on Broadway for most of the previous year to dance the night away in a bacchanalian haze. This night was no different, until at one point a beautiful man, an Adonis actually, came out of the shadows and kissed me. Now, being kissed by a beautiful stranger was not so unusual a thing to have happened to me at the Roxy, but this was different. We made out for hours and stumbled out into the dawn light together. The last time I had done so, my exit had been a surreal and sobering experience. It was the night before my final performance of *Cabaret* and strewn everywhere on the sidewalk outside the club were copies upon copies of discarded *HX* magazines that had been handed out to the departing revellers, with my face looking up wistfully from the cover and the headline "Alan Cumming's curtain call". Of course, by the time I witnessed this sight, many hundreds of revellers had, quite literally, stamped on my face, so I was looking a little worse for wear, as indeed I was in real life.

That Thanksgiving Eve night, though, there was no such narcissistic impediment, and I took Adonis home. We manoeuvred past the half-unpacked boxes and I christened my new murphy bed with this God, who was as beautiful without his clothes as you might have imagined. We had sex. I think we may have even made love. I generally hate the phrase "making love". It's just a euphemism for fucking that denies the darker, baser, rawer traits of sexual union with another human that I feel we should embrace and exalt. I don't approve of "making love". To me, it's the pale, sickly older brother of "fooling around". But that night I think we did, because while we fucked, I fell in love with him. Maybe it had already happened. I think I might have fallen in love the moment he appeared out of the shadows.

When I try to describe the car crash of the next few months of my life with the Adonis, I always say it was like I was the victim of a chemical weapons attack. I was powerless, completely intoxicated, and without any filter or ability to see how insane my behaviour, and indeed this relationship, was.

For example, after two weeks we had each other's names tattooed on our bodies. Just above the groin on the right side. Another man's name was now *tattooed* on my body, a man I didn't even know existed fourteen days before—*and* I thought this was the most sensible thing I had ever done.

Immediately after the tattoo, Adonis and I took a road trip across America together. Oh, and we both thought it would be a good idea to stop smoking cold turkey on said trip, therefore spending entire days jonesing for a cigarette, in a car with—let's face it—basically a stranger. I mean we had covered a lot during those two weeks, but we didn't really know the important aspects about one another. Biographical details are easy to cram. It's someone's character that takes a while to reveal itself.

It is obvious now that this relationship had its basis, its core, its raison d'être (à la lettre!) in sex. Immediately sex was the best way we communicated. Shortly after it became the only way we communicated. Conjoining in a sexual act was the only time I could be certain I was properly understood by this man. Afterwards, we went back to constantly missing each other, sending out and receiving messages on different planes. When we were able to engage on a sexual level, things were great. Sex quickly became a bandage for the wounds in our relationship, and they were many.

I could be all bitchy and hoity-toity here and say that we were not intellectual equals, but that somehow assumes knowledge gives you superiority. I don't agree with that notion. I think education makes you superior only in that it proves you have perseverance and commitment. And in my relationship with the Adonis, I made decisions that definitely caused people to question my intellectual capacity, and indeed my sanity: I had always practised safe sex but with him I willingly exposed myself to risk and, worse, found this rolling of the dice an erotic thrill. I was maddened by him. He was my succubus.

I spent New Year's Eve of the millennium with him, in Dollywood. For those of you who don't know, Dollywood is Dolly Parton's theme park near Pigeon Forge, Tennessee. Please let me state that I have nothing against Dolly Parton. In fact, I adore Dolly Parton. I would love to meet her and if I did, I would completely fangirl on her. I think if you don't like Dolly, it's like saying you don't like seals.

But I still didn't want to be in Dollywood on the New Year's Eve of the millennium, the most important and exciting New Year's Eve any of us will ever experience! The party of the century! Two centuries! The New Year's Eve when the world was possibly going to end! Of course, that was crazy religious cant, but just in case, I didn't want to potentially end my time on earth in Dollywood!!

It was actually even more tragic. Dollywood, of course, closed way before midnight, so I did not actually take in the new millennium in the park. But while I was still actually there, I received a call from a previous lover threatening to kill himself. Yes! No one should get suicide calls at Dollywood. Not on New Year's Eve of the millennium. Oh, no. He didn't go through with it, but still.

Then Adonis and I drove back to the—I'm sorry—hideous hotel room that had been all we had managed to snag for the night and before we went upstairs to begin our inevitable carnal eruption, we sat in our car for a while because the audiobook of Dolly Parton's autobiography, read by (yes, of course and why wouldn't it be?) Dolly Parton herself, was nearing its climax and there was no CD player in that hideous room. The clock was ticking to . . . who knew what, Armageddon? The Rapture? A lot of ATMs not working and that being really annoying? And there I was, cold, sitting in the car park of a dingy Tennessee hotel wanting to strangle a beloved national icon for her verbosity.

When Dolly's aural life reached its inexorable and triumphant climax (I mean, duh, it's Dolly!), Adonis and I went upstairs to do what we did best. We took Ecstasy and we rutted. Oh yes, our sexual chemistry now required chemical enhancement. I brought in the twenty-first century high and fucking, definitely not making love. It wasn't so bad.

Of course, the only possible outcome was a hideous and messy breakup. I braced myself for it. Every nonsexual moment was damage control. Despite my mostly happy, home-oriented lifestyle—the great friends, the apartments, the ability to partake in a pretty hectic and tumultuous work life yet still make it look easy, speak my mind, and have fun all at the same time—in this relationship with Adonis, I was a hot fucking mess. And he was with me, too. We were like each other's worst nightmares that we just wanted to constantly bang.

Four and a half months after that first night at the Roxy, it was over.

———

Naturally, I was plucked from the cesspit of the breakup by, you guessed it, Hollywood. This time it came in the form of an invitation from Robert Rodriguez to come to Austin, Texas, to make *Spy Kids*, a family movie about two kids who discover their parents are spies and in order to rescue them from fiendish danger (moi!), they become spies, too. It was just what the doctor ordered.

Spy Kids was one of those magical films where everything seemed to go right. The cast was lovely. Antonio Banderas, Carla Gugino, Tony Shalhoub, and Danny Trejo were among the grown-ups, and Alexa PenaVega and Daryl Sabara were the eponymous kids.

One day I was shooting a scene with little Daryl and we got chatting between takes.

"What do you think happens to you when you die?" he asked, apropos of absolutely nothing.

"Well," I began rather nervously. "I think you just sort of go back into the earth, into the air. . . ."

"You don't think we go to heaven?" Daryl asked, slightly alarmed.

"No," I replied. "I don't think heaven exists. But I think you leave behind your spirit in the way you've interacted with people and through the things you've done and said."

I suddenly worried I was going to make a little boy cry with my atheist ways.

"What do you think?" I diverted, but also because I was genuinely interested in what he might say.

Quite promptly and assuredly he answered, "I think you die and then two weeks later your body stays here but your soul goes to heaven."

"Why two weeks?"

"That's just how long it takes," answered the seven-year-old.

Then the first AD called the next take, and our little theological debate was over.

Each morning I would get picked up by my driver Sissy, a laconic Texan woman. Drivers, as well as makeup and hair artists, form very intimate relationships with actors. Perhaps it's because we usually see each other so early in the morning when our guard is down. During our predawn drives to the studio, Sissy and I would go pretty deep about things. I told her all about Adonis and the fallout from our recent split. She would occasionally ask me a question, but mostly she just listened and allowed me to talk, and vent. Then, at the end of the day, when I was tired again and a little vulnerable, my thoughts returning to the real world once more on leaving Floop's magical kingdom, we would pick up where we left off.

One morning I was on a tear about some new development in our messy untangling.

"I just wish he would . . . I just wish, I wish . . ." I struggled to find the words to express my frustration and disappointment.

"Alan," said Sissy in her slow and wise drawl. "If wishes were fishes, we'd all take a swim."

None of us had a clue *Spy Kids* was going to become such a

monster hit. If the studio had known it was going to be the blockbuster it became, I fear I would not have been offered the role of Fegan Floop, the magical, island-dwelling TV host who turned people into puppets for his children's programme. No, probably Johnny Depp or someone of his status would have been given first dibs. But *Spy Kids* was a sleeper, and then suddenly we were number one at the box office, in Happy Meals at McDonald's, I was on the back of orange juice cartons, and a franchise was born.

But the best part of the *Spy Kids* legacy did not occur around the film's launch or its subsequent success, or even the two sequels for which I returned for brief cameos. It took years before I knew the true blessing of having been in that film. It was the way in which young adults began to react to me.

Around the end of the 2010s, the children who had been nine or ten when the film came out were now young adults, perhaps at college but certainly making their way in the world. Previously I had always found that age bracket a little awkward to deal with when they recognised me—too cool for school to gush, not sophisticated enough to function normally. But then those awkward interactions stopped, and young men and women would approach me as though they were meeting Mickey Mouse at Disneyland, or about to sit on Santa's knee in a department store. Floop's magical quality, his sense of innocence and mischief all at the same time, had seemingly struck a chord with a generation of children, and still does to this day. *Spy Kids* is a perennial favourite.

"Floop! You were a part of my childhood."

"I grew up watching you." (That actually makes me feel I was the one being spied on.)

My current favourite, in terms of being totally hilarious in its unintended inappropriateness, was when the young camera assistant on the set of a recent TV show I shot in Albuquerque approached me one day as I was walking back to set from my trailer, and said, very sincerely and with a slightly breathless, nervous delivery, "Alan, I want to tell you that you touched me a lot when I was a little boy!" Oops!

After the relative calm of a few months in Texas, existential con-
versations notwithstanding, life returned to its maniacal norm. To wit,
I wrapped *Spy Kids* and left Austin on a Sunday, flew back to New
York to spend my first night alone in my flat there, that is, sans Adonis,
then left for LA the next morning for some reshoots, then on to San
Francisco, where I hosted the Webby awards, and from there I flew to
Berlin, where I arrived on Saturday to start a new film, Alan Rudolph's
Investigating Sex. So, in one week I had slept in Austin, New York, Los
Angeles, San Francisco, and Berlin.

I flung myself into the local nightlife and found the topsy-turvy
Berlin social mores of having sex first (in the bar), then having a drink,
and maybe after that planning dinner, to really suit me. I've never
been a big dater. I'm either all in or it's a sex thing.

The Berliners' open attitude towards sex and public nudity really
connected with me then because, in addition to the enormous grief
and confusion I was dealing with in the aftermath of Adonis, for the
very first time I was actually ashamed of my behaviour in a relationship. Not the actual sexual acts but the risks I took, the abandonment
of self-care and self-worth I willingly engaged in. I'm all for role-play
and consensual anything, but this was beyond that. I had given up my
power to someone who wasn't just undeserving, but also hadn't actually asked for it. I needed to feel good about myself again. Mentally,
sexually. I needed to rediscover abandon that wasn't dangerous, but
joyful. Berlin was the perfect antidote.

There remained, however, the matter of the tattoo. That old
thing. The rather strange, stranger's name I had marked on my body,
appropriately within grabbing distance of my genitals.

When I left Berlin for LA to start prepping and shooting *The Anniversary Party*, a film I wrote and directed with Jennifer Jason Leigh,
I found out there was a top-of-the-range laser tattoo removal clinic
at Cedars-Sinai hospital in Beverly Hills, so off I went and began
the excruciating and repetitive process of having someone's name
wrenched from my body by laser. (And you could hear it happening.

When I asked the nurse what the buzzing noise was, she told me it was the laser actually exploding the ink *in my body*!)

After one of the removal sessions we had a night shoot in Runyan Canyon, the only part of the movie that wasn't set in the house of my and Jennifer Jason Leigh's characters. In the scene Jennifer and I, as Sally and Joe, got into a huge fight and were literally screaming at each other about the abortion Sally had hidden from her husband, who was desperate to have a child with her. The fact my groin was pulsating with pain, as the local anaesthetic had worn off and the laser's incineration of my skin was fully and truly palpable, certainly helped in connecting with Joe's despair that night.

The Anniversary Party was one of those projects that only came into being because of a rare confluence of luck and chutzpah. We told

the studios we pitched it to that we only had the cast for a month. And we'd told the cast that was the month they would work. If anything changed the whole thing was potentially off.

I think Jennifer and I believed in the movie so much we just made it happen, insisted it should happen. It would just be stupid for it not to happen.

After the shoot I planned to stay on in LA for the editing process. However, before the film had been green-lit, I had accepted a role in *Josie and the Pussycats* that would shoot in Vancouver and clash with the editing time. As *The Anniversary Party* became a reality and I began to understand the huge task in front of me, I told my agents I thought it best that I regretfully withdraw from *Josie*, citing my directorial commitments. Alas, that did not go down well with the lawyers at Universal, who threatened to sue if I was not in Vancouver ready for shooting on the morning of Monday, August 28, 2000. Jennifer understood that I could not afford to take on the legal might of a major Hollywood studio and so off I went to Vancouver.

And I loved making *Josie and the Pussycats*, a witty script by the directors Harry Elfont and Deborah Kaplan, way ahead of its time in terms of its parodying of product placement and the commercialisation of our culture. I played a neurotic music manager named Wyatt Frame, whom I based completely on my old friend Richard E. Grant. I basically did my version of his role in *Spice World*. And I adored sparring with Parker Posey, who had just been so brilliant in *The Anniversary Party*.

All that summer I continued with the voracious priapic adventures I'd begun in Berlin. It didn't quite strike me just how sexually active I was during that time until a few years ago—in my defence a good fifteen years after the actual events—when I met someone who I didn't recognise but who gently reminded me we had had sex together in the house I rented in the Hollywood Hills that *Anniversary Party* summer. Always a little embarrassing not to remember someone you have put your penis inside, but it got worse. In his attempts to jog my memory, the gentleman in question told me he had left his watch behind on my nightstand after our encounter.

"Oh yes," I said, the clouds of reminiscence beginning to clear. "I remember! But I mailed it back to you, didn't I?"

"Yes," said my former swain. "But you sent me someone else's watch!"

About nine months later, back in New York, I met up with Adonis. After an awkward forty-five minutes or so of wounded flirting, he asked me a question.

"Do you still have your tattoo, honey?"

I should point out that Adonis used words like "honey" frequently, as there was a good deal of the cowboy about his persona.

"No," I scoffed. "I had it wrenched from my body by laser. You?"

From the corner of his mouth a smirk began to form. Such a simple movement of his lips had once given me cause to draw breath. Now I just ignored it and persevered.

"You?" I repeated. "Do you still have your tattoo?"

"Kinda," he drawled, half seductive, half embarrassed. Annoyingly still a winning combo.

"What do you mean?" I demanded.

He slowly popped the buttons of his fly and pulled the right flap down a little. There, where once had been "Alan", there now was . . .

"Balance."

If I had been a part of bringing balance to one of the least balanced people I'd ever known, then that seemed a perfect coda to our time together.

And then I went back to London and, well, you can guess what happened there.

insanity

15

The first plane hitting the twin towers woke me up on 9/11.

I was in my studio apartment on Fourteenth Street, in bed with my dog, Honey. We both jerked awake, listened for a second, then drifted back to sleep.

You get used to waking up with a start living in New York City. Sirens, of course, permeate the air constantly, but you can also be shaken from your slumber by the rumbling of the subway, weird bangs and shudders from roadworks blocks away, booming bass from the stereo system of cars idling nearby, random screams, opera singers, the screams of opera singers, or the cracking of electrical wires and cables against the sides of buildings when the wind snakes across from the Hudson to the East River. It's an aural cornucopia, and for true-blue New Yorkers, familiar and comforting.

When I was seventeen and left home to go to Glasgow for drama school, I lived in digs on a side street in the city's West End, quiet by anyone's standards. But my entire life up to then had been spent inside what was essentially a forest. Any sound that was not born of nature registered as shrilly as a referee's whistle or a pneumatic drill.

Glasgow was like immediate and excruciating tinnitus for me. The sound of the night buses creeping up Great Western Road kept me awake for many months, but eventually they became my new aural normal. The howl of the wind, the grunt of a distant deer, and the creaking and crunching of a tree faded from memory, and I transformed into a city boy.

I don't remember the second plane hitting. Perhaps my brain had fully switched to Manhattan mode and let me slumber on. But soon, I heard my name being called. I opened my eyes. Honey's ears pricked up and she let out a sleepy growl. We could hear a man's voice and he seemed to be outside on our terrace. He was crying hysterically and, through his tears, calling for me.

It was my next-door neighbour Eddie, who at that point was also working as my assistant. He'd turned on the television after being awakened by the explosions and saw that our city was under attack. Together we watched the first tower collapse on TV, and then the second, while through the open terrace door we heard distant thunder that was the actual sound of them dropping, and the city's screams of disbelief.

Nothing can prepare you for an experience like that, other than it actually happening. We were utterly and truly incredulous. Of course, in the face of such chaos some sort of primal need for order kicks in. I took Honey out for a walk and sent Eddie to the supermarket to buy food because it was anyone's guess how long we might be stranded. I tried to call my family in Scotland, and my boyfriend back in London, but there was no mobile phone service. I stumbled out of my building, bleary-eyed and dazed, onto Fourteenth Street and started walking east. There was a crowd gathered at the corner, staring down Seventh Avenue. I gasped when I realised what they were looking at: the massive plumes of dust and smoke that were, mercifully, blowing south off the island for now, which were all that remained of the twin towers. They were the very spectre of them. Those towers had been my guide whenever I was lost or drunk, or both: the World Trade Center was at the bottom of Manhattan, so I knew to steer away from them to go north. Daily, they were what saved me and so many New Yorkers. Now what would we do?

Later Eddie and Honey and I went out to try to find somewhere open for lunch. We ended up at a table outside Les Deux Gamins on Waverly Place. The world seemed dazed, the act of doing something so commonplace now utterly surreal. The constant wail of so many sirens filling the air almost became white noise. It was a beautiful day, too beautiful for this to have happened. Occasionally a car would drive slowly by covered in gray ash, wipers frantically trying to scrape away the noxious reality that could never be erased. Then suddenly a person would appear, eyes bulging, similarly encased in powder, as though trying to walk themselves back in time. One woman looked like a stone statue that was about to topple: she had lost a shoe but limped on, clutching her handbag, clinging to some sliver of order.

Whenever one of these visions appeared, a hush would descend, but soon the chatter would start up again, people frantically connecting, exchanging information, rumour, panic. Someone said they'd heard that one of the passengers on the hijacked Flight 93 that crashed in Pennsylvania had been able to call his family on his mobile phone from the plane to say good-bye.

"Wow," said a wisecracking New York broad at the table next to us. "I wonder who his carrier was? There's a commercial waiting to happen."

The thing I remember most about that day, and the many following, was the smell. A toxic mix, like nothing I'd ever known before or since, that seemed to consist equally of scorched industrial waste and burning flesh.

Later that night I ate dinner at a Greek place on Eighth Avenue with Eddie and a couple of friends. The streets were deserted. All the bridges and tunnels were closed, so Manhattan was effectively a sealed ghetto. Eddie, the boys, and I took advantage of this once-in-a-lifetime opportunity and ran screaming up the middle of Eighth Avenue. It felt awful and amazing and vital at the same time. We arrived at Barracuda, a bar on Twenty-Second Street, where Eddie immediately went to the men's loo and vomited up his dinner. He said he hadn't exercised so much in years. We then got drinks and went to the back part of the bar, where we had been told that, incredibly, the drag show was still going ahead. Talk about New York Strong! The lights dimmed and the drag queen Cashetta took the stage. *Now this,* I remember thinking to myself, *is a tough gig.*

That morning of September 11, 2001, was the first I'd woken up in New York for some time. I'd been working in LA the previous week and before that I'd spent most of August in London, and Edinburgh for a film festival. I'd landed at JFK in the early hours, then rushed home to an ecstatic Honey and a mound of mail.

When I permanently moved to New York City, suddenly I saw everything in my life making sense: the overwhelming welcome, the relief of no longer being an outsider, that amazing feeling that the energy on the streets wasn't just something I was entering into but what had lain long dormant inside of me, and was now gurgling up, so powerfully I wanted to perpetually hiccup. Once I had experienced that feeling, I only left the city when I absolutely had to, almost always for work. And while the drive from any of the airports back onto the island of Manhattan is still for me as exciting and magical as Dorothy and her cohorts' advance towards the Emerald City, conversely, the journey out to JFK, LaGuardia, or Newark is the most dreary— emotionally as well as aesthetically—that I know.

Even on the hottest, sweatiest, slowest, beastliest of summer nights, when no ceiling fan or clanky air conditioner brought relief, I still couldn't imagine anywhere on earth I'd rather be. I couldn't comprehend the complaints of acquaintances yearning "to get out of the city". Why would you ever want to leave this place? I pondered.

But I suppose the newness of something, whether a person or a city, is always romantic. Not that I have ever doubted my passion for Manhattan, but as time goes on and circumstances change and we get a little older, we naturally start to take our love for granted. It's a given. Then sometimes something happens that jolts us into a new way of thinking.

And we'd all just had a very big jolt.

Don't get me wrong. My love for Manhattan has only increased since that horrible day. The way the city bounced back, the way it rallied and blossomed and *lived* (Auntie Mame would be so proud!) only increased my desire to be a citizen of this weird little island floating off the coast of America, and even proud to have been there when the awfulness happened.

For a few days I spent my time wandering around the West Village, mesmerised by the hundreds of "missing" pictures that were stuck to lampposts and fences and walls by desperate families who could not accept the terrible truth. As the days went by, these signs became memorials, ways for us to process the magnitude of what had occurred, and to slowly embrace the denial of *missing*. These people who smiled out at us, in pictures from family gatherings and office outings, were dead, vaporised. They were missed, but not missing. I recognised a lady who had served me in the Windows on the World restaurant when I had taken my mum on a visit to the towers a few months before. We had chatted, laughed. It was jarring to think she very well might be among the ashes that were now drifting onto my terrace each day.

Just as there were no missing, the initial call for blood to be donated had quickly abated. I had gone around the corner to St. Vincent's hospital that first afternoon, but soon discovered my blood was not acceptable. Three of the questions on the blood bank form I was given were:

Have you lived in England between the mid-eighties to late nineties?

Have you had sex with a man in the last ten years?

Are you a recreational drug user?

Yes, yes, and yes. Sex, drugs, and mad cow disease. Three strikes. I was out. But I tried.

On the Saturday after the Tuesday, when the bridges and tunnels were all open again, a friend invited me to drive with him to his place upstate. I jumped at the chance. Suddenly, not being allowed to leave Manhattan had made me desperate to get out of it, no matter how devoted I was.

We set off, knocked sideways and dazed, amazed the farther we travelled north at the ever-increasing number of signs we saw proclaiming revenge and death to those who had dared threaten American sovereignty. Maybe because we'd been where it had happened, maybe because we were still in shock, maybe because we hadn't worked out our feelings yet, but these public declarations of violence outside churches and fire stations and schools just didn't tally with what was going on inside our heads and hearts. We just wanted some peace.

And we got it. First of all, it was the silence. I hadn't appreciated how insanely noisy New York had been. Post-9/11 there were endless bomb scares and the streets ranged from being utterly empty to being full of people screaming and running in every direction. The Empire State Building is about to be blown up! There's a chemical attack on the subway! Don't drink the water! Get a gas mask before stocks run out!

To be away from it all—in this quiet, balmy, beautiful, leafy wilderness—was shocking, and forced me to process everything I'd been merely living through for the last five days. I wept and grieved. I looked around me and for the first time ever understood what those people meant when they said they had to get out of my beloved city.

It just so happened that the land that abutted my friend's property was for sale. A twelve-acre parcel of forest with a little hunting lodge at a price that seemed too good to miss. Honey and I got in my car and drove up to have a look. That moment is crystallised forever in my mind. The track up to the little house was so overgrown it was like entering a tunnel of mottled green. Rufus Wainwright's *Poses* was blasting from my car stereo. A flicker of breeze rushed by, allowing the sun to sneak through the parting tree limbs above and momentarily blinding us. When the breeze stopped, there stood a perfect little wooden cottage on stilts. A sanctuary. A dream to usurp the nightmare. It was mine by Tuesday morning, a week to the day after the twin towers had fallen. In case you haven't realised, I'm an instant gratification kind of guy.

I went back to the city to record a duet of "Baby, It's Cold Outside" with Liza Minnelli. Yes, clang, thank you very much! It was for a

Christmas album to benefit the New York City firefighters and Broadway Cares/Equity Fights AIDS. Liza had come directly from singing
"New York, New York" on that morning's *The Rosie O'Donnell Show*
and before we got started, there was a film crew from *Entertainment
Tonight* set to interview us about the duet and also to ask us about our
9/11 experiences. Liza, as always an endearing, shaky ball of chutzpah
and nerves, grabbed both my hands as I sat next to her and began
to tell the *ET* reporter she'd initially thought the whole thing was
a movie when she turned on her TV the week before. I didn't say very
much at all. Indeed, a friend who saw the piece when it was aired
told me I looked like a ventriloquist's dummy sitting on Liza's knee.

"Then I started to get angry," she proclaimed, referring to the
hijackers and squeezing my hands even harder. "And now I'm just
really angry! How dare they! I don't want these guys thinking 'we
closed six Broadway shows!'"

———

Later that day I flew to Paris. The airport was, literally, a war zone.
Armed guards at every turn. Lines of people out the doors and down
the kerb. The security checks were insanely, retrospectively thorough.
On the third time I was pulled aside for a random check, I questioned
if it could still be defined as random. *Where were you ten days ago?* I
wanted to scream.

Finally, I made it to the Air France lounge. All the televisions in
the room were blaring competing news channels. It was deafening.
Also, the events of 9/11 heralded the advent of the constant scrolling
news ticker on TV screens, which added to the audiovisual onslaught.
I truly believe these now-omnipresent tickers have encouraged Americans to stay in a constant state of heightened anxiety about politics,
foreigners, and just the world in general. This has only helped those
who have sought power by preying on our insecurities and fears. On
that day, America was about to invade Afghanistan. It was inexorable,
the required gesture of revenge. The United States is just so big and
unwieldly a collection of ideas that it can't be wrangled intellectually
or analytically, so gesture is often the compromise, I suppose.

I love an airline lounge. I am a self-confessed lounge whore. I see any unexpected delay at check-in or security as eating into my lounge time, a roadblock between me and a Bloody Mary, nuts, and a moment of repose. But that day I couldn't wait for my lounge time to be over. Much as I dreaded the flight—and remember, everyone was understandably terrified of flying at that time—I longed for the journey to begin. I actually longed to be outside of New York, of America, at that moment. The signs of vengeance on the drive upstate, the mob mentality and rising violence against Muslims—and indeed anyone with a vaguely Middle Eastern skin colour—all pointed to a country bubbling out of control. Of course, little did I know it would take another fifteen years, and a ban on all Muslims entering the country, for some quarters to feel true reparations had been made.

I arrived at Charles de Gaulle Airport and wept in my waiting boyfriend's arms. We took a few days to drive to Italy for the wedding of two dear friends, Fay and Daniel. For everyone present it was a relief to have something else to occupy our thoughts. Life could go on, and here we were to celebrate and prove it.

Most of the commitments I had around this time had been cancelled. Earlier that year *The Anniversary Party* had premiered at the Cannes Film Festival and we were scheduled to attend several other festivals to coincide with the film's staggered release around the globe. I was particularly looking forward to travelling to Rio de Janeiro but due to security concerns we were told our trip there was cancelled. I was expected at the Flanders film festival in Belgium in a few weeks' time, and that was still on, so I decided to just stay in Europe and see what happened.

As per the norm in my life, quite a lot happened.

After a couple of days in Florence, my boyfriend and I took a train south and then a moonlit taxi ride along the Amalfi coast that was both the most terrifying and most beautiful car journey I'd ever had. We rode along the winding, precipitous clifftop road with the Mediterranean far below, almost phosphorescent in the lunar glare.

This journey was befitting the destination, for we were on our way for a weekend stay with Gore Vidal at his villa in Ravello!

I had met Gore earlier that year in New York when I took part in a reading of his play *Visit to a Small Planet*. I wasn't really a fan of the play, but it isn't every day you get to meet someone like Gore. The whole thing was very glittery, with Tony Randall and Lily Tomlin among the cast, as well as my old chum Kristin Chenoweth—who had played Lily St. Regis to my Rooster in the Disney remake of *Annie* the previous year—and Christine Baranski, whom I'd go on to have many years of fun with in *The Good Wife*.

Like many people I was both fascinated and slightly scared of Gore. I loved his stories and he loved that I loved them. I was flattered by his attention, and the invitation to visit him in Italy, but at the same time I would never want to be on the wrong side of him. He was a legendary drinker, but the few meetings we had between the play reading and my visit to Ravello were usually breakfasts or lunches, with maybe a glass of white wine the extent of the alcoholic consumption. So, I had never seen the other side of Gore's personality. All of that was about to change.

When we arrived, Gore had greeted us in a shaft of moonlight at the door of the villa, ice cubes clinking in the whisky glass he held aloft, and ushered us into his rococo study, where Howard, Gore's longtime partner, was completely plastered.

"We started drinking at six and so your tardiness is the reason for us being a little buzzed," Gore slurred.

I asked Howard how he was doing. He peered up at me out of a huge armchair next to the drinks table that made him seem even more diminutive and impish than he actually was.

"I'm floating," came the reply.

I really liked Howard. It must have been hard to get a word in edgewise living with Gore Vidal, and so perhaps that gave him the time to hone his one-liners down to such a degree that every single one was a gem. Gore had once described Howard to me—not in his presence, of course—as "a wisecracker" and smiled with a rare fondness. And that is exactly what he was, especially that evening.

Gore showed us upstairs to our room. Golden yellow drapes hung at the huge windows and the walls were festooned with slightly menacing gilt eagles. Behind the two voluminous sofas that abutted the marble fireplace was a four-poster bed, and books, books everywhere.

"This is gorgeous," I gasped.

"It was Princess Margaret's room," Gore said over his shoulder as he stepped unsteadily out onto a terrace with the most beautiful view I had ever seen. We were so high up that the sparkling lights from the ships moored up and down the coast for miles looked like fireflies. There was another little room off the terrace that Gore told us had been the maid's quarters but now housed all of his foreign editions.

"I am published in sixty-two languages," he almost moaned. "They keep sending them to me. I have to have somewhere to put them."

We freshened up quickly then went back downstairs, where Gore and Howard, doing their well-worn double act, were on a roll.

"I once spent two successive Christmas Eves in Paris, in the company of the Duke and Duchess of Windsor," Gore declared.

Howard, fixing us cocktails from his seated position next to the drinks table, deadpanned, "Just lucky I guess!"

We all roared with laughter. Howard handed me my drink and winked.

"There was some little French accordionist playing and the Duke didn't know the words of the hymns in English. He kept lapsing into German. He was a supporter of Hitler, but I don't think he was intelligent enough to know what Nazism was," Gore continued undeterred.

By the time we sat down to dinner, prepared by a famous Japanese chef who was vacationing nearby, the mood was quite raucous. Gore and Howard were not very au fait with Japanese food and at one point, Gore, who had refused chopsticks, forked up a huge mound of the hottest wasabi I had ever tasted, and was about to swallow it whole. The table exploded in cries of panic, especially from the chef, who had just regaled us with the list of ingredients in every dish and was obviously acutely aware of the consequences of a drunk seventy-six-year-old ingesting this thermogenic condiment.

But Gore, who was seated next to me at the head of the table in a very low chair ("Have you shrunk?" Howard had quipped), refused to heed anyone's advice, and like the wilful, wicked schoolboy he was, held the forkful of wasabi in front of his mouth, his eyes darting around the table to be sure we were all watching, then swallowed the lot of it. We all waited for something to happen but miraculously he did not explode. He gave a silent toast with his sake glass and we all followed suit, but then, under the cover of the nervous, stilted conversation that finally resumed at the other end of the table, I heard him emit a series of weird grunts.

Howard was being charming and getting a lot of attention and I could tell Gore was becoming a little jealous. He asked me what I was working on and I told him I was trying to finish off my first book, a novel, but what with all that had been going on over the last few weeks, I was having a little trouble.

"Well of course you are, you're not a novelist," he snapped, without looking at me.

I said nothing. I knew exactly what was happening. Sadly, a response like this was an old standby for bitter old queens of a certain age. They show you kindness that you mistake as respect, then they bring you down or humiliate you when they know you can't—or wouldn't—retaliate because, actually, you want to protect them, not embarrass them. I knew this was in Gore's lexicon and I had even imagined something along these lines happening during this visit. In a way it was a sign that he liked me enough, or trusted my kindness, to be that cruel. And also, of course, in a way he was right. I wasn't a novelist. Yet.

There was a rather long pause that I wasn't going to break. Not with Gore's belly full of whisky and sake and wasabi, and his speech slurring and his eyes straining to focus. Also, at that moment, I actually held the upper hand. I found Gore boring and wished I was farther up the table listening to Howard being witty and hilarious—which I knew would be a dagger to Gore's heart.

"Write about what you know," he said quietly.

I wanted to say that was exactly what I was doing, that my novel was a thinly veiled roman à clef about my debaucherously fun deep dive a few years prior, overlaid with my still very present physical yearnings for fatherhood.

But I didn't have a chance. He was off.

"You get around the world, you meet interesting people, you have ideas. Write them down! And *analyse*," he said, with great emphasis.

"Write about this weekend," he continued, looking over his sake glass at Howard. "Write about two men who have been together for over fifty years and yet have hardly ever had sex. Analyse it."

Their relationship did indeed fascinate me. They had been together at that point for fifty-two years and seemed completely dependent on, and loyal to, each other. But Gore had written copiously about his other lovers, his fear of commitment, and that he had never been in love except once, briefly, with his fellow schoolboy named Jimmy Trimble, whose death soon after their teenage love affair ended haunted him and his work—*Palimpsest*, Gore's memoir, was both a paean, and dedicated, to Jimmy. I wondered how Howard felt about all of that.

I had finished reading *Palimpsest* just a couple of hours earlier, rushing through the last chapters on the train that afternoon like a guilty schoolboy cramming for a tutorial. And now here I was, listening to the man himself recount many of the anecdotes I'd so recently read. It was like having drinks with a living audiobook. When he started the one about Greta Garbo saying to Cecil Beaton that she wished her genitals got smaller as she got older, it was all I could do to stop myself from chiming in with the punch line.

Gore and Howard had met in the aptly named Everard Baths on Twenty-Eighth Street in New York City in the late forties, where they had had some sexual contact ("mostly in the presence of others" as Gore delicately put it). Gore talked fondly of those halcyon days when

men of all sexualities gathered in bathhouses ("it was cheaper than a
hotel and they could get blown") and where, he said, you could have
anyone.

Even sitting down, Gore was swaying now, and beginning to nee-
dle me. He could feel I was taking him up on his challenge and by
questioning him about his views and past adventures I was indeed
trying to analyse his and Howard's relationship. So, he kept throwing
challenges back.

"Don't you hate commitment?" he asked wickedly, knowing my
boyfriend was within earshot.

"No," I said, thinking carefully. "I don't hate it."

"But you obviously aren't that fond of it by the way you responded."

"Well . . ." I was beginning to feel a little uncomfortable and Gore
could tell and was loving it.

"It's not that I'm not fond of it. When I make a commitment, I like
it. I just don't like to feel trapped."

Gore's eyes sparkled and he flashed a vulpine smile, no doubt
honing his next salvo. I decided to retaliate. The hunted became the
hunter.

"*You* seem to be the one with the commitment issues, Gore."

There was a pause for a moment. He slurped more sake. "Oh yes."

Suddenly Gore reminded me of Tommy, the eponymous hero of
my unfinished novel, shagging everything he could and refusing to be
pinned down or defined. But unlike Tommy, he had enjoyed all that
in his life *and* commitment. Gore had no commitment issues. He had
been committed to Howard for more than half a century. What he
had a problem with was *admitting* his commitment.

He then started to talk about never having loved.

"What about Jimmy Trimble?" I asked.

"Ah yes." I could tell he was torn—half pleased I had done my
homework and read his memoir; half pissed-off I was interrupting his
lament. "I didn't realise how much he meant to me," Gore conceded.

"But you were never really in love with him, were you?" I pounced,
knowing the answer already, but wanting to hear him say it aloud.

"How could I have been? We were so young. We were just friends fooling around."

Of course, Gore would be an exponent of my least favourite American phrase.

"He was just a teenage infatuation?" I pushed.

"Yes."

"So, you have never loved, Gore?"

"No."

I suppose I should have been outraged that Gore Vidal had just confessed to me that the central theme of his memoir was a lie, but I wasn't. A human being in his seventies sitting in front of me asking me to believe he had never been in love was far more outrageous. Just as he had never properly acknowledged the commitment he had made to Howard, he couldn't admit to ever having been in love.

I couldn't understand it. The usual recipe of shame and self-loathing you might attribute to a man of his generation in such a scenario just didn't wash: he'd been very vocal about his male partners. And his female ones. In fact, let's face it, Gore was pretty vocal about everything. His first novel, *The City and the Pillar*, is very graphic in its description of a gay relationship and caused a sensation when it was first published. It's not as if he had a problem with admitting he liked cock. He just had a problem admitting to liking the rest of the person a cock belongs to.

"You Brits are more prone to affection in sex," he said, reaching for the sake bottle.

"You make that sound like a bad thing," I replied.

The subject was closed. Gore was finished.

Later, with yet more sake sloshed into our glasses, Gore launched into another elabourate and racy story. Things were getting pretty woozy by now, but I seem to recall this one was about a youthful Prince Philip and the coterie of European aristocrats on whose kindness he had depended. Howard interrupted with another wisecrack that made us all howl, and the next thing we knew Gore was up and out of his seat, staggering against the kitchen door frame as he exited stage right. A big, huge baby in a big, theatrical huff. He did not return.

Everyone was a little embarrassed, and Howard seemed genuinely worried, but then someone suggested a nightcap, and the promise of alcohol numbed his anxiety.

When the other guests had left to drive home to their villa, I told Howard to go to bed and that I would clean up.

"Well, it can't be too bad, he must quite like me, we have been together for fifty-two years," he said, his ever-present cigarette wobbling in his mouth as he spoke. I thought it both sad and strangely sweet to be that insecure, after all that time. And with that, Howard bade us good night.

As we climbed the stairs to the Princess Margaret room, I heard voices coming from the study, where Gore had retreated and Howard had now joined him. They were bickering. Through the open door I saw Gore hunched over in a chair, balancing a tumbler of whisky on his knee. He glanced up and our eyes met.

"Good night, children," he said sadly.

As we reached the bedroom door, I could hear their argument continue. I sat down on the top step and listened. Suddenly I was taken back to my childhood home, and the many times I sat on our stairs attuned to the raised voices of my parents, my stomach clenched in anguish, wondering if it was anything I had said or done that had sparked this latest conflict.

"You weren't using your brain, Howard, you didn't know what you were doing, you were so drunk," growled Gore, who at this point was barely intelligible himself.

"This is not working, Gore, it's not working, period. I have got to get out of here." I heard Howard leave and start down the stairs to their bedrooms below.

Oh, good, I remember thinking, he only means he has to get out of that room.

But then, after a few seconds came Howard's final, departing cry:

"I am putting the lights out now, Gore, and don't worry, in the morning I will be *so* out of here."

Oh my God, I thought. *They are splitting up! I was present on the very night a fifty-year relationship ended, and all because I was late, and they got so drunk before dinner! I am partly to blame for Howard and Gore breaking up!*

(Please note I had been drinking heavily myself.)

In the morning, my boyfriend and I crept downstairs, fearful of the carnage we might find. At first, we couldn't find anyone at all, but then a little Italian lady appeared and ushered us out to a terrace overlooking the Amalfi coast and a table set for breakfast, where Gore and Howard were sitting, crashingly hungover. But when they saw us, they perked up immediately.

"Wasn't that a fantastic evening?" asked Gore.

"I really needed a blowout after the tension of the last few weeks," agreed Howard.

Considering I had expected Howard to be gone, his appearance as well as their glowing review of the previous night's shenanigans left me stunned.

We sat down and our breakfast order was taken. Under the table, I absentmindedly slid my hand into my boyfriend's. The table was glass and so Howard saw this gesture and immediately swatted his napkin at me.

"Not in front of Maria," he hissed.

I quickly withdrew my hand, confused, suddenly ashamed, but not sure why. Already following Gore's advice of the previous evening, I began to analyse what had just happened, and I was filled with sadness—that not just love but tenderness or even touch had no place here, even under the table, in a home two men had shared for thirty years.

———

We left Ravello and took the train all the way up to Milan, where fashion week had just begun. My friend Glenda Bailey, the recently minted editor of *Harper's Bazaar*, had suggested we come up and join her for some frivolity. Before I knew it, I was invited to the Versace show and a party afterwards at Donatella's villa on Lake Como. Alas, our train delay meant we missed the actual show, but we had time to get to our hotel and for me to change into the Versace ensemble that was waiting in a garment bag in my room.

The party was as opulent and hilarious as you might have wished, dreaded, or assumed it to be. The villa and gardens were stunning. The mist was wafting across the moonlit lake. Except it wasn't. As I walked along the terrace to the porta-potties (Donatella very wisely did not allow a bunch of drunk fashionistas to clog up her neoclassical plumbing), I saw that in fact the mist was actually supplied by a dry-ice machine and the moonlight by a cleverly secreted series of theatrical lights. *Ah well, all art is artifice*, I mused as I headed back inside to the party.

I saw Donatella by the door and went over to thank her for inviting me and also for sending the clothes I was currently wearing.

Donatella has talked openly of her eighteen years of cocaine addiction. I can confirm that this evening was during those years. I have known of a certain numbness of the upper lip that can occur when one has over-imbibed in the blow department, and Donatella was certainly experiencing it at that moment, too. As we say in Scotland: the lights were on but there's naebody in.

But it was a fun party. Fashion week in New York had been cancelled a few weeks earlier, and so everyone was making up for it, as well as letting off steam—like Howard—in response to the new awfulness we had all experienced. On 9/11 itself I'd been scheduled to attend the opening of a new Tom Ford/YSL store on Madison Avenue. I remember wondering if a terrorist attack would be enough to halt the juggernaut of fashion commerce. It was.

A little while later that evening, I was laughing with Glenda, when suddenly our drinks were snatched from our hands. We looked around in surprise at a table that had miraculously materialised in the centre of the room. Suddenly waiters streamed in with trays of champagne, and a huge white cake was carried aloft and placed on the table, around which a procession of beautiful people gathered, and I realised they included Donatella, Jennifer Lopez, and a lovely dancer named Cris, whom she had married a few days earlier.

"Oh my God," I whispered to Glenda. "We're at J-Lo's wedding reception!"

And indeed, as the happy couple began to cut the cake, we were encouraged to raise our glasses in a toast, and Donatella shouted, "To Jenneefer and Crees!"

There then followed that sort of embarrassing lull in the evening as nobody knew quite what was supposed to happen next, but mercifully the DJ kicked in again and the table was removed and the party went back to some semblance of normality, well, normal for a Versace fashion after-party in Donatella's schloss on Lake Como. With fake mist.

I couldn't quite countenance what had just happened and found myself continuing to stare at the happy couple. Then something crazy occurred.

"Oh wow, J-Lo's coming this way," I warned my group. "Oh wow, she's coming straight towards us," I said. Then, "Holy shit, she is actually coming right over here . . ."

"Hello, Alan," said Jennifer Lopez, standing in front of me, looking utterly bewitching.

"Oh gosh, hi Jennifer. I totally forgot I knew you," I stammered, and I actually had.

"How *do* you two know each other?" someone thoughtfully intervened.

"We did *SNL* together." Jennifer smiled, seeming slightly embarrassed that everyone didn't know. Particularly me, of course, I suppose.

"Yes, that's right." I tried to regain some credibility. "When I was the host of *Saturday Night Live*, Jennifer was the musical guest. I got to say, 'Jennifer Lopez is in the hoooouuuuusssseee!'"

There was another awkward lull. We all sipped our champagne.

"I really liked the video for your song 'Ain't It Funny'," I ventured.

Jennifer's eyes lit up.

"You did, really?" she said.

"Yes," I spluttered, amazed she would doubt me on this.

"Would you tell Cris, my husband, that you liked it? He directed it and it would really mean a lot to him."

Now, I am no relationships guru, and back then I was even less qualified to pass judgement on a couple's chance of longevity, but a superstar bride asking an acquaintance to go over and boost the confidence of her new husband (who until recently had been her backup dancer) mere days after they'd tied the knot did not scream that the relationship was on a secure footing to me. It was a loving and lovely gesture on J-Lo's part, but also, alas, portended doom.

I duly walked over to Cris, introduced myself, and congratulated him on the video.

"Oh, you really liked it?" He seemed pleased.

"Yes. I loved how on one side of the washing line Jennifer was a plain country girl and then when she went under the washing line to the other side she became all glam." It was true. I did.

Cris's smile seemed a little frozen. I thought he must be a little overwhelmed. And jet-lagged. I made my excuses and went back to my gang.

It is only now, twenty years later, having done some online research in order to remember which particular J-Lo song it was I liked all those years ago, that I have discovered the video I described in such glowing detail to the groom was not in fact the one he directed at all. I now know Cris directed the "Ain't It Funny" remix that also featured Ja Rule and Cadillac Tah and contained not even a hint of a washing line. An easy mistake to make perhaps, but nonetheless, no doubt a doubly bitter pill for Cris to swallow considering I was congratulating him, at his wife's behest, for something he had not only not done, but which was actually the work of the legendary photographer Herb Ritts. Oops.

———

Herb Ritts had recently shot me for that year's *Vanity Fair* Hollywood issue. It's one of my favourite pictures ever taken of me.

But, like most things I truly like, it did not turn out at all as planned. Herb was a lovely, gentle man and wanted to buck the trend of me wearing more makeup than clothes that had become the norm in pictures of me. He called me up to discuss his idea.

"This will be the Alan nobody has seen," he said excitedly. "No makeup, natural light, just a classic handsome portrait."

I baulked initially at the idea of no makeup, but of course this was Hollywood and no makeup actually meant "a natural look", created by, well, makeup. My favourite ever variation of this was a makeup artist who once told me she wanted to create for me a "natural smoky eye". Huh?

I'm always game to try something new, and of course when a genius like Herb Ritts is asking you to get on board, you jump. Plus, he called me handsome. Things started to go wrong, however, when I couldn't do the shoot in daylight due to my commitments on *The Anniversary Party*, which was in the very crucial last stages of postproduction. So, it was to be a studio shoot one evening after work. And with the stable door opened, the horse duly bolted.

I ended up spending four hours in makeup, having hooves, horns, nails, and ears attached to me and eventually hobbling into a studio (hooves aren't easy) that had been transformed into a bucolic forest. So much for the natural look. I was now the god Pan, complete with flute. For the last few years there had rarely been an interview that did not use one of the words "imp", "sprite", or "nymph" to describe me, and now here I was, the living embodiment of all that nomenclature.

"Should I just sit against that tree trunk, Herb?" I asked innocently.

"No!" Herb exclaimed, aghast at my naïveté. "Lie down across the forest floor! That way we get two pages in the magazine!"

———

New York City was still reeling but defiantly fighting back. Mayor Giuliani regularly appeared on TV and encouraged us to go out and shop and dine and imbibe. Basically, his message was: spend money, you'll feel better.

That's the American way, I suppose. Somehow even getting drunk became a sanctioned, positive act of political and patriotic defiance. And so, I duly obliged. People were almost bullishly pretending they were okay, that life had to go on. It was a supreme, collective effort of mind over matter, and utter positivity. Of course, inside we were all volcanoes of PTSD waiting to happen.

But one night, shortly after I returned from Europe, I went to an event that brought me both a strange calm as well as the biggest laugh I had had in months.

Tina Brown, then editor of the recently launched *Talk* magazine, threw a dinner party at her home to celebrate the publication of a new book by English author Simon Schama, *A History of Britain, Volume 2*. After a lovely meal we wandered out to the garden, where the author made an amazing speech that drew an allusion between the sudden, recent example of religious fundamentalism that had occurred just a few miles south of where we all stood and some of the political and religious extremism that stemmed from the English Civil Wars, a period detailed in his book. It was strangely comforting to hear that what had happened in our beloved city was, of course, awful, but not unusual by history's standards. This fracture of cultures and religious ideologies had happened before. Simon placed it contextually for us in a way that made us all breathe a little easier.

However, we all may have been breathing easier due to what had happened immediately before he began to speak: Tina, her husband, Harold Evans, and Simon Schama all lined up in front of a little hedge, facing us, their audience, as we looked on. Martha Stewart, America's reigning domestic goddess, was a guest that night as well and for some reason she joined Tina, Howard, and Simon in the official lineup.

Remember, this was 2001. This was pre-prison Martha, this was omnipotent Martha, this was the Martha whom I'd met out and about on the town and who, like me, clearly enjoyed a few drinks. Now, perhaps there was a logic for her joining the illustrious literary threesome that evening, but it did not seem to be apparent, judging by their expressions as she sidled up to them as they waited for the last of the guests to settle and the speeches to begin.

Just then Martha—perhaps in an attempt to make a little more room on the already crowded patio edge—took a step backward, lost her footing, and suddenly disappeared from view. There was a gasp from the crowd as I strained on my tiptoes over the man in front of me to see Martha's legs sticking up from behind the miniature hedge like the witch in *The Wizard of Oz*. Then those very legs began to pedal as she vainly tried to get up, but almost instantly a gaggle of damage control experts rushed in, righted her, and swept Martha away, never to be seen again, that night anyway. A shimmer of incredulity rippled through the crowd. "Did that actually just happen?" one of my table mates gasped as she turned to me, openmouthed.

"What?" said someone too slow to have witnessed the act.

The speeches started and the matter was never mentioned again. But I was there, and I saw it, and it signalled that New York, in all its insanity, was back.

mutancy

16

I entered my late mid-thirties in Isla Mujeres, a little island off the coast of Mexico, where I had gone to learn to scuba dive. It seemed like a good idea at the time, but there is a moment from that trip that has seen much repeat viewing in the relatively small repertoire of my nightmares.

One day towards the end of my course we took a field trip to Tulum to do some cave diving. This involved strapping a little torch to my head and diving far underwater but also far underground—which meant that if for some reason you suddenly needed to get back to the surface, you could not. Swimming upwards would mean banging your head against the rock of the cave wall ceiling and then slowly and painfully drowning. But it was so beautiful! These underground caves were like drenched, deserted ballrooms of some sunken villa, and I became mesmerised by the magical troves my torch revealed with each flick of my head.

Scuba diving is predicated on always keeping visual contact with other divers, but I was so bewitched by what I was seeing around me that all safety protocols were quickly forgotten. I soon found myself alone, deep inside a dark cave full of water. The thing is, at the time, I didn't really care, or even notice. The thrill and sensory overload I was experiencing overrode any fear. It was only when I noticed, far in the

distance at the very edge of my periphery and through many subter-
ranean chambers, the intermittent gleams of a fellow diver's torch that
I realised I had strayed from my group and was potentially lost.

Even then I didn't panic. I kicked my fins, made for the lights
ahead of me, and fell into line without any of them noticing I had
been missing.

My dreams, however, have been riddled with a re-creation of that
moment with the appropriate fear of what might have happened—that
I would never have found my group or made it to the surface, breathed
my last oxygen alone in the dark and then shrivelled into an aqueous
cadaver. Indeed, many of my nightmares are built around magical
real-life happenings whose risks and consequences are only revealed
to me in catatonic retrospection. An internal equilibrium, perhaps, to
counter my conscious insouciance?

I doubt I will ever scuba dive again. But scuba diving is not the
only precarious experience I look back on from 2002 with the need
to reassure my retroactive superego that I will not put myself in such
a position again. Another was playing Nightcrawler in X2: *X-Men
United*. Yes, Hollywood called again, and I became a superhero. It
wasn't so super.

I flew from New York to Vancouver to begin filming the morning
after the closing night of a play, Jean Genet's *Elle*, which had been one
of the most exciting and fulfiling adventures I had had in quite some
time. I had almost turned down the movie because of it, but the studio
offered a compromise that allowed me to do a shortened run of the
play before heading immediately to the world of mutants.

Elle had never been performed in English before and so I adapted
the text from the French and took on the leading role of the pope.
The play is a tale of a photographer who comes to take a picture of the
pope, only to discover that, as the pope is only ever seen from the front,
the back of him is bare, literally: his arse sticks out of his robes. Genet
posits the notion that the pope only really exists when he is being photographed, when he is being presented to the world. This idea really

chimed with me for I'd recently been struck by a conversation I'd had with an acquaintance about a swanky awards party I'd gone to.

"Are you sure you were there?" he asked me suspiciously.

"Yes," I replied. For it was true. I had been.

"It's just that I saw the pictures from that party in *InStyle* magazine and I didn't see you."

So, because I wasn't in the magazine, to my conversation partner I hadn't been to the party at all. And this was exactly the same existential dilemma Genet was wrestling with in *Elle*!

Around this time is when phones with high-quality cameras were introduced. This changed the life of every celebrity in the world overnight, because now the marking of an encounter with one of us was no longer merely our signature on a napkin or a piece of paper. Now an image of a celeb could be captured on a phone and prove, beyond a shadow of a doubt, that the meeting had occurred. The ephemeral was no more! Anything and everything could be digitally commemorated forever! And conversely, if you didn't get the picture with the celebrity, did you actually meet them? Were they even really there? Were you? Perhaps even more prescient is Genet's speculation that the pope only actually exists when he is being photographed, for surely the lives we present to the world in our Instagrammed existence nowadays do not *really* exist, either, given they have all been staged and airbrushed and filtered.

I loved playing the pope. It was challenging on all levels. I was on roller skates (Genet's idea, not mine!) in a Vivienne Westwood-designed robe and mitre, and I played him dripping with ancient Eastern European ennui! The whole process of adapting the play, forming a company to get the play on, then seeing it come together was incredibly satisfying and fulfiling, but not easy: here was a play that had never before been performed in English, in which the pope takes a shit onstage (sorry, I forgot to mention that part!). This does not immediately scream bums on seats, as it were. But it worked and we became a bona fide hit, and all the more of a cult success because the

run was so short due to my *X-Men* dates. But going immediately from papal nakedness to shoot a superhero movie was exactly how I liked to roll: on to the next! Cancel, continue!

———

I now think of myself as someone unafraid of confrontation, but I was not as brave before I made the X-men movie. Back then, I would speak up and be an ally and an advocate, but I had never instigated an intervention.

As actors we are constantly reminded of our expendability. No matter how beloved we become, how bankable, how much power we wield, it's still difficult to unlearn the ingrained and omnipresent message that we should be grateful to be working at all. Lawyers and agents and business affairs people may haggle, sometimes for months, over the minute details of elabourate business deals based on our perceived worth, crafting ironclad contracts that commodify our place at the table and ensure our rights are respected and our voices heard. Yet rarely do we actors use those voices.

Often, our experience on a set can be quite insular. Bad behaviour is hidden from us. We are protected from the excesses of those who are abusing their place and others'. The system is designed to keep us in a cocoon, the precious cargo penned in our trailers until the set is absolutely ready for us, ensuring we are fresh and rested and able to be slotted efficiently into the assembly line. It can sometimes be years before we are fully cognizant of some drama that was occurring mere feet from us on set as we worked. But on X2, everyone knew. Everyone could see it, felt it, was damaged by it.

The director, Bryan Singer, has himself admitted he was using painkillers at the time, and he definitely exhibited corresponding behavioural patterns during filming: mood swings, tantrums, paranoia. Many mornings I would have been in the makeup trailer for up to five hours being transformed into a blue, teleporting mutant, only to be told I would not be shooting that day after all. Bryan had changed his mind, or Bryan was having some back-pain issues. I would sometimes not even leave my seat in the trailer. The two special effects makeup artists responsible for my transformation would simply begin the process of undoing all their work and we would all be sent home.

Perhaps this sounds as if I am complaining. And boo hoo, maybe that's why I was being paid so handsomely. Yes, of course. I hear that. But the level of disregard on a regular basis, along with a general air of unpredictability and tension that engulfed the set, combined with insane working hours and constant physical discomfort that comes with playing such a role was enough to make anyone resort to uncharacteristic behaviour. So, yes, I am complaining.

When I first began shooting on the movie, it was for the opening scene in which Nightcrawler attacks the Oval Office and attempts to assassinate the president. That sequence took weeks to achieve and involved a multitude of stunts and special effects but little acting from me aside from a few snarls and bookends to my stuntmen's acrobatics. But there was also great secrecy and paranoia surrounding the look of my character, because I was a new X-man. Comic book fans were agog to find out how one of their favourite superheroes would be manifested onscreen and there was a bounty for the first picture of me in costume and makeup. I had zero previous knowledge of the Marvel Universe (indeed, the night before the audition for the role I was disabused by a friend of my belief that Nightcrawler was green and not blue!) and so it felt even more surreal to find myself at the centre of this media storm, with paparazzi lurking in the bushes outside the studio fences trying to get a snap of me. This meant that I was not allowed to leave my trailer without wearing a huge black cloak that covered my entire body and face. It was very fine material so I could sort of see through it, but nonetheless it was weird and rather humiliating to take my dog out for a pee looking like the Grim Reaper.

Soon a photo shoot I had done in character was leaked from 20th Century Fox's publicity department, and pictures of me as Nightcrawler flooded the internet. From then on I took my first stand and refused to wear the cloak, my burka as I had come to call it. Also, hilariously, I had not been wearing my tail in the publicity pictures as they were going to photoshop it on afterwards, and so in the leaked picture you could see my Calvin Klein undies through the hole where the tail was usually attached. "They're making Nightcrawler gay!" came the cry from the blogosphere.

Actually, *X2: X-Men United* is probably the gayest film I have ever been in. Bryan and his writers made such a clever and sensitive allusion of mutancy and otherness with gayness. The movie was also directed by a gay man, written by gay men, and several of its stars were queer. In that respect, I felt we were putting a really positive message into the world.

On one of my first days I remember being in a harness hanging from wires high in a corner of the Oval Office set, assuming that any second we would go for a take because, well, I was in a harness hanging from wires. Surely they would not have hauled me up into such an uncomfortable and dangerous position if we were not about to go?

"Why aren't we rolling?" I asked the first AD.

"Bryan's not on set," he replied.

"Why not?" I asked innocently.

Crickets.

I then inquired, quite politely, that if he wasn't coming soon, perhaps I could be let down from the painful position. I was, and I was grateful.

Finally, Bryan arrived, and I was hauled up again to shoot the fleeting moment that appeared onscreen.

After a few days when this became an obvious pattern, I began to get frustrated. Again, I was hauled up on wires, again left dangling there. Again, I asked to be taken down.

"Why aren't we rolling?"

"Bryan's not on set" came the reply once more.

"Why not? Does he know we're all waiting?"

"Yes."

"Someone's gone to tell him?" I asked.

"We've told him three times," came the reply.

I started towards the exit.

"Where are you going, Alan?" asked a PA nervously.

"I'm going to find Bryan."

I arrived outside Bryan's trailer and banged on the door, still dressed as Nightcrawler: blue face, pointy ears, yellow contact lenses, hooves, tail missing but the harness for it under my costume awaiting its reconnection.

No answer. I banged again.

"Bryan!" I cried. "It's Alan!"

The door opened out towards me and there he was, looking a little sheepish.

"Oh, hey, Alan," he said, as though I was a friendly neighbour he hadn't seen for a while, making a surprise visit.

"What's going on, Bryan? Everyone's waiting on set for you, and I'm in a harness, dangling in the air. I'm being told you're not coming out of your trailer!"

"What? Nobody told me," he replied, suddenly indignant.

"Seriously? The ADs told me they've asked you three times!" I said, bemused.

"Nobody told me!" said Bryan, "I'll be right there."

He closed the door and I returned to the sound stage, pissed off with the ADs, who I assumed had been spinning me a line or were responsible for some breakdown in the communication chain.

I had believed him.

None of the other X-men were involved in this White House sequence, so I did not come into contact with my fellow actors immediately. I had no bellwether as to how things had played out on the set before I arrived. When I began to do scenes with the rest of the cast, I saw how they, having literally been through this movie before (the first X-men film had been shot in Toronto two years prior), had learned from that experience that keeping their heads down and getting on with it was the best and sadly perhaps the only way to navigate the chaos of our working environment.

As months and months of filming stretched out in front of me, I could see that I too needed to formulate a survival plan. In the same way that I tried to meditate and stay calm during the hours and hours I sat in the makeup chair, on set I also battened down my hatches and tried to be impervious to the culture of conflict and unease that was being created by this man. I did not always succeed. One such day I had been picked up at 2:12 a.m. for my hours of makeup only to be told yet again I would not be used that day. I could go home but was asked to keep the makeup on (!) to help with turnaround times for the next day of filming! At first I thought it was a joke.

"You want me to keep my makeup on all night? Go to bed with it on?" I exclaimed.

I was answered with a mortified nod.

This was too much. I snapped. "What if I want to have sex?"

"I am so over this fucking movie!" I cried to the heavens. Sanity was restored. I went off to have my makeup removed and be sent home once more.

One day, about halfway through the shoot, I started to develop a severe toothache. I could barely move my head because of the thumping pain and begged to be wrapped early so I could see an emergency dentist. I was certain, and I was correct, that I needed a root canal. The nerve was infected, and I had never felt pain like it. As often happens on sets in such situations, I was asked if I could possibly wait until the end of shooting, as my leaving early would necessitate an extra day of tattoo application and airbrushing of my face at 3 a.m. I was promised that a dentist would be waiting for me as soon as I

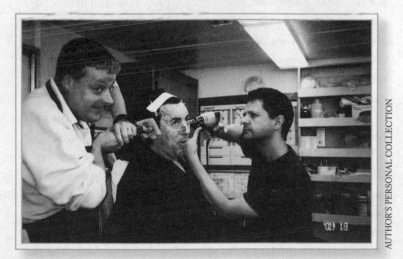

wrapped. What I hadn't counted on was that I would have to go to the dentist still in my Nightcrawler makeup! To expedite my arrival in the chair, Charles, one of the makeup artists, would accompany me to the appointment and remove everything at my home afterwards. As I lay back to be examined, the only part of my Nightcrawler look that wasn't in place was the prosthetic teeth. The dentist was very jovial about it all and, by that point, so was I.

Earlier in the day, Bryan, upon hearing I was in terrible pain, summoned his assistant to bring over to me his tray of painkillers. It was one of those large plastic boxes with many compartments that I had only ever seen used by old people. Bryan explained to me the properties of the various pills he was offering, but all I wanted was something that would allow me to function until the end of the day. I don't know the name of the one he eventually recommended—all I know is that the unimaginable pain went away. Before there had been chaos and pain and now, with the pill, I was detached from everything, floating inside a cocoon of calm, looking out at the world as, presumably, Bryan saw it. Everything made sense for a few hours.

Films with a budget the size of X2's can often be, by their very nature, rather dissociative experiences. Massive sets and hugely complex special effects sequences can dwarf any feeling of creativity or even individuality for performers. But when that experience is presided over by someone volatile, it can quickly come to feel like an ordeal. Add to this the fact that with such films, the distant, faceless monolith of *the studio* is always looming.

I would go home each night, my face red and sore from the toxic blue makeup, my spirit crushed from feeling I was part of a system that ignored, enabled, and seemingly venerated such abusive practises. I would eat, drink wine, have a good cry then fall into bed exhausted, dreading my alarm and the repetition of the whole demeaning process. Finally, out of sheer desperation that the film would never end, fear that someone might get badly hurt, and that Bryan would even do some permanent damage to himself, we did something. The cast staged an intervention with our director.

It did not go well.

On that fateful morning, I was told that filming was halted once again. When I asked why, I was told Bryan was refusing to come out of his trailer. It is telling that this news did not seem so out of the ordinary, but then I was told the reason for today's delay was that Bryan had earlier fired one of the producers, Tom DeSanto, and refused to resume shooting until Tom had left Canadian airspace. Throughout the morning we heard stories of an office having been trashed, and a physical altercation.

I remember standing at craft services with Halle Berry as she munched on cheesy Wotsits. We were both numb and exhausted, and we talked of how galling it was that none of the big producers or *the studio* seemed to be prepared to challenge Bryan or even offer him the help he so clearly needed. We decided right there to call a meeting of the cast to discuss the idea of making a joint statement to the studio, expressing how deeply we were concerned and how untenable the situation was. We all gathered in my trailer.

I will never forget it. Ian McKellen and Rebecca Romijn weren't working that day, but the rest of us were all in our full X-men drag. Halle, Patrick Stewart, Hugh Jackman, James Marsden, Famke Janssen, and I all gathered in the lounge part of my trailer. Anna Paquin, Shawn Ashmore, and Aaron Stanford—the baby X-men—sat on the end of my bed in the adjoining room, nervously looking down the corridor towards us. We all agreed something needed to be done. A stunt had gone wrong due to Bryan's insistence it go ahead without the proper oversight. Bryan had gone MIA one day, only to be discovered asleep or zoned out on the X jet. People did not feel safe, and we were also genuinely concerned for Bryan's health. But we agreed that before we shared such a statement with the studio, we should explain our actions to Bryan in person so that he heard it from us first. As we were forming what we should say and how to approach it, we heard Bryan approaching our trailer area, screaming for Hugh.

He sounded quite demented and I think it's fair to say we were all a little scared. Hugh leapt up and went outside to talk to him. Before we could properly form what we wanted to say to our director, the door opened, and Hugh ushered Bryan inside. He looked crazed, hunched, swaying, his eyes bloodshot. Suddenly we were in the intervention and we hadn't rehearsed.

Halle went first. She spoke movingly of people she had known with drug issues, and whether heroin or painkillers, addiction was addiction, always potent and pervasive and that it must be confronted. I followed up, explaining we were worried about safety on set and genuinely worried about him, too, as well as wondering whether the film would ever, in fact, end. I offered up some of the scenarios we had begun to discuss before he crashed the party—that another director could be brought on to share the burden to get us to the finish line to allow him to rest, to deal with his health issues.

When I finished, there was a long pause. We all stared at Bryan, who now sat looking down at the floor, breathing heavily, shaking his head. Perhaps, understandably, he couldn't comprehend the absurdity of a trailer full of superheroes staging an intervention—please remember we were all in full costume and makeup. The silence was broken by a low and sonorous voice behind me that said, "And Halle and Alan speak for aaaaawwllll of us, Bryan." It was Patrick. For the win.

We all held our breath. Bryan slowly lifted his head towards us.

"You people . . ." he began ". . . are full of fucking shit!"

He went on to tell us how lucky we were to be working with him and how none of us had ever made a decent film between us. This no doubt contributed to Halle, who had earlier that year won Best Actress at the Academy Awards for *Monster's Ball*, delivering her much-quoted line as she exited my trailer.

"I've heard enough," she said, her Storm cape wafting behind her in her wake. "You can kiss my Black ass!"

Production was halted. Lawyers were flown in. Many, many phone calls went back and forth between agents and managers and producers and publicists and *the studio*, but ultimately the message that came down to cast and crew on the ground was just to keep our heads down and muddle through. We were almost done, we were told. There were only a few weeks left, maybe a month. Plus, the film was going to be a big hit and make lots of money! Certainly, everyone understood and commiserated with our predicament, but we *were* under contract, after all.

So basically, nothing happened except our attempt to repair a toxic situation had only prolonged it. Bryan went on to direct two further X-men films.

Several weeks later, on the snowy banks of a lake near Kananaskis in Alberta, I shot my last scene. Storm and Nightcrawler had to carry Professor X (in his wheelchair) away from a dam that was about to burst and potentially wipe out all the X-men, and on one take we slipped on the ice and fell. One minute I was looking towards the imaginary X jet, standing by to whisk us away to safety, the next I saw only white and then the faces of Patrick Stewart and Halle Berry very, very close to mine.

We were all freezing and exhausted, and as wardrobe and makeup rushed in to brush our costumes and faces free of lumps of snow, I found myself openly bemoaning the logic of the scenario.

"I don't know why we are even carrying you, Patrick. I could just teleport you straight to the X jet!" I said in all seriousness.

"Well, I could just change the weather and make all this snow and ice go away!" added Halle, equally exasperated.

At the end of the scene, my wrap was called and for the first time ever in my career I did not shake the hand of or embrace the director of a project. Bryan was nowhere to be seen.

"Are you guys nearly done?" a Canadian man in a park ranger uniform asked me as I passed him on my way back to the makeup trailer for the last time.

"Ah, I'm done but they're still shooting," I replied, exhausted and relieved.

The man looked slightly worried.

"Why?" I asked.

"Well, we have seen some activity on the radar," he said enigmatically.

"What do you mean?"

"We tag all our bears with chips so we can identify and track them electronically," he began. "And I think it might be because of all the catering trucks and the smell of food, but we are seeing a couple of them headed this way."

Being mauled by a hungry grizzly just as I stepped into the waiting car to take me to Calgary airport would have been the perfect ending to this experience.

———

It took me a long while to recover from this film. And it was a recovery in that I had to regain something I had lost: my dignity. I felt I was complicit in a structure that enabled and ratified a value system that went against everything I believed in, and I saw myself on a career trajectory that would undoubtedly lead me to more such situations, more Bryans, more having to keep my head down. I didn't want to feel bad about myself for simply going to work. I also realised that our cast intervention had affected me profoundly. Confronting Bryan had many resonances with confronting my father. With the latter I had dared to challenge the world order I had grown up with because I felt there was no other option if I wanted to move forward. On the set of X2, although I didn't realise it right away, I was challenging the world order because it was a world I no longer wanted to be a part of, a world that placed financial gain and preservation of the machine over the treatment or respect of any of the cogs involved in it.

I think X2: X-Men United is a great film and I'm proud to be in it. It sits next to *Titus* in the miserable experience/great movie category of my career. I learned so much about myself while making it. I would no longer be afraid of confrontation in the workplace, or indeed in life, and for that I am very grateful—to the movie, to Bryan, even to *the studio*.

I once expressed my fears of failure about another performance to a wise woman named Patti Smith.

"But how can it be a failure, Alan, if you've tried your best?" she answered.

The fallout of the discussion in my trailer left me shaken and upset but somehow cleansed of this particular fear, because what we had done felt honest, authentic, and the right thing to do. We tried our best. And although that day I looked like a blue, tattooed mutant, I was never more myself.

Like scuba diving, I will likely never play a superhero again. And that is totally fine.

But never say never.

agency

17

I am totally and utterly drenched and standing at the side of the out-door stage of the Domain in Sydney. A young, tanned Aussie boy, similarly waterlogged and rather perilously wearing a headset, is about to give me the signal to walk onstage and present an award at Tropfest, the short-film festival that had been interrupted only minutes before with one of those huge, all-encompassing, life-affirming Australian summer thunderstorms.

"You're up next, Alan!" he shouted through the deluge.

The rain lessened for a moment and I heard the host say, "And now, please welcome . . . Jamie Foxx!"

"And cue!" said the headsetted Aussie.

"That's not me!" I replied.

The smattering of applause from the remaining few audience members waiting for the awards to be doled out had ceased. Aussie headset boy gestured again for me to get onstage.

"Cue! You're on!" he hissed.

Jamie Foxx was, like me, in town shooting a movie, and like several actors from both casts we had been asked to be judges or present-ers for the evening, as a means of encouraging and supporting new, young Australian filmmakers. But I think Jamie had gone home and no one had told the host.

Aussie headset boy was positively vibrating now.

"Go!" he pleaded. Except it sounded more like "Gahooh!"

There are times when mistakes are made—honest, innocent ones—and I sometimes just ignore them and pretend they haven't happened. For example, people often add an *s* to my surname. It is a total pet peeve of mine, and I normally correct the person who does it, as kindly as possible, but sometimes I just let it go. Choose your battles and all that. But being introduced as a man who is not only not me but a totally different race I thought needed to be addressed.

"I'm not Jamie Foxx!" I remonstrated.

Aussie boy looked back at me with a mixture of pity and contempt.

"Nobody cares!" he replied.

––––––––

I had come to Australia a few months prior, an exultant refugee from yet another ugly and painful divorce. I was playing Loki, God of Mischief in *Son of the Mask*, a prequel to the original Jim Carrey film. I had a glorious time making that movie but alas, this good fortune did not extend to the movie's reception. It bombed at the box office and went on to receive eight nominations at that year's Razzie Awards, that prestigious organisation that honours the worst of cinematic underachievement. Both the late, great Bob Hoskins, who played my father, Odin, and I, as Loki, were nominated for Worst Supporting Actor. My fellow co-stars were nominated for Worst Onscreen Chemistry and the film itself won Worst Remake or Sequel. Hey, if you're going to go down, go down in flames, I say!

Jamie Foxx, along with Josh Lucas and Jessica Biel, was shooting a film called *Stealth* on the soundstage next to ours at Fox Studios. That film also starred Sam Shepard, whom I met one day just after shooting a scene in which I had been in an explosion, and in keeping with the comic book aesthetic of the movie I was wearing a massive fright wig and my entire face and body were caked in post-detonation cartoon dust and debris. It was not the look I had imagined I would be giving as I was introduced to a living legend of the American theatre.

I had first been to Australia at the very end of 1988, to perform *See Victor and Barry and Faint!* at the Sydney Opera House during the Festival of Sydney, followed by a country-wide tour. It was a magical time. I turned twenty-four during our run at the Opera House and I will never forget the incongruous sight of watching Dame Joan Sutherland, the Australian superstar soprano known as "La Stupenda", sitting alone in the corner of the canteen, knitting, as I ate my dinner before a show.

I fell in love with Australia on that trip. I love its fusion of trop-
ics, desert, and merry old Britain. I love its light and its hugeness and
openness and the very possibility of the country. And perhaps because
it is such a commitment to get to, or because I have twice spent con-
siderable periods of time there, I have had quite life-changing epipha-
nies during my visits. The first one, I can see now, set the pattern for
many actions that followed: the decision to walk away.

In 1989 I decided to walk away from *Victor and Barry*, the double
act with my drama school friend Forbes that had grown in only a few
short years from a student skit to national treasure. This feeling had
been brewing deep inside me for several months, since the launch in
Glasgow of our album (*Hear Victor and Barry and Faint!*) had been a
major story on every Scottish TV channel's nightly news. *We shouldn't
be on the news!* I remember thinking. We were just a couple of daft
laddies who made up our best material late at night while inebriated
or stoned! Now a new collection of our songs and ramblings was *news*!
Something about that just did not feel right to me. I know now that this
was deeply based in insecurity and lack of confidence and self-worth,
but also a kind of fear. The characters were beginning to become, and
could be forever, my full-time job.

When it was all going well there was nothing better: that feeling
of free-falling onstage with someone you knew would always catch
you, combined with the excitement and connection of entering your
country's zeitgeist. But we had already begun to feel the pressure. Too
soon the roller coaster morphed into a treadmill. And it's difficult to
be in a double act: juggling the offers we were getting as a duo with
solo acting work. I felt trapped, and worried that *Victor and Barry*
would overwhelm my acting career before it had really begun.

I decided to accept a role in a play at Bristol Old Vic on our return
to the United Kingdom, which meant Victor and Barry would have to
cancel dates, and that was the beginning of my walking away from the
act altogether. But I wasn't as strong or confident then as I am now. I
didn't realise the kindness of a clean break versus a slow demise. Victor and Barry finally died as they would have wanted—onstage—at a

benefit concert at the London Palladium in 1992. Their friend and mystic Brenda Turk had mistakenly told them to beware a couple with the names Ella and Sam, though she later realised she had misordered the names and what Victor and Barry should fear was in fact salmonella! The fish she had recently gifted them, and which Victor and Barry had made into soup and eaten onstage earlier as a mid-show snack, was riddled with it! They sang one last song, their mantra for how to live life the "Most Dramatic Way", then Forbes, as Victor, slumped onto the piano keys and I, as Barry, fell into a theatrical hamper. Curtain!

Forbes and I used to love to go swimming at an outdoor pool named after the Olympic swimmer Andrew "Boy" Charlton during our stay in Sydney. We also discovered the joys of the Australian pie there at the poolside café. The hole in the ozone layer above Australia had been discovered a few years prior and everyone was rightly very paranoid about the damage the sun's rays could cause. This, combined with our Scottish pasty whiteness, caused several locals to stop us in the street and give us counsel. One day as I was walking alone, a woman took one look at me, stopped in her tracks, and screamed, "Skin cancer!" and then walked on. I appreciated her thoughtfulness.

Fifteen years later, during filming of *Son of the Mask*, I returned to the Boy Charlton many times. Towards the end of the shoot I would swim and then read potential scripts for my next project, and one day, as I looked up and out across Woolloomooloo Bay, I decided I needed to walk away again from the direction my career was taking me. I needed a direction that made sense for me. The cookie-cutter progression to more money and better billing with each project wasn't, well, cutting it. I needed to start forging my own destiny, and so came the birth of my concept of the Hollywood Bank.

Each job I do in film and television I think of as either making a deposit or a withdrawal at the imaginary Hollywood Bank. A more commercial, mainstream film or TV project (like *Son of the Mask*) would be a deposit to the Hollywood Bank. That deposit enables me to make a future withdrawal to subsidise my involvement in a play in the theatre or in smaller, independent screen projects, often about subjects I feel more personally invested in, and sometimes to help them get made at all because of the bankability (or interest accrued!) by doing the "deposit" jobs.

I had been doing too many—maybe only—deposit jobs for a long time. I enjoyed the spoils of that labour, of course. I was certainly very grateful for the lifestyle I could afford because of them. But I felt it was time to stand back and reassess what it was I actually wanted. Over the past few years, I had more than dipped my toe into the world of franchises and blockbusters—I was part of the swim team. I wanted to feel passionate about my work again. I wanted to have more experiences like *The Anniversary Party*, where I felt truly artistically fulfiled. I wanted to try different things, to be challenged in ways that didn't just involve dealing with difficult, even destructive people or being in a harness. I wanted to walk away.

But I realised that walking away was something I had done before. I walked away from Forbes and *Victor and Barry* and the increasing fame I was experiencing in Scotland. A few years later I walked away from him again and our sitcom, *The High Life*. I walked away from my marriage. I walked away from fatherhood. I walked away from being a London theatre starlet. I walked away from London itself. I walked away from Los Angeles. I walked away from the idea of a conventional relationship being possible for me.

But then walking away was my template, my familiar. My childhood was merely killing time until I could walk away from my father.

One of the scripts I had brought to the pool to read was *Reefer Madness: The Movie Musical*, based on the 1936 anti-marijuana propaganda film which highlighted how we are all ruled by fear and how much it is in our governments' interests to keep us in that state. It was hilarious, weird, politically provocative, and I had been offered the role of the lecturer who comes to town to warn parents of the evils of marijuana who also pops up in many different guises throughout the film. And it was a *musical*! And he sings the title song! I decided it was the perfect subversive antidote I needed, and I signed on immediately.

Reefer Madness would premiere at the Sundance Film Festival on my fortieth birthday, and I suppose that impending birthday milestone had much to do with my decision to begin forging my own path that sunny day in Sydney. A midlife crisis, to be reductionist. Over the next few years, I made several television projects and many films, some that never saw the light of day, some that I wish hadn't, a few that I am incredibly proud of. But all were fascinating and enriching and I was doing them because I wanted to. Yes, I made many withdrawals from the Hollywood Bank!

I produced several films, I directed another. And the eclecticism in the roles I chose—a contemporary vicar, a 1920s Minnesotan farmer, a taxi driver in love with a lesbian, a pansexual manager of a lesbian bar, a deranged hitchhiker, a ditzy TV production assistant, a mental patient, a murderous cello teacher—was mirrored in the other forms of my work: I had my own interview series, *Eavesdropping with Alan Cumming*; I was the poster boy for a brand named Fuck Yoga; I designed wallpaper, wrote forewords for several books, and articles for magazines; I hosted a film show on the Sundance Channel with my dogs; I voiced a cat, a goat, a bear; I even launched a fragrance— Cumming—and reenacted iconic images from fragrance ads of the past for the promotional campaign as well as shot a commercial with me rolling around on a bed talking about what sexy meant to me, that was both an homage and a parody of the whole notion of celebrity endorsement. And then we launched ancillary products like a lotion (Cumming All Over) and my personal favourite, a soap (Cumming in a Bar)!

In short, I made my career fun! I became the eclectic version of myself that I now know and love. Finally I wasn't walking away from anything. I was walking *towards* things.

sanctuary

18

On April 25, 2000, I met my second saviour.

I had boarded a plane at Newark airport bound for Austin (where I was shooting *Spy Kids*), having made a discovery minutes before that truly wrenched my guts.

A week before, Adonis had left me an uncharacteristically weepy, loving, apologetic-ish voice mail that was marred somewhat by the announcement in the background for a departing United flight to a destination I did not get to hear as he quickly cut the call short. But now I knew. A simple question to the lady at the desk in the lounge confirmed my worst suspicion: there was a nightly United flight to Rome shortly after the time Adonis had left me the message.

I was glad, for sure, to have the mystery revealed, though there was little solace in having it confirmed. Adonis had, very shortly after our breakup, flown to Rome into the arms and presumably the bed of another man, one who had been recently circling us like a vulture and who would now be gorging on the remains of our tainted love.

I'm not sure there is a word to sum up the feelings this news engendered. I was sure I had made the right decision to end it. But the speed with which he fled from me to this older wealthy man, well-known in the fashion industry, only made me further doubt the veracity of our passion. I was sick to my stomach to think he had seen me as a similar, convenient celebrity meal ticket.

As I waited for takeoff to Austin, imbibing the first of many in-flight cocktails that evening, a man sat down in the seat next to me and smiled. This kind stranger let me spill out my heart to him over the next few hours, intuiting my need to vent such a maelstrom of emotions. By Austin we had formed a firm bond, and later that week we met for lunch, our first date.

There have been three people who have come into my life at a time when meeting them was what I needed most—their goodness, kindness, and beauty to rescue me from the toxic seas of my immedi-ately previous relationship. My former fiancée was the first and now this man on the plane was the second.

We had a short love affair that glided into becoming great friends and eventually neighbours—it was his house in the Catskills I visited after 9/11 and he is the reason I have my home there today. I have so much to be grateful to him for. He introduced me to my sanctuary— both of them.

One evening later that summer, I went to a pre-clubbing drinks party at the man on the plane's apartment in New York City, and when I arrived I realised I was being given the once-over by his peer group. It may sound a little daunting, but I liked the care and protection of him this moment demonstrated. They were right to be concerned. I was the wild child, the Broadway bad boy, recently crowned the city's *frolicky pansexual sex symbol for the new millennium* by the *New York Observer*. I would've been concerned about my friend dating me. And so that night, for the first time, I felt the scrutiny of the man who was to eventually become my husband, as he was the best friend of the man on the plane.

Over the next few years, I would see the man who would become my husband sporadically, at parties or in bars. I always found him funny and kind and sexy. Then in 2003, I went through another epic rupture of a coupling I had thought was for life. By chance, my for-mer fiancée (we call each other ff for short now!) was in town and we went out to drown my sorrows. It was a Tuesday, and so we ended up at Beige, a legendary weekly party at B Bar on the Bowery and East Fourth Street. Beige was one of those gatherings where you were guaranteed to run into old friends and make new ones, a sort of queer *Cheers*.

As I unpacked my battered heart to ff, someone tapped me on the shoulder. It was a very sheepish Adonis. He looked like a child who knew he had done wrong but was betting heavily he might avoid being scolded by looking cute.

In that instant I decided to start smoking again.

"Do you have an American Spirit Yellow?" I asked him, knowing he would.

Later on, I ran into the man who would become my husband. I was drunk and horny and after some initial chivalrous prevaricating on his part, I assuaged his moral dilemma (still a beautiful/utterly annoying trait of his) and convinced him I was indeed very single. And so, we went back to his apartment.

The next morning it was clear to both of us that the timing was not right to pursue any kind of *thing*. I snuck away, and wandered through the then-unfamiliar East Village, hungover and wretched, vying with the morning commuters for a cab home. There was no way I could know that the apartment I had just left would be my home one day.

Oh great, I thought to myself. *Is this my life now? I'm going to sleep with all my friends and ruin everything.* This downward spiral continued the next evening when Adonis called me late at night and caught me a little tipsy and at a particularly low self-esteem moment.

He was driving through the night to Knoxville, Tennessee, transporting a van of furniture for a friend who'd moved there.

"I wish I was going to Tennessee," I lamented. And I did. Anything to be lifted from the carnage of my life at that moment.

"I've only got as far as Jersey. I could come back and pick you up," he said.

I could hear my brain screaming at me to stop right there, that driving through the night to Tennessee with my ex in a van packed with someone else's possessions was a terrible idea. And we didn't exactly have a good track record with road trips.

"Aw, thanks," I replied. "It does sound really appealing but I can't. I have stuff to do this weekend."

"Me too," he replied. "I have to be back in the city by Sunday at noon. Should I turn back for you . . . ?"

Naturally I said yes. My dog Honey and I were soon wedged awkwardly into the passenger seat of a rickety old van for the next nine hours, aside from a few pit stops for Adonis to top up with caffeine— and a mysterious substance that turned out to be speed but was branded as Trucker's Friend. It was the combination of coffee and speed that enabled us to make this marathon journey, spend a night in Knoxville, and drive through the night again to have me back in my Manhattan apartment by late Sunday morning. It did me a world of good. I completely disappeared from my life for forty-eight hours. I was light. Invisible. There were no mistakes to be made because the entire venture was a huge mistake. The irony that it was Adonis who helped bring some balance back into my life did not escape me.

At our last stop before we drove through the Holland Tunnel back into Manhattan, I switched on my phone and it immediately rang. Why not, I thought? I'll answer.

"Hello?"

"Alan? This is Faye Dunaway. Would you happen to be free to come with me to the Grammys this evening?"

Of course it was Faye.

I had met Faye when she came to see *Elle* and she had expressed interest in working with the Art Party, the company I'd helped form to mount that production. She had also asked me to play Maria Callas's accompanist in a film version of Terrence McNally's play *MasterClass* that she was trying to put together. Faye would of course be giving her Callas, and she told me she had spoken to Alicia Keys about playing the young student soprano in the film. As Alicia was presenting at the

Grammys that night, she thought it a good idea to go and try to woo her. I was apparently a necessary part of the lure.

Naturally, again, I said yes. And why not? After making an unscheduled round-trip dash to Tennessee with a man whose name I had tattooed and then lasered off my body, the idea of attending the Grammys on the arm of an old-school movie legend seemed totally in keeping with the vibe of the weekend.

A few hours later I was sitting *in the front row* at Madison Square Garden next to Faye Dunaway. A succession of superstars old and new appeared in front of us—Simon and Garfunkel, No Doubt, Lou Reed, Tony Bennett, Justin Timberlake, P. Diddy. I felt I was in some kind of musical fever dream, which I suppose I was. In my pocket I could feel my phone manically buzzing as friends watching the show at home could not believe their eyes each time the camera cut to us.

A couple of hours in, Faye and I were taken backstage to see Alicia. She received us very cordially and we made polite chatter. I excused myself to have a cigarette. I had rejoined the ranks of smokers upon seeing Adonis just five days before, which now felt like ten years ago.

Those were the days when you could still smoke inside, but I didn't want to fog up Alicia's dressing room, so I popped out into a passageway and had a quiet moment to myself, trying to process everything that had gone on since Tuesday. Suddenly a door flew open and a panting, sweating Bruce Springsteen appeared, guitar slung round on his back, fresh from performing on the MSG stage. He bounded towards me, his clomping cowboy boots echoing through the corridor, and I felt compelled to say something to him.

"Bravo, Bruce!" I gushed, as though I had somehow managed to witness his performance and then rush back to greet him, having miraculously smoked half a cigarette in the process.

"Thanks, man!" said the Boss as he brushed by me.

Back in Alicia's room I saw that Faye was at the food table, trans-ferring some sandwiches into a napkin and then to her bag. Just then a stage manager came to tell us that if, as I'd requested, we wanted to see Eminem perform, we needed to get back to our seats during the next commercial break. We bade Alicia farewell.

"Sixty seconds to air!" came the announcement as we relieved our seat fillers in the front row.

What happened next felt to be in excruciating slow motion, though clearly it must all have happened in the space of a minute.

I had eaten out with Faye a couple of times, so I was aware she weighed her food. Yes. She had a system, which obviously served her very well as she was in great shape, of keeping a strict count on her calorie intake by carrying a little set of scales around with her, much like ones I have seen drug dealers use in movies. She also used a little silver cup, almost like the top of a cocktail shaker, that she stuffed so full of salad that when she turned it upside down, out plopped a veritable sand castle of greens. Luckily there was no sign of the salad holder tonight. But the scales were now sitting on Faye's knees and I could feel hysteria rising from deep within me.

"Forty-five seconds to air. Please take your seats!"

She then began peeling the bread from the sandwiches she had pilfered from Alicia's dressing room and placing the fillings—a combo of tuna and egg salad, I deduced from my proximity to both the sight and smell—onto the scales, all the while peering through her reading glasses that she held aloft with her other hand.

"Thirty seconds to air." If my friends who had been messaging me thought it was crazy that I was at the Grammys sitting next to Faye Dunaway, I could not compute what they—or indeed the rest of the world—would think if they saw Faye myopically depositing globs of tuna and egg salad onto a set of grubby drug dealer scales.

My aching discomfort must have been palpable because Faye glanced over at me and said, "Is this weird?"

"Fifteen seconds to air!"

"It is a little weird, Faye, yes. I mean I know this is what you do and everything and I really think weighing your food works for you so, so well, but I just wonder, what with the show about to start again, if you really, you know, want to be on camera doing . . . this . . . right now!"

Faye considered this for a moment.

"Five seconds to air! Please take your seats!"

"Should I wait and do it in the limo on the way to the party?"

"I think you should, Faye, yes!"

Somehow as the lights went down and the camera zoomed past us and up the stairs and Eminem's "Lose Yourself" began to fill the auditorium, Faye had removed her glasses, shoved all her paraphernalia into her bag, and it was as though nothing had happened. I, though, had aged another ten years.

———

A few months later the man who would become my husband and I ran into each other again but neither of us mentioned our night together. I thought we were on track towards an easy "nothing ever happened" kind of friendship. That maybe one day, years in the future, over a glass of wine at some friend's dinner table, we would laugh about our youthful horny selves.

But then that Christmas, when I was back in New York from Australia for the holidays, we ran into each other again in another of our favourite haunts, Barracuda in Chelsea. Above the noise and the dancing and the seasonal cheer the subject was broached.

"I can't talk about this right now," I said, shutting the conversation down. I was not alone, you see. I was then with my third saviour, a beautiful man who had guided me back towards the light after the fallout of my most recent dark uncoupling.

The following summer, when I had returned from my travels and the renovations on my house in the Catskills were finally finished, I decided to throw a joint housewarming and Fourth of July party with my dear friend and neighbour down the hill—the man on the plane. As we chatted one night on the phone about who we were each going to invite up for the weekend, he told me he had asked his best friend and my heart skipped a beat.

On the balmy Saturday night of July 3, 2004, as we all had drinks on the spanking new deck and looked out across the rolling hills, something happened. I looked across and met the gaze of the man who would become my husband. Maybe it's because we have the same hazel eyes and so looking into his feels like looking into myself. But I don't think I was aware of that yet. I just knew I felt safe and calm and at home. And ready.

That night was our second together, and the next morning it was his turn to sneak away, back down the hill to the house of the man on the plane before he and his guests woke up.

We've been together ever since.

We were both thirty-nine and had both been around the block a few times. For the first time ever in my life I entered a relationship having a frank discussion about my needs as well as my shortcomings. I didn't want to make false promises about what I was capable of. I did not want to disappoint. I wanted to be looked after but not smothered. I wanted to feel rooted but also free. I knew I wasn't easy. Being in my life wasn't always easy. I recognised patterns in myself and in those I attracted, and I needed to know I was desired for the right reasons.

Most of all I did not want drama. It seemed to have engulfed me for so long. The absence of drama was what I craved more than anything.

For the first time I felt I was meeting an equal, someone as caring of me as he was uncaring of all the glittery detritus that surrounded Alan Cumming. Finally, I had a partner who did not want to change me.

I walked towards him.

finally

19

In 2006 I made further withdrawals from the Hollywood Bank when I returned to the theatre. The first half of the year I spent on Broadway, prowling the stage of my old haunt, Studio 54, as that Brechtian bad boy, Mac the Knife in *The Threepenny Opera*; the latter half as a gay concentration camp inmate pretending to be a Jew because he thinks it will ensure him better treatment in Martin Sherman's epic *Bent* in London's West End.

It was a great year. I felt fulfiled and happy and in love.

We rehearsed *Bent* in Bloomsbury and I visited the nearby Gay's The Word bookshop many times on my walk home after work to browse their amazing collection of LGBTQ+ material, and specifically books about the Holocaust. I wanted to understand the huge changes people like my character, Max, would have encountered going from the heady days of Weimar Berlin, with its sexual liberation, clubs like the one I had overseen in *Cabaret*, and even a burgeoning gay rights movement under the sexologist Magnus Hirschfeld, to the sudden fugitive status that homosexuals encountered after the Night of the Long Knives in 1934.

One day as I was browsing I picked up a leaflet titled "Everything You Need to Know about Civil Partnerships". The first same-sex civil partnerships had taken place in the United Kingdom about six months earlier. I had been working with various American organisations that were campaigning for same-sex marriage (including the Empire State Pride Agenda, the Human Rights Campaign, and the American Civil Liberties Union) so I was well-versed with what was happening (or not happening) on the issue stateside, but I was a little out of the loop about it all on this side of the pond.

I did realise that the campaign for same-sex marriage and other LGBT rights issues, like equalising the age of consent and the freedom to serve openly in the military, had been kick-started during Tony Blair's New Labour reign. He had become Britain's prime minister in 1997 in a landslide election that heralded a new dawn (his words, actually!) of social justice and equality, much needed after the seemingly endless years of Thatcherism and its *every man for himself* mentality. I was very excited by the prospect of New Labour, and indeed in 1997 I hosted a rally for Tony Blair in Edinburgh's Usher Hall.

My job that night was to introduce various speakers and keep things rolling along. At the climax of Blair's keynote speech (that night his focus was education) I had been instructed to join the rest of the evening's participants in applauding and cheering him. However, as the host, I had an extra and very important duty. I was tasked with giving Blair the signal to leave the stage once the band—who would perform the campaign anthem—had finished setting up behind us and certain security protocols were in place so that he could be rushed out to a waiting car and off to his next campaign engagement. I was to be given the go-ahead to give Blair the signal by one of his security detail standing in my eyeline just offstage. I found being a part of the mechanics of power in this way incredibly exciting. However, there must have been some sort of unusual delay that evening, because as we all went onstage and joined the packed crowd at the Usher Hall in a very long and rousing standing ovation, I kept receiving a very firm shake of the head and a stand-down gesture from my informant. I, in turn, would then give Tony Blair a similar signal (but more subtle— we were onstage, after all). Eventually Blair's looks over became more questioning. This went on for what seemed like an eternity, and I could see Blair trying to resist the temptation to keep turning to me, and so instead he was giving me sideways glances, basically the equivalent of prime minister side-eye. He was sweating quite profusely at that point, and with each increasingly panicked look from him, I tried to imbue my head shake back with an exhortation to remain calm. Eventually I was giving him a "believe me, I want this to end, too" sort of look.

I began to feel a little crazed with power. Here I was, exerting utter control over the next prime minister of Britain. I started to slightly enjoy being his captor, of having him in my thrall. Tony Blair was my bitch! Mercifully, finally, the ordeal ended. I got the nod, and gave him the nod. He scampered offstage and the strains of "Things Can Only Get Better" blasted out across the hall.

For me the same-sex marriage fight was part of a bigger movement for legal equality for queer people in the workplace, health care, the military, the tax system, in fact in all areas of society. I had of course heard the horror stories of lifelong partners being banned from hospital rooms as their other half lay dying or evicted from their homes once a partner died because under the law as it stood they had no rights or legal protections. I was angry about being considered a second-class citizen in America, a country that constantly trumpeted itself as the land of the free where anything was possible. It blatantly wasn't either.

In Britain, the path to same-sex civil unions was not as fast as the Blair administration had promised, and there are many who felt that giving same-sex couples all the same legal rights as straight marriage but naming it civil partnership instead said more about the administration's fear of upsetting middle England than its commitment to equality. Ironically, in 2014 when same-sex marriage did finally pass in the United Kingdom, seven years after Blair had left office, it was a Conservative government that saw that #LoveWon.

But I realised it wasn't just my desire to compare and contrast the LGBT civil rights struggles in the United States and the United

Kingdom that had caused me to devour all the information in the leaflet that day. I had begun to think that I should propose during the six months we would be spending in London during the run of *Bent*.

The man who would become my husband and I were perfectly happy the way we were. Obviously we wanted the same legal rights as other citizens and we both fought for them, but I felt we were married in that we were totally committed, we had bought an apartment together, and we shared our resources. There was nothing I felt lacking in our relationship that marriage or civil union would bring.

But that's how you think when you have no choice. And maybe the subject matter of *Bent* was making me feel we should seize hard-won rights when they were offered, for history showed they could easily be snatched from us, and worse. Perhaps it was also the endless galas back in America, the marches and meetings with politicians and the speeches that had blurred my vision. Perhaps I had forgotten the other purpose of marriage: the celebration, the opportunity for family and friends, everyone from all aspects of your lives, to come together and celebrate your love. It is such an intrinsic, spiritual part of the whole idea of why we get married. But gay people had never known it. Legal rights are palpable, solid, and bureaucratic. But it's impossible to imagine communal emotion and joy about your love and life together if that has never been an option for you, and if you have never seen your elders or peers experience it, either.

I knew that emotion, of course. I had been married before and I knew of the rite of passage you experience when your granny is giving you marital advice as you sashay round a dance floor that is filled with everyone you love. And I wanted that again. I was ready for it. That leaflet had opened my eyes and my mind, and again, I walked towards it.

I hid the leaflet behind a picture that was propped up on a shelf next to the bed in my flat in London that looked down on to Leicester Square. The flat was close to the theatre and therefore the venue for many rowdy nights with my *Bent* castmates, laughing and dancing and filling our beings with joy to enable us to go back the next evening and become the vessels for such utter despair, the very worst of humanity. I felt bad for my friends coming to see the play. I tried to warn them it would be disturbing, but there is nothing that can really prepare you for an evening of theatre that grabs your very soul. My mum came and the first thing she said when she walked into my dressing room was "Everyone should see this play." Nailed it, Mary Darling. Joan Collins, whom I'd met years before on *The Flintstones* movie, also made the pilgrimage up the four flights of stairs to say hello and was very moved.

"How do you do this every night, Alan?" she asked through tears.

"By not talking about it after, Joan," I replied gaily but firmly.

"Yes, but how do you do this every night?"

"Well, Joan, as I said . . . !"

It might seem weird to some that I would choose to propose to my husband at a party in the home of my former fiancée. But it shouldn't. I have always tried to embrace my past, and of my past loves only one is no longer in my life. Considering my aggregate, that's a pretty good average, don't you think?

I hadn't intended to propose that night. It just sort of happened, like all of the good things in my life. But it was obviously on my mind as I was talking to someone I hadn't seen for ages and ribbing him about why he still hadn't made an honest woman out of his girlfriend.

"Well, why haven't you proposed to your boyfriend?" he touchéd back.

Everything stopped.

"I'm going to," I said.

"When?" The old friend laughed.

"Right now!" I exclaimed and left the room to look for the man who would very soon become my fiancé.

Apparently when I found him, I clasped my hands to either side of my head, like a fortysomething Macaulay Culkin, entirely appropriate, really, as like Macaulay in his iconic pose, I too was overwhelmed by the magnitude of what life had just thrown at me. Also, like Mac, I was in a situation of my own making.

As I asked him, I suddenly remembered we had never discussed the matter before. Why would you talk about something that had never been an option? At one point in the past I am sure I had even voiced my leeriness of formalised unions altogether, both due to my bad track record in that area but also the couple of really spectacularly bitter and gouging processes of disentanglement I'd suffered through. And we were happy, secure, calm. I didn't need ceremony to quantify my love for this man. And then suddenly I did. Right now, that very moment I did.

"Yes," he replied. "But ask me again when you're sober!"

Did I mention he is a wise man, too? I did and again, he said yes.

We were married eleven weeks later (I don't mess around), surrounded by family and friends in the Painted Hall of the Old Royal Naval College in Greenwich. My mum walked me down the aisle, his dad walked him. A string quartet played pop hits we'd had them arrange. We walked back up the aisle, married, to Queen's "You're My

Best Friend". Outside, the courtyard had been iced over for the winter and so we rented the rink and instead of a first dance we had a first skate. Many guests had panicked about the dress code for a same-sex wedding that involved skating. "Layer" was my advice. Later that night we all danced on a barge that took us back up the Thames to Embankment, and then we went out clubbing.

The next day my husband and I woke up with faces aching from smiling.

"How are you?" he asked me.

"Still alive!" I replied, grateful.

EPILOGUE

I did more research on Alan Cumming for the writing of this book than I have done for any character I have ever portrayed. But then I have never had such total access to the archives of someone I have played.

Some of the events I reviewed took place up to forty years ago. My recall of them is understandably a bit dim and based predominantly on preexisting memories. Revisiting them felt like questioning my belief in my own press.

By delving through old diaries and datebooks, and more recently, like some retro digital stalker, being able to track my every move via the internet, I have not only realigned what I thought happened in many instances in my past but also posited new interpretations to whole periods of my life by seeing them from this privileged vantage point: the gift of objectivity that only time passing (and Google) can provide.

Not everything made sense. I saw repeated appointments with names I still do not recognise. I marvelled at the closeness of tumultuous events that I had remembered happening years apart. I saw how quickly good intentions faded, lessons hard-learned forgotten. I saw the subtle shifts in my demeanour, my confidence, my hair, my voice, my teeth.

The older I saw myself become, the more I relaxed. I saw not just the wisdom of age, but the vigilance that comes with embracing the idea that nothing is ever completely sure. Conversely the earlier in my life I delved, the more I worried for my younger self, and eventually my worries were justified: Freud would classify it as *Nachtraglichkeit* or afterwardsness, where an early experience that didn't register as negative or damaging at the time can be transcribed much later as traumatic. It's not a delayed reaction because there was no trauma to begin with, but rather a similar experience occurring or, in my case, new information being revealed that can retroactively construct trauma: as a young man I was the product of years of lack of respect— of my mind as well as my body—by my father, and then, of course, by me. I practised what I had been taught. Later I projected my lack of self-respect into the world and allowed my still-boyish body to be the touchstone of my worth. I did this with several people, and all the interactions were pleasurable and consensual, even empowering. But only recently I discovered that one of those partners worshipped young men's bodies like mine habitually. Now my youthful emancipa- tion seemed less glorious. I realise I was groomed by a predator. Other interactions were tinged as well.

I had focused for so long on the recovery from my childhood abuse from the point I fully discovered and accepted it, but now I began to trace its fallout in the years up to the recognition. It was another example of the necessity of vigilance. There is nothing to be done. There is no one to blame. The time that separates full enlightenment and comprehension of an event from the event itself will continue to expand the older I get. And that's okay. I actually look forward to it, for it will contribute to my completeness.

Understanding there may be trauma ahead in my life from events that hitherto have not registered also led me to question the notion of breaking cycles. Can a cycle ever truly be broken if we continue to add to its root cause in this way? Maybe what we need to focus on is to continue *breaking* the cycle, not having broken it.

One of the cycles I realise I have actually broken is having children, which was, let's not forget, the genesis of all my troubles in the first place.

I will be thankful to my dying day that my wife and I could not have a child. Our lives together would have become even more bitter, painful, and complicated. I am actually grateful I have never had kids with any of the people I entertained the idea with. My sperm has been much vaunted and petitioned at times, but the right moment never, well, came.

I love kids. I wanted one really badly for a long while. I heard the ticking clock and had the physical and mental yearning to nurture the fruit of my loins. But I sometimes wonder if I was too scared to have children. I think we are all a bit scared of becoming our parents, but my genetic predisposition gives me more pause than most. The idea that I would somehow be powerless to avoid treating my child as my father treated me was unconscionable. And so, I broke that cycle.

And I got older and I got content. I don't want to disrupt my life with kids any more. Both my husband and I like our life too much as it is. The moment has passed for me. And I trust my body when it tells me that. If it made me have a nervous breakdown to stop me having kids, to remember and come to terms with my own childhood all those years ago, I think I can safely say it is not betraying me now when I feel happy to be enjoying my life as it is. I'm asked often if I think I'll ever regret not becoming a father or, worse, "Who will look after you when you're old?" as though having children is just a way to ensure free future geriatric care. But I have come to realise I have many people in my life young enough to be my children, and many for whom I am very much a father figure. I am at peace with the idea that I have become the kind of father I wish I'd had, and perhaps it is not an accident that he is childless.

And in addition to my worries that I might be predestined to repeat my father's transgressions, the scientific community added to my woes when I stumbled across epigenetics, the study of how what happens to us in our lives can actually change our DNA. The cells and behaviour of our future children and grandchildren can be altered because of experiences we have before they exist. So even if I managed to break the cycle of abusive behaviour in the childhood of any future offspring, they could still inherit the PTSD from mine.

But surely, if what psychologists call the intergenerational transmission of trauma can alter our very DNA, then can't we equally—by therapy, by breaking cycles—change our DNA to ensure a sunnier disposition for our progeny?! If trauma can be transferred molecularly, surely so can positivity?

If life has taught me anything, it's that change is a given. Change is hard and scary but inexorable. The sooner we embrace its possibility, the sooner we can really start living.

The more my life has changed, the closer I have come to a place of authenticity. Although I began this book by refuting the notion of having triumphed, I do see great victory in becoming yourself. So does Shakespeare . . .

> *This above all: to thine own self be true,*
> *And it must follow, as the night the day,*
> *Thou canst not then be false to any man.*
> *Farewell: my blessing season this in thee!*

ACKNOWLEDGEMENTS

Thanks to my agent, Luke Janklow, and everyone at Dey Street books who contributed to birthing this book—Peter Kispert, Ploy Siripant, Andrea Molitor, Paula Szafranski, Eliza Rosenberry, Joseph Papa, Kell Wilson, Ben Steinberg, Liate Stehlik, Andrew Jacobs—and especially my editor, Carrie Thornton, for, above all, her patience (my original delivery date was October 3, 2016. I hope it's been worth the wait!). Special thanks to my manager, Nikola Barisic, and my assistant, Matt Brown, who I know always have my back and somehow keep the train on the tracks.

I'd like to acknowledge that my life has been a series of mixed messages. From my father telling me I was useless and my mother telling me I was precious, to my high school English teacher who encouraged me to join her after-school drama group and my drama school acting teacher telling me I would never make it as a professional actor. The result of these and many other inconsistencies was for me to make up my own mind—about myself, about them, about the world.

I have forged my own idiosyncratic path in both my work and my personal life. At times it's a little lonely, but not having peers is a small price to pay for a truly autonomous existence. I want to thank all my friends and family who support me, care for me, worry about me, and, most importantly, understand me. And to my husband, Grant Shaffer, who was once asked by a friend if he was nervous watching the videos appearing on social media of me intoxicatedly crowd surfing in a monkey suit on another continent and replied, "Of course. But Alan is a butterfly and we have to let him fly." I am a feisty, strong butterfly, but that statement means so much to me and reminds me why you truly are my better half.

ALAN CUMMING

Not My Father's Son

A Family Memoir

'Both heart-breaking and brave . . . A thoroughly
gripping read' *Sunday Times*

CANON‖GATE